British Railw

C000142863

ELE
MULTIPLE UNITS

THIRTY-THIRD EDITION
2020

The Complete Guide to all
Electric Multiple Units which operate on
the national railway network

Robert Pritchard

ISBN 978 1909 431 57 7

© 2019. Platform 5 Publishing Ltd, 52 Broadfield Road, Sheffield, S8 0XJ, England.

Printed in England by The Lavenham Press, Lavenham, Suffolk.

CONTENTS

PROVISION OF INFORMATION

This book has been compiled with care to be as accurate as possible, but some information is not easily available and the publisher cannot be held responsible for any errors or omissions. We would like to thank the companies and individuals who have been helpful in supplying information to us. The authors of this series of books are always pleased to receive notification of any inaccuracies that may be found, to enhance future editions. Please send comments to:

Robert Pritchard, Platform 5 Publishing Ltd, 52 Broadfield Road, Sheffield, S8 0XJ, England.

e-mail: robert.pritchard@platform5.com   **Tel:** 0114 255 2625.

This book is updated to information received by 11 October 2019.

UPDATES

This book is updated to the Stock Changes given in **Today's Railways UK 215** (November 2019). The Platform 5 railway magazine **"Today's Railways UK"** publishes Stock Changes every month to update this book. The magazine also contains news and rolling stock information on the railways of Great Britain and Ireland and is published on the second Monday of every month. For further details of **Today's Railways UK**, please contact Platform 5 Publishing Ltd.

Front cover photograph: LNER "Azuma" 800 113 passes Sunderland Bridge, Durham, with a 5Q07 15.50 York–Heaton test run on 23/07/19. **Dave McAlone**

BRITAIN'S RAILWAY SYSTEM

INFRASTRUCTURE & OPERATION

Britain's national railway infrastructure is owned by a "not for dividend" company, Network Rail. In 2014 Network Rail was reclassified as a public sector company, being described by the Government as a "public sector arm's-length body of the Department for Transport".

Most stations and maintenance depots are leased to and operated by Train Operating Companies (TOCs), but some larger stations are controlled by Network Rail. The only exception is the infrastructure on the Isle of Wight: The Island Line franchise uniquely included maintenance of the infrastructure as well as the operation of passenger services. As Island Line is now part of the South Western Railway franchise, both the infrastructure and trains are operated by South Western Railway.

Trains are operated by TOCs over Network Rail tracks (the National Network), regulated by access agreements between the parties involved. In general, TOCs are responsible for the provision and maintenance of the locomotives, rolling stock and staff necessary for the direct operation of services, whilst Network Rail is responsible for the provision and maintenance of the infrastructure and also for staff to regulate the operation of services.

The Department for Transport (DfT) is the franchising authority for the national network, with Transport Scotland overseeing the award of the ScotRail franchise and the Welsh Government overseeing the Wales & Borders franchise.

A franchise is the right to run specified services within a specified area for a period of time, in return for the right to charge fares and, where appropriate, to receive financial support from the Government. Subsidy is payable in respect of socially necessary services. Service standards are monitored by the DfT throughout the duration of the franchise. Franchisees earn revenue primarily from fares and from subsidy. They generally lease stations from Network Rail and earn rental income by sub-letting parts of them, for example to retailers.

TOC's and open access operator's main costs are the track access charges they pay to Network Rail, the costs of leasing stations and rolling stock and of employing staff. Franchisees may do light maintenance work on rolling stock or contract it out to other companies. Heavy maintenance is normally carried out by the Rolling Stock Leasing Companies, according to contracts.

TOCs can take commercial risks, although some franchises are "management contracts", where ticket revenues pass directly to the DfT. Concessions (such as London Overground) see the operator paid a fee to run the service, usually within tightly specified guidelines. Operators running a concession would not normally take commercial risks, although there are usually penalties and rewards in the contract.

Note that a railway "reporting period" is four weeks.

DOMESTIC PASSENGER TRAIN OPERATORS

The majority of passenger trains are operated by Train Operating Companies on fixed-term franchises or concessions. Expiry dates are shown in the list below:

Franchise	*Franchisee*	*Trading Name*
Caledonian Sleeper	Serco (until 31 March 2030)	**Caledonian Sleeper**
Chiltern	Arriva (Deutsche Bahn) (until 11 December 2021)	**Chiltern Railways**

There is an option to extend the franchise by 7 months to July 2022.

Cross Country	Arriva (Deutsche Bahn) (until 17 October 2020)	**CrossCountry**

In 2018 competition for the next franchise was stopped, pending the publication of a Rail Review by the Government.

Crossrail	MTR (until 27 May 2023)	**TfL Rail**

There is an option to extend the concession by 2 years to May 2025.

East Coast		**London North Eastern Railway**

Franchise awarded to Stagecoach/Virgin Trains in 2015 but was terminated just over 3 years later in 2018 (having originally been due to operate until 2023) after the franchise failed. Currently operated on an interim basis by the DfT's "Operator of Last Resort". It is due to be relet in the future as part of a new public/private East Coast partnership.

East Midlands	Abellio (until 21 August 2027)	**East Midlands Railway**

There is an option to extend the franchise by 2 years to August 2029.

East Anglia	Abellio (Netherlands Railways) (60%)/Mitsui Group (40%) (until 11 October 2025)	**Greater Anglia**

There is an option to extend the franchise by 1 year to October 2026.

Essex Thameside	Trenitalia (until 10 November 2029)	**c2c**

There is an option to extend the franchise by 6 months to May 2030.

Great Western	First Group (until 31 March 2020)	**Great Western Railway**

Direct Award extension expected to March 2022, with the option of a further 2 year extension to March 2024.

London Rail	Arriva (Deutsche Bahn) (until 25 May 2024)	**London Overground**

This is a concession and is different from other rail franchises, as fares and service levels are set by Transport for London instead of by the DfT. There is an option to extend the concession by 2 years to May 2026.

Merseyrail Electrics Serco (50%)/Abellio (Netherlands Railways) (50%) **Merseyrail**
(until 22 July 2028)
Under the control of Merseytravel PTE instead of the DfT. Franchise reviewed every five years to fit in with the Merseyside Local Transport Plan.

Northern Arriva (Deutsche Bahn) **Northern**
(until 31 March 2025)
There is an option to extend the franchise by 1 year to March 2026.

ScotRail Abellio (Netherlands Railways) **ScotRail**
(until 31 March 2022)
There is an option to extend the franchise by 3 years to March 2025.

South Eastern Govia (Go-Ahead/Keolis) **Southeastern**
(until 1 April 2020)
The franchise competition was scrapped in 2019. It will either be restarted (in which case another extension to Govia will be required) or the DfT will take over as "Operator of Last Resort" from 2020.

South Western First Group (70%)/MTR (30%) **South Western Railway**
(until 17 August 2024)
There is an option to extend the franchise by 11 months to July 2025.

Thameslink, Southern & Govia (Go-Ahead/Keolis) **Govia Thameslink Railway**
Great Northern (TSGN) (until 18 September 2021)
There is an option to extend the franchise by 2 years to September 2023.

Trans-Pennine Express First Group **TransPennine Express**
(until 31 March 2023)
There is an option to extend the franchise by 2 years to March 2025.

Wales & Borders KeolisAmey **Transport for Wales**
(until 15 October 2033)
Franchise procured by the Welsh Government.

West Coast Partnership Virgin Rail Group (Virgin/Stagecoach Group) **Virgin Trains**
(until 7 December 2019)
In August 2019 a consortium of First Group and Trenitalia won the new West Coast franchise, which will run until March 2031 and also include the first years of the planned HS2 services.

West Midlands Trains Abellio (70%)/JR East (15%)/Mitsui (15%) **West Midlands Railway/**
(until 31 March 2026) **London Northwestern**

There is an option to extend the franchise by 2 years to March 2028.

NON-FRANCHISED SERVICES

The following operators run non-franchised, or "open access" services
(* special seasonal services):

Operator	Trading Name	Route
Heathrow Airport Holdings	Heathrow Express	London Paddington–Heathrow Airport
Hull Trains (part of First)	Hull Trains	London King's Cross–Hull
Grand Central (part of Arriva)	Grand Central	London King's Cross–Sunderland/ Bradford Interchange
Locomotive Services (TOC)	Locomotive Services	
North Yorkshire Moors Railway Enterprises	North Yorkshire Moors Railway	Pickering–Grosmont–Whitby/ Battersby, Sheringham–Cromer*
South Yorkshire Supertram	Stagecoach Supertram	Meadowhall South–Rotherham Parkgate
Tyne & Wear PTE	Tyne & Wear Metro	Pelaw–Sunderland
Vintage Trains	Vintage Trains	Birmingham Snow Hill–Stratford-upon-Avon*
West Coast Railway Company	West Coast Railway Company	Fort William–Mallaig* York–Settle–Carlisle* Carnforth–York–Scarborough*

INTERNATIONAL PASSENGER OPERATORS

Eurostar International operates passenger services between London St
Pancras and mainland Europe. The company, established in 2010, is jointly
owned by SNCF (the national operator of France): 55%, SNCB (the national
operator of Belgium): 5% and Patina Rail: 40%. Patina Rail is made up of
Canadian-based Caisse de dépôt et placement du Québec (CDPG) and UK-
based Hermes Infrastructure (owning 30% and 10% respectively). This 40%
was previously owned by the UK Government until it was sold in 2015.

In addition, a service for the conveyance of accompanied road vehicles
through the Channel Tunnel is provided by the tunnel operating company,
Eurotunnel. All Eurotunnel services are operated in top-and-tail mode by
the powerful Class 9 Bo-Bo-Bo locomotives.

INTRODUCTION

This book contains details of all Electric Multiple Units, usually referred to as EMUs, which can run on Britain's national railway network.

The number of EMUs in operation has been steadily increasing in recent years as both more lines have been opened or have been electrified and as the number of passengers travelling on the network has increased. EMUs work a wide variety of services, from long distance Intercity (such as the Class 390 Pendolinos) to inter-urban and suburban duties.

LAYOUT OF INFORMATION

25 kV AC 50 Hz overhead EMUs and dual voltage EMUs are listed in numerical order of set numbers. Individual "loose" vehicles are listed in numerical order after vehicles formed into fixed formations.

750 V DC third rail EMUs are listed in numerical order of class number, then in numerical order of set number. Some of these use the former Southern Region four-digit set numbers. These are derived from theoretical six digit set numbers which are the four-digit set number prefixed by the first two numbers of the class.

Where sets or vehicles have been renumbered in recent years, former numbering detail is shown alongside current detail. Each entry is laid out as in the following example:

Set No.	Detail	Livery	Owner	Operator	Allocation	Formation
5912	*	**SS**	P	*SW*	WD	77835 62837 67400 77836

Codes: Codes are used to denote the livery, owner, operator and depot allocation of each Electric Multiple Unit. Details of these can be found in section 9 of this book. Where a unit or spare car is off-lease, the operator column is left blank.

Detail Differences: Detail differences which currently affect the areas and types of train which vehicles may work are shown, plus differences in interior layout. Where such differences occur within a class, these are shown either in the heading information or alongside the individual set or vehicle number.

Set Formations: Regular set formations are shown where these are normally maintained. Readers should note set formations might be temporarily varied from time to time to suit maintenance and/or operational requirements. Vehicles shown as "Spare" are not formed in any regular set formation.

Names: Only names carried with official sanction are listed. Names are shown in UPPER/lower case characters as actually shown on the name carried on the vehicle(s). Unless otherwise shown, complete units are regarded as named rather than just the individual car(s) which carry the name.

GENERAL INFORMATION

CLASSIFICATION AND NUMBERING

25 kV AC 50 Hz overhead and "Versatile" EMUs are classified in the series 300–399. 750 V DC third rail EMUs are classified in the series 400–599. More recently dual-voltage units have been numbered in the 700+ series and Hitachi IEP units in the 800–802 series Classes 800 and 802 are bi-mode units which can operate under both diesel or electric power.

Until 2014 EMU individual cars were numbered in the series 61000–78999, except for vehicles used on the Isle of Wight – which are numbered in a separate series, and the Class 378s, 380s and 395s, which took up the 38xxx and 39xxx series'.

For all new vehicles allocated by the Rolling Stock Library since 2014 6-digit vehicle numbers are being used.

Any vehicle constructed or converted to replace another vehicle following accident damage and carrying the same number as the original vehicle is denoted by the suffix[II] in this publication.

WHEEL ARRANGEMENT

A system whereby the number of powered axles on a bogie or frame is denoted by a letter (A = 1, B = 2, C= 3 etc) and the number of unpowered axles is denoted by a number is used in this publication. The letter "o" after a letter indicates that each axle is individually powered.

UNITS OF MEASUREMENT

Principal details and dimensions are quoted for each class in metric and/or imperial units as considered appropriate bearing in mind common UK usage.

All dimensions and weights are quoted for vehicles in an "as new" condition with all necessary supplies (eg oil, water, sand) on board. Dimensions are quoted in the order Length – Width. All lengths quoted are over buffers or couplers as appropriate. Where two lengths are quoted, the first refers to outer vehicles in a set and the second to inner vehicles. All width dimensions quoted are maxima. All weights are shown as metric tonnes (t = tonnes).

Bogie Types are quoted in the format motored/non-motored (eg BP20/BT13 denotes BP20 motored bogies and BT non-motored bogies).

Unless noted to the contrary, all vehicles listed have bar couplers at non-driving ends.

Traction motors power details refer to each motored car per unit.

Vehicles ordered under the auspices of BR were allocated a Lot (batch) number when ordered and these are quoted in class headings and sub-headings. Vehicles ordered since 1995 have no Lot Numbers, but the manufacturer and location that they were built is given.

OPERATING CODES

These codes are used by train operating company staff to describe the various different types of vehicles and normally appear on data panels on the inner (ie non driving) ends of vehicles.

A "B" prefix indicates a battery vehicle.
A "P" prefix indicates a trailer vehicle on which is mounted the pantograph, instead of the default case where the pantograph is mounted on a motor vehicle.

The first part of the code describes whether or not the car has a motor or a driving cab as follows:

DM Driving motor   DT Driving trailer   M Motor   T Trailer

The next letter is a "B" for cars with a brake compartment.
This is followed by the saloon details:

F First   S Standard   C Composite

Finally vehicles with a buffet or kitchen area are suffixed RB or RMB for a miniature buffet counter.

Where two vehicles of the same type are formed within the same unit, the above codes may be suffixed by (A) and (B) to differentiate between vehicles.

A composite is a vehicle containing both First and Standard Class accommodation, whilst a brake vehicle is a vehicle containing separate specific accommodation for the conductor.

ACCOMMODATION

The information given in class headings and sub-headings is in the form F/S nT (or TD) nW. For example 12/54 1T 1W denotes 12 First Class and 54 Standard Class seats, one toilet and one space for a wheelchair. A number in brackets (ie +2) denotes tip-up seats (in addition to the fixed seats). Tip-up seats in vestibules do not count. The seating layout of open saloons is shown as 2+1, 2+2 or 3+2 as the case may be. Where units have First Class accommodation as well as Standard Class and the layout is different for each class then these are shown separately prefixed by "1:" and "2:". TD denotes a universal access toilet suitable for use by a disabled person.

ABBREVIATIONS

The following abbreviations are used throughout this publication:
AC   Alternating Current.
BR   British Railways.

BSI	Bergische Stahl Industrie.
DC	Direct Current.
EMU	Electric Multiple Unit.
Hz	Hertz.
kN	kilonewtons.
kW	kilowatts.
LT	London Transport.
LUL	London Underground Limited.
m	metres.
mph	miles per hour.
SR	BR Southern Region.
V	volts.

NEW EMUS ON ORDER

Where possible all EMUs for which firm orders have been placed are
listed in this book, where numbers have been allocated. However there
are several orders for new EMUs for which the unit number and/or vehicle
number series' have not yet been confirmed. EMUs or bi/tri-mode units that
are on order but <u>are not shown in this book</u> are summarised in the table
below:

Class	Manufacturer	Operator	Quantity	Delivery dates
711[1]	Bombardier	c2c	6 x 10-car	2021
tbc[2]	Stadler	Transport for Wales	36 x 3-car	2021–22
tbc[3]	Stadler	Transport for Wales	17 x 4-car	2023
tbc[3]	Stadler	Transport for Wales	7 x 3-car	2023
tbc[4]	Hitachi	East Midlands Railway	33 x 5-car	2021–22
tbc[5]	Hitachi	First Group	5 x 5-car	2021

[1] Aventra units. Funded by Porterbrook.
[2] FLIRT bi-mode electric/battery multiple units.
[3] FLIRT tri-mode diesel/electric/battery multiple units.
[4] These units will be similar to the GWR and LNER IETs/Azumas but with
24 m bodies.
[5] On order for First Group's planned open access service on the East Coast
Main Line between King's Cross and Edinburgh.

1. 25 kV AC 50 Hz OVERHEAD & DUAL VOLTAGE UNITS

Except where otherwise stated, all units in this section operate on 25 kV AC 50 Hz overhead only.

CLASS 313   BREL YORK

Inner suburban units. All remaining Great Northern units withdrawn from normal service, and following a farewell tour are due for disposal by late 2019.

Formation: DMS–PTS–BDMS or DMS–TS–BDMS.
Systems: 25 kV AC overhead/750 V DC third rail.
Construction: Steel underframe, aluminium alloy body and roof.
Traction Motors: Four GEC G310AZ of 82.125 kW.
Wheel Arrangement: Bo-Bo + 2-2 + Bo-Bo.
Braking: Disc & rheostatic.   **Dimensions:** 20.33/20.18 x 2.82 m.
Bogies: BX1.   **Couplers:** Tightlock.
Gangways: Within unit + end doors. **Control System:** Camshaft.
Doors: Sliding.   **Maximum Speed:** 75 mph.
Seating Layout: Various, see sub-class headings.
Multiple Working: Within class.

Class 313/0. Standard Design. Refurbished with high-back seating (3+2 facing). Fitted with tripcocks for operating between Moorgate and Drayton Park.

DMS. Lot No. 30879 1976–77. –/74. 36.0 t.
PTS. Lot No. 30880 1976–77. –/83. 31.0 t.
BDMS. Lot No. 30885 1976–77. –/74. 37.5 t.

313033	**FU**	E	*GN*	HE	62561	71245	62625
313039	**FU**	E	*GN*	HE	62567	71251	62631
313047	**FU**	E	*GN*	HE	62575	71259	62639
313048	**FU**	E	*GN*	HE	62576	71260	62640
313049	**FU**	E	*GN*	HE	62577	71261	62641
313060	**FU**	E	*GN*	HE	62588	71272	62652
313061	**FU**	E	*GN*	HE	62589	71273	62653
313064	**FU**	E	*GN*	HE	62592	71276	62656

Class 313/1. Former London Overground unit. Original low back seating (3+2 facing). Fitted with tripcocks for operating between Moorgate and Drayton Park. Details as Class 313/0.

313134	**FU**	E	*GN*	HE	62562	71246	62626

Name (carried on PTS): 313134   City of London

Class 313/2. Southern units. Refurbished for Brighton Coastway services. Fitted with 2+2 mainly facing high-back seating. 750 V DC only (pantographs removed).

DMS. Lot No. 30879 1976–77. –/64. 37.0 t.
TS. Lot No. 30880 1976–77. –/64(+2). 31.0 t.
BDMS. Lot No. 30885 1976–77. –/64. 37.0 t.

313201	(313101)	**BG**	BN	*SN*	BI	62529	71213	62593
313202	(313102)	**SN**	BN	*SN*	BI	62530	71214	62594
313203	(313103)	**SN**	BN	*SN*	BI	62531	71215	62595
313204	(313104)	**SN**	BN	*SN*	BI	62532	71216	62596
313205	(313105)	**SN**	BN	*SN*	BI	62533	71217	62597
313206	(313106)	**SN**	BN	*SN*	BI	62534	71218	62598
313207	(313107)	**SN**	BN	*SN*	BI	62535	71219	62599
313208	(313108)	**SN**	BN	*SN*	BI	62536	71220	62600
313209	(313109)	**SN**	BN	*SN*	BI	62537	71221	62601
313210	(313110)	**SN**	BN	*SN*	BI	62538	71222	62602
313211	(313111)	**SN**	BN	*SN*	BI	62539	71223	62603
313212	(313112)	**SN**	BN	*SN*	BI	62540	71224	62604
313213	(313113)	**SN**	BN	*SN*	BI	62541	71225	62605
313214	(313114)	**SN**	BN	*SN*	BI	62542	71226	62606
313215	(313115)	**SN**	BN	*SN*	BI	62543	71227	62607
313216	(313116)	**SN**	BN	*SN*	BI	62544	71228	62608
313217	(313117)	**SN**	BN	*SN*	BI	62545	71229	62609
313219	(313119)	**SN**	BN	*SN*	BI	62547	71231	62611
313220	(313120)	**SN**	BN	*SN*	BI	62548	71232	62612

CLASS 314   BREL YORK

Inner suburban units. All remaining units to be withdrawn by the end of 2019.

Formation: DMS–PTS–DMS.
Construction: Steel underframe, aluminium alloy body and roof.
Traction Motors: Four GEC G310AZ (* Brush TM61-53) of 82.125 kW.
Wheel Arrangement: Bo-Bo + 2-2 + Bo-Bo.
Braking: Disc & rheostatic.   **Dimensions:** 20.33/20.18 x 2.82 m.
Bogies: BX1.   **Couplers:** Tightlock.
Gangways: Within unit + end doors.   **Control System:** Thyristor.
Doors: Sliding.   **Maximum Speed:** 70 mph.
Seating Layout: 3+2 low-back facing.
Multiple Working: Within class and with Class 315.

DMS. Lot No. 30912 1979. –/68. 34.5 t.
64588[II]. DMS. Lot No. 30908 1978–80. Rebuilt Railcare Glasgow 1996 from Class 507 No. 64426. The original 64588 was scrapped. –/74. 34.5 t.
PTS. Lot No. 30913 1979. –/76. 33.0 t.

314202	*	**SC**	SR	*SR*	GW	64585	71451	64586
314203	*	**SR**	SR	*SR*	GW	64587	71452	64588[II]
314204	*	**SR**	X		ZG	64589	71453	64590
314205	*	**SC**	SR	*SR*	GW	64591	71454	64592
314209		**SR**	SR	*SR*	GW	64599	71458	64600
314210		**SC**	SR	*SR*	GW	64601	71459	64602
314214		**SR**	SR	*SR*	GW	64609	71463	64610
314215		**SC**	SR		YO	64611	71464	64612
314216		**SC**	SR	*SR*	GW	64613	71465	64614

CLASS 315   BREL YORK

Inner suburban units.

Formation: DMS–TS–PTS–DMS.
Construction: Steel underframe, aluminium alloy body and roof.
Traction Motors: Four Brush TM61-53 (* GEC G310AZ) of 82.125 kW.
Wheel Arrangement: Bo-Bo + 2-2 + 2-2 + Bo-Bo.
Braking: Disc & rheostatic.   **Dimensions:** 20.18 x 2.82 m.
Bogies: BX1.   **Couplers:** Tightlock.
Gangways: Within unit + end doors.   **Control System:** Thyristor.
Doors: Sliding.   **Maximum Speed:** 75 mph.
Seating Layout: 3+2 low-back facing.
Multiple Working: Within class and with Class 314 and 317.

DMS. Lot No. 30902 1980–81. –/74. 38.2 t.
TS. Lot No. 30904 1980–81. –/86. 27.4 t.
PTS. Lot No. 30903 1980–81. –/75(+7) 2W. 33.8 t.

315 801	**LO**	E	*LO*	IL	64461	71281	71389	64462
315 802	**LO**	E	*LO*	IL	64463	71282	71390	64464
315 803	**LO**	E	*LO*	IL	64465	71283	71391	64466
315 804	**LO**	E	*LO*	IL	64467	71284	71392	64468
315 805	**LO**	E	*LO*	IL	64469	71285	71393	64470
315 806	**LO**	E	*LO*	IL	64471	71286	71394	64472
315 807	**LO**	E	*LO*	IL	64473	71287	71395	64474
315 808	**LO**	E	*LO*	IL	64475	71288	71396	64476
315 809	**LO**	E	*LO*	IL	64477	71289	71397	64478
315 810	**LO**	E	*LO*	IL	64479	71290	71398	64480
315 811	**LO**	E	*LO*	IL	64481	71291	71399	64482
315 812	**LO**	E	*LO*	IL	64483	71292	71400	64484
315 814	**LO**	E	*LO*	IL	64487	71294	71402	64488
315 815	**LO**	E	*LO*	IL	64489	71295	71403	64490
315 816	**LO**	E	*LO*	IL	64491	71296	71404	64492
315 817	**LO**	E	*LO*	IL	64493	71297	71405	64494
315 818	**TF**	E	*XR*	IL	64495	71298	71406	64496
315 819	**TF**	E	*XR*	IL	64497	71299	71407	64498
315 820	**TF**	E	*XR*	IL	64499	71300	71408	64500
315 821	**TF**	E	*XR*	IL	64501	71301	71409	64502
315 822	**TF**	E	*XR*	IL	64503	71302	71410	64504
315 823	**TF**	E	*XR*	IL	64505	71303	71411	64506
315 824	**TF**	E	*XR*	IL	64507	71304	71412	64508
315 825	**TF**	E	*XR*	IL	64509	71305	71413	64510
315 826	**TF**	E	*XR*	IL	64511	71306	71414	64512
315 827	**TF**	E	*XR*	IL	64513	71307	71415	64514
315 829	**TF**	E	*XR*	IL	64517	71309	71417	64518
315 830	**TF**	E	*XR*	IL	64519	71310	71418	64520
315 831	**TF**	E		ZN	64521	71311	71419	64522
315 833	**TF**	E	*XR*	IL	64525	71313	71421	64526
315 834	**TF**	E	*XR*	IL	64527	71314	71422	64528
315 836	**TF**	E	*XR*	IL	64531	71316	71424	64532
315 837	**TF**	E	*XR*	IL	64533	71317	71425	64534

315838		TF	E	XR	IL	64535	71318	71426	64536
315839		TF	E	XR	IL	64537	71319	71427	64538
315842	*	TF	E		ZN	64543	71322	71430	64544
315843	*	TF	E	XR	IL	64545	71323	71431	64546
315844	*	TF	E	XR	IL	64547	71324	71432	64548
315847	*	TF	E	XR	IL	64553	71327	71435	64554
315848	*	TF	E	XR	IL	64540	71328	71436	64556
315849	*	TF	E	XR	IL	64557	71329	71437	64558
315851	*	TF	E	XR	IL	64561	71331	71439	64562
315852	*	TF	E	XR	IL	64563	71332	71440	64564
315853	*	TF	E	XR	IL	64565	71333	71441	64566
315854	*	TF	E	XR	IL	64567	71334	71442	64568
315856	*	TF	E	XR	IL	64571	71336	71444	64572
315857	*	TF	E	XR	IL	64573	71337	71445	64574
315858	*	TF	E	LO	IL	64575	71338	71446	64576
315859	*	TF	E	XR	IL	64577	71339	71447	64578

Names (carried on DMS):

315817   Transport for London
315829   London Borough of Havering Celebrating 40 years

CLASS 317   BREL YORK/DERBY

Outer suburban units.

Formation: Various, see sub-class headings.
Construction: Steel.
Traction Motors: Four GEC G315BZ of 247.5 kW (except 317 722, see below).
Wheel Arrangement: 2-2 + Bo-Bo + 2-2 + 2-2.
Braking: Disc.   **Dimensions:** 19.83/20.18 x 2.82 m.
Bogies: BP20 (MS), BT13 (others).   **Couplers:** Tightlock.
Gangways: Throughout   **Control System:** Thyristor.
Doors: Sliding.   **Maximum Speed:** 100 mph.
Seating Layout: Various, see sub-class headings.
Multiple Working: Within class & with Classes 315, 318, 319, 320, 321, 322 and 323.

Class 317/1. Pressure ventilated.

Formation: DTS–MS–TC–DTS.
Seating Layout: 1: 2+2 facing, 2: 3+2 facing.

DTS(A). Lot No. 30955 York 1981–82. –/74. 29.5 t.
MS. Lot No. 30958 York 1981–82. –/79. 49.0 t.
TC. Lot No. 30957 Derby 1981–82. 22/46 2T. 29.0 t.
DTS(B). Lot No. 30956 York 1981–82. –/71. 29.5 t.

317337	TL	A	GA	IL	77036	62671	71613	77084
317338	TL	A	GA	IL	77037	62698	71614	77085
317339	TL	A	GA	IL	77038	62699	71615	77086
317340	TL	A	GA	IL	77039	62700	71616	77087
317341	TL	A	GA	IL	77040	62701	71617	77088
317342	TL	A	GA	IL	77041	62702	71618	77089

317343	**TL**	A	*GA*	IL	77042	62703	71619	77090
317344	**GA**	A	*GA*	IL	77029	62690	71620	77091
317345	**GA**	A	*GA*	IL	77044	62705	71621	77092
317346	**GA**	A	*GA*	IL	77045	62706	71622	77093
317347	**GA**	A	*GA*	IL	77046	62707	71623	77094
317348	**TL**	A	*GA*	IL	77047	62708	71624	77095

Names (carried on TC):

317345 Driver John Webb | 317348 Richard A Jenner

Class 317/5. Pressure ventilated. Units renumbered from Class 317/1 in 2005 for West Anglia Metro services. Refurbished with new upholstery and Passenger Information Systems. Details as Class 317/1.

The original DTS 77048 was written off after the Cricklewood accident of 1983. A replacement vehicle was built at Wolverton in 1987 and given the same number.

* Fitted with a universal access toilet to comply with the 2020 accessibility regulations. Full details awaited.

317501	*	**GA**	A	*GA*	IL	77024	62661	71577	77048^{II}
317502		**GA**	A	*GA*	IL	77001	62662	71578	77049
317503		**GA**	A	*GA*	IL	77002	62663	71579	77050
317504	*	**GA**	A	*GA*	IL	77003	62664	71580	77051
317505		**GA**	A	*GA*	IL	77004	62665	71581	77052
317506	*	**GA**	A	*GA*	IL	77005	62666	71582	77053
317507		**GA**	A	*GA*	IL	77006	62667	71583	77054
317508		**GA**	A	*GA*	IL	77010	62697	71587	77058
317509		**GA**	A	*GA*	IL	77011	62672	71588	77059
317510		**GA**	A	*GA*	IL	77012	62673	71589	77060
317511		**GA**	A	*GA*	IL	77014	62675	71591	77062
317512		**GA**	A	*GA*	IL	77015	62676	71592	77063
317513		**GA**	A	*GA*	IL	77016	62677	71593	77064
317514		**GA**	A	*GA*	IL	77017	62678	71594	77065
317515		**GA**	A	*GA*	IL	77019	62680	71596	77067

Name (carried on TC): 317507 University of Cambridge 800 Years 1209–2009

Class 317/6. Convection heating. Units converted from Class 317/2 by Railcare, Wolverton 1998–99 with Chapman seating.

Formation: DTS–MS–TS–DTC.
Seating Layout: 2+2 facing.

77200–219. DTS. Lot No. 30994 York 1985–86. –/64. 29.5 t.
77280–283. DTS. Lot No. 31007 York 1987. –/64. 29.5 t.
62846–865. MS. Lot No. 30996 York 1985–86. –/71. 49.0 t.
62886–889. MS. Lot No. 31009 York 1987. –/71. 49.0 t.
71734–753. TS. Lot No. 30997 York 1985–86. –/60(+3) 2T. 29.0 t.
71762–765. TS. Lot No. 31010 York 1987. –/60(+3) 2T. 29.0 t.
77220–239. DTC. Lot No. 30995 York 1985–86. 24/36. 29.5 t.
77284–287. DTC. Lot No. 31008 York 1987. 24/36. 29.5 t.

317649	**GA**	A	*GA*	IL	77200	62846	71734	77220

317650	**GA**	A	*GA*	IL	77201	62847	71735	77221
317651	**GA**	A	*GA*	IL	77202	62848	71736	77222
317652	**GA**	A	*GA*	IL	77203	62849	71739	77223
317653	**GA**	A	*GA*	IL	77204	62850	71738	77224
317654	**GA**	A	*GA*	IL	77205	62851	71737	77225
317655	**GA**	A	*GA*	IL	77206	62852	71740	77226
317656	**NC**	A	*GA*	IL	77207	62853	71742	77227
317657	**NC**	A	*GA*	IL	77208	62854	71741	77228
317658	**GA**	A	*GA*	IL	77209	62855	71743	77229
317659	**GA**	A	*GA*	IL	77210	62856	71744	77230
317660	**GA**	A	*GA*	IL	77211	62857	71745	77231
317661	**GA**	A	*GA*	IL	77212	62858	71746	77232
317662	**GA**	A	*GA*	IL	77213	62859	71747	77233
317663	**GA**	A		EP	77214	62860	71748	77234
317664	**GA**	A	*GA*	IL	77215	62861	71749	77235
317665	**GA**	A	*GA*	IL	77216	62862	71750	77236
317666	**NC**	A	*GA*	IL	77217	62863	71752	77237
317667	**GA**	A	*GA*	IL	77218	62864	71751	77238
317668	**GA**	A	*GA*	IL	77219	62865	71753	77239
317669	**NC**	A		EP	77280	62886	71762	77284
317670	**GA**	A	*GA*	IL	77281	62887	71763	77285
317671	**NC**	A	*GA*	IL	77282	62888	71764	77286
317672	**GA**	A	*GA*	IL	77283	62889	71765	77287

Name (carried on DTC): 317654   Richard Wells

Class 317/7. Units converted from Class 317/1 by Railcare, Wolverton 2000 for Stansted Express services between London Liverpool Street and Stansted. Air conditioning. Fitted with luggage stacks. Displaced from Stansted services in 2011 by Class 379s – most units are now operated by London Overground. Toilets have been locked out of use.

* 317722 received new Bombardier MJA 280-8 AC traction motors as part of an Angel trial. Two vehicles (77021 and 62682, now in **GA** livery) also received an interior refurbishment with new Fainsa seating whilst the other two vehicles were left in their Stansted Express condition (still in **NX** livery).

Formation: DTS–MS–TS–DTC.
Seating Layout: 1: 2+1 facing, 2: 2+2 facing.

DTS. Lot No. 30955 York 1981–82. –/52 + catering point. 31.4 t.
MS. Lot No. 30958 York 1981–82. –/62 (* –/64). 51.3 t.
TS. Lot No. 30957 Derby 1981–82. –/42(+5) 1TD 1T 1W. 30.2 t.
DTC. Lot No. 30956 York 1981–82. 22/16 + catering point. 31.6 t.

317708		**LO**	A	*LO*	IL	77007	62668	71584	77055
317709		**LO**	A	*LO*	IL	77008	62669	71585	77056
317710		**LO**	A	*LO*	IL	77009	62670	71586	77057
317714		**LO**	A	*LO*	IL	77013	62674	71590	77061
317719		**LO**	A	*LO*	IL	77018	62679	71595	77066
317722	*	**GA/NX**	A		EP	77021	62682	71598	77069
317729		**LO**	A	*LO*	IL	77022	62683	71599	77070
317729		**LO**	A	*LO*	IL	77028	62689	71605	77076
317732		**LO**	A	*LO*	IL	77031	62692	71608	77079

Class 317/8. Pressure Ventilated. Units refurbished and renumbered from Class 317/1 in 2005–06 at Wabtec, Doncaster for use on Stansted Express services. Displaced from Stansted services in 2011. Toilets have been locked out of use on London Overground units.

Formation: DTS–MS–TC–DTS.
Seating Layout: 1: 2+2 facing, 2: 3+2 facing.

DTS(A). Lot No. 30955 York 1981–82. –/66. 29.5 t.
MS. Lot No. 30958 York 1981–82. –/71. 49.0 t.
TC. Lot No. 30957 Derby 1981–82. 20/42 2T († –/62 2T). 29.0 t.
DTS(B). Lot No. 30956 York 1981–82. –/66. 29.5 t.

317881		**GA**	A	*GA*	IL	77020	62681	71597	77068
317882		**GA**	A	*GA*	IL	77023	62684	71600	77071
317883		**GA**	A	*GA*	IL	77000	62685	71601	77072
317884		**GA**	A	*GA*	IL	77025	62686	71602	77073
317885		**GA**	A	*GA*	IL	77026	62687	71603	77074
317886		**GA**	A	*GA*	IL	77027	62688	71604	77075
317887	†	**LO**	A	*LO*	IL	77043	62704	71606	77077
317888	†	**LO**	A	*LO*	IL	77030	62691	71607	77078
317889	†	**LO**	A	*LO*	IL	77032	62693	71609	77080
317890	†	**LO**	A	*LO*	IL	77033	62694	71610	77081
317891	†	**LO**	A	*LO*	IL	77034	62695	71611	77082
317892	†	**LO**	A	*LO*	IL	77035	62696	71612	77083 Ilford Depot

CLASS 318   BREL YORK

Outer suburban units. Fitted with a universal access toilet to comply with the 2020 accessibility regulations.

Formation: DTS–MS–DTS.
Construction: Steel.
Traction Motors: Four Brush TM 2141 of 268 kW.
Wheel Arrangement: 2-2 + Bo-Bo + 2-2.
Braking: Disc.   **Dimensions:** 19.83/19.92 x 2.82 m.
Bogies: BP20 (MS), BT13 (others).   **Couplers:** Tightlock.
Gangways: Within unit.   **Control System:** Thyristor.
Doors: Sliding.   **Maximum Speed:** 90 mph.
Seating Layout: 3+2 facing.
Multiple Working: Within class & with Classes 317, 319, 320, 321, 322 and 323.

77240–259. DTS. Lot No. 30999 1985–86. –/55 1TD 2W. 32.0 t.
77288. DTS. Lot No. 31020 1987. –/55 1TD 2W. 32.0 t.
62866–885. MS. Lot No. 30998 1985–86. –/79. 53.0 t.
62890. MS. Lot No. 31019 1987. –/79. 53.0 t.
77260–279. DTS. Lot No. 31000 1985–86. –/69(+2). 31.6 t.
77289. DTS. Lot No. 31021 1987. –/69(+2). 31.6 t.

318250	**SR**	E	*SR*	GW	77240	62866	77260
318251	**SR**	E	*SR*	GW	77241	62867	77261
318252	**SR**	E	*SR*	GW	77242	62868	77262
318253	**SR**	E	*SR*	GW	77243	62869	77263
318254	**SR**	E	*SR*	GW	77244	62870	77264

318255	**SR**	E	*SR*	GW	77245	62871	77265
318256	**SR**	E	*SR*	GW	77246	62872	77266
318257	**SR**	E	*SR*	GW	77247	62873	77267
318258	**SR**	E	*SR*	GW	77248	62874	77268
318259	**SR**	E	*SR*	GW	77249	62875	77269
318260	**SR**	E	*SR*	GW	77250	62876	77270
318261	**SR**	E	*SR*	GW	77251	62877	77271
318262	**SR**	E	*SR*	GW	77252	62878	77272
318263	**SR**	E	*SR*	GW	77253	62879	77273
318264	**SR**	E	*SR*	GW	77254	62880	77274
318265	**SR**	E	*SR*	GW	77255	62881	77275
318266	**SR**	E	*SR*	GW	77256	62882	77276
318267	**SR**	E	*SR*	GW	77257	62883	77277
318268	**SR**	E	*SR*	GW	77258	62884	77278
318269	**SR**	E	*SR*	GW	77259	62885	77279
318270	**SR**	E	*SR*	GW	77288	62890	77289

CLASS 319   BREL YORK

Express and outer suburban units. Units shown * or † have a universal access toilet to comply with the 2020 accessibility regulations. Some units are being rebuilt as bi-modes and are now numbered in the Class 769 or Class 799 series.

Formation: Various, see sub-class headings.
Systems: 25 kV AC overhead/750 V DC third rail.
Construction: Steel.
Traction Motors: Four GEC G315BZ of 268 kW.
Wheel Arrangement: 2-2 + Bo-Bo + 2-2 + 2-2.
Braking: Disc.   **Dimensions:** 20.17/20.16 x 2.82 m.
Bogies: P7-4 (MS), T3-7 (others).   **Couplers:** Tightlock.
Gangways: Within unit + end doors. **Control System:** GTO chopper.
Doors: Sliding.   **Maximum Speed:** 100 mph.
Seating Layout: Various, see sub-class headings.
Multiple Working: Within class & with Classes 317, 318, 320, 321, 322 and 323.

Class 319/0. DTS–MS–TS–DTS. 319002/003/006/007/008 (plus four other units to be identified) are being converted to Class 769 bi-mode units for Transport for Wales.

Seating Layout: 3+2 facing.

DTS(A). Lot No. 31022 (odd nos.) 1987–88. –/82 (* –/79). 28.2 t (* 30.7 t).
MS. Lot No. 31023 1987–88. –/82 (* –/81). 49.2 t (* 50.9 t).
TS. Lot No. 31024 1987–88. –/77 2T (* –/63 1TD 2W), † –/64 1TD 2W). 31.0 t (*† 32.5 t).
DTS(B). Lot No. 31025 (even nos.) 1987–88. –/78 (* –/79). 28.1 t (* 30.0 t).

319003	*	**TL**	P		LB	77295	62893	71774	77294
319004		**TL**	P		LM	77297	62894	71775	77296
319005	*	**TL**	P	*WM*	NN	77299	62895	71776	77298
319006	*	**TL**	P		LB	77301	62896	71777	77300
319007	*	**TL**	P		ZN	77303	62897	71778	77302

319009		**TL**	P		LM	77307	62899	71780	77306
319010		**TL**	P		LM	77309	62900	71781	77308
319011		**TL**	P		LM	77311	62901	71782	77310
319012	*	**TL**	P	*WM*	NN	77313	62902	71783	77312
319013	†	**LM**	P	*WM*	NN	77315	62903	71784	77314

Names (carried on TS):

319001 Driver Mick Winnett	319011 John Ruskin College
319009 Coquelles	

Class 319/2. DTS–MS–TS–DTC. Units converted from Class 319/0.

Seating Layout: 1: 2+1 facing, 2: 2+2/3+2 facing.

DTS. Lot No. 31022 (odd nos.) 1987–88. –/64. 30.0 t.
MS. Lot No. 31023 1987–88. –/73. 51.0 t.
TS. Lot No. 31024 1987–88. –/52 1TD 1T. 31.0 t.
DTC. Lot No. 31025 (even nos.) 1987–88. 18/36. 30.0 t.

319214	*	**TL**	P	*WM*	NN	77317	62904	71785	77316
319215	*	**TL**	P	*WM*	NN	77319	62905	71786	77318
319216	*	**LM**	P	*WM*	NN	77321	62906	71787	77320
319217	*	**TL**	P	*WM*	NN	77323	62907	71788	77322 Brighton
319218	*	**TL**	P	*WM*	NN	77325	62908	71789	77324
319219	*	**TL**	P	*WM*	NN	77327	62909	71790	77326
319220	*	**TL**	P	*WM*	NN	77329	62910	71791	77328

Class 319/3. DTS–MS–TS–DTS. Converted from Class 319/1 by replacing First Class seats with Standard Class seats.

Refurbished with a new universal access toilet to comply with the 2020 accessibility regulations, except 319373.

Seating Layout: 3+2 facing.

DTS(A). Lot No. 31063 1990. –/79. 29.0 t.
MS. Lot No. 31064 1990. –/81. 50.6 t.
TS. Lot No. 31065 1990. –/64 1TD 2W. 31.0 t.
DTS(B). Lot No. 31066 1990. –/79. 29.7 t.

319361	*	**NR**	P	*NO*	AN	77459	63043	71929	77458
319362	*	**NR**	P	*NO*	AN	77461	63044	71930	77460
319363	*	**NR**	P	*NO*	AN	77463	63045	71931	77462
319364	*	**NR**	P	*NO*	AN	77465	63046	71932	77464
319365	*	**NR**	P	*NO*	AN	77467	63047	71933	77466
319366	*	**NR**	P	*NO*	AN	77469	63048	71934	77468
319367	*	**NR**	P	*NO*	AN	77471	63049	71935	77470
319368	*	**NR**	P	*NO*	AN	77473	63050	71936	77472
319369	*	**NR**	P	*NO*	AN	77475	63051	71937	77474
319370	*	**NR**	P	*NO*	AN	77477	63052	71938	77476
319371	*	**NR**	P	*NO*	AN	77479	63053	71939	77478
319372	*	**TL**	P	*NO*	AN	77481	63054	71940	77480
319373		**TL**	P	*NO*	AN	77483	63055	71941	77482
319374	*	**NR**	P	*NO*	AN	77485	63056	71942	77484
319375	*	**NR**	P	*NO*	AN	77487	63057	71943	77486

319376	*	NR	P	NO	AN	77489	63058	71944	77488
319377	*	NR	P	NO	AN	77491	63059	71945	77490
319378	*	NR	P	NO	AN	77493	63060	71946	77492
319379	*	NR	P	NO	AN	77495	63061	71947	77494
319380	*	NR	P	NO	AN	77497	63062	71948	77496
319381	*	NR	P	NO	AN	77973	63093	71979	77974
319382	*	NR	P	NO	AN	77975	63094	71980	77976
319383	*	NR	P	NO	AN	77977	63095	71981	77978
319384	*	NR	P	NO	AN	77979	63096	71982	77980
319385	*	NR	P	NO	AN	77981	63097	71983	77982
319386	*	NR	P	NO	AN	77983	63098	71984	77984

Class 319/4. DTC–MS–TS–DTS. Converted from Class 319/0. Refurbished with carpets. DTS(A) converted to composite.

Eight units (319424/431/434/442/448/450/456/458) have been or are being converted to Class 769 bi-mode units for Northern (see Class 769).

319422/423/425/427/428/430/432/435–440/443/445/447/449/452/459 are to be converted to Class 769 bi-mode units for Great Western Railway.

Non-standard livery: 319 454 Porterbrook Innovation Hub (blue).

Seating Layout: 1: 2+1 facing 2: 2+2/3+2 facing.

77331–381. DTC. Lot No. 31022 (odd nos.) 1987–88. 12/51 (* 12/50). 30.0t (* 31.0 t).
77431–457. DTC. Lot No. 31038 (odd nos.) 1988. 12/51 (* 12/50). 30.0t (* 31.0 t).
62911–936. MS. Lot No. 31023 1987–88. –/74 (* –/75). 49.2 t (* 52.4 t).
62961–974. MS. Lot No. 31039 1988. –/74 (* –/75). 49.2 t (* 52.4 t).
71792–817. TS. Lot No. 31024 1987–88. –/67 2T (* –/58 1TD 2W). 31.0 t (* 33.7 t).
71866–879. TS. Lot No. 31040 1988. –67 2T (* –/58 1TD 2W). 31.0 t (* 33.7 t).
77330–380. DTS. Lot No. 31025 (even nos.) 1987–88. –/71 1W (* –/73). 28.1 t (* 30.7 t).
77430–456. DTS. Lot No. 31041 (even nos.) 1988. –/71 1W (* –/73). 28.1 t (* 30.7 t).

319421	*	TL	P		LM	77331	62911	71792	77330
319422	*	TL	P		LB	77333	62912	71793	77332
319423	*	TL	P		ZN	77335	62913	71794	77334
319425	*	TL	P		LM	77339	62915	71796	77338
319426	*	NR	P		LB	77341	62916	71797	77340
319427	*	TL	P		ZN	77343	62917	71798	77342
319428	*	TL	P		LM	77345	62918	71799	77344
319429	*	LM	P	WM	NN	77347	62919	71800	77346
319430	*	TL	P		LM	77349	62920	71801	77348
319432	*	TL	P		LM	77353	62922	71803	77352
319433	*	LM	P	WM	NN	77355	62923	71804	77354
319435	*	TL	P		ZN	77359	62925	71806	77358
319436	*	TL	P		LM	77361	62926	71807	77360
319437	*	TL	P		LB	77363	62927	71808	77362
319438	*	TL	P		LM	77365	62928	71809	77364
319439	*	TL	P		ZN	77367	62929	71810	77366
319440	*	TL	P		RG	77369	62930	71811	77368
319441	*	LM	P	WM	NN	77371	62931	71812	77370
319443	*	TL	P		LB	77375	62933	71814	77374
319444	*	TL	P		ZA	77377	62934	71815	77376

319445	*	TL	P		ZN	77379	62935	71816	77378
319446	*	TL	P		ZN	77381	62936	71817	77380
319447	*	TL	P		ZN	77431	62961	71866	77430
319449	*	TL	P		RG	77435	62963	71868	77434
319451		FU	P		LM	77439	62965	71870	77438
319452	*	TL	P		LM	77441	62966	71871	77440
319453		FU	P		LM	77443	62967	71872	77442
319454		O	P		LM	77445	62968	71873	77444
319455		FU	P		LM	77447	62969	71874	77446
319457	*	LM	P	*WM*	NN	77451	62971	71876	77450
319459	*	TL	P		ZN	77455	62973	71878	77454
319460	*	LM	P	*WM*	NN	77457	62974	71879	77456

Name (carried on TS): 319444   City of St Albans

CLASS 320   BREL YORK

Suburban units. All 320/3s refurbished 2011–13 and fitted with a new universal access toilet to comply with the 2020 accessibility regulations. In 2016–19 ScotRail received 320401/403/404/411–418/420 (ex-Class 321s), reformed as 3-cars and also refurbished with a new universal access toilet.

Formation: DTS–MS–DTS.
Construction: Steel
Traction Motors: Four Brush TM2141B of 268 kW.
Wheel Arrangement: 2-2 + Bo-Bo + 2-2.
Braking: Disc.   **Dimensions:** 19.95 x 2.82 m.
Bogies: P7-4 (MS), T3-7 (others).   **Couplers:** Tightlock.
Gangways: Within unit.   **Control System:** Thyristor.
Doors: Sliding.   **Maximum Speed:** 90 mph.
Seating Layout: 3+2 facing.
Multiple Working: Within class & with Classes 317, 318, 319, 321, 322 and 323.

Class 320/3. Original build.

DTS(A). Lot No. 31060 1990. –/51(+4) 1TD 2W. 31.7 t.
MS. Lot No. 31062 1990. –/78. 52.6 t.
DTS(B). Lot No. 31061 1990. –/73(+2). 31.6 t.

320301	SR	E	*SR*	GW	77899	63021	77921
320302	SR	E	*SR*	GW	77900	63022	77922
320303	SR	E	*SR*	GW	77901	63023	77923
320304	SR	E	*SR*	GW	77902	63024	77924
320305	SR	E	*SR*	GW	77903	63025	77925
320306	SR	E	*SR*	GW	77904	63026	77926
320307	SR	E	*SR*	GW	77905	63027	77927
320308	SR	E	*SR*	GW	77906	63028	77928
320309	SR	E	*SR*	GW	77907	63029	77929
320310	SR	E	*SR*	GW	77908	63030	77930
320311	SR	E	*SR*	GW	77909	63031	77931
320312	SR	E	*SR*	GW	77910	63032	77932
320313	SR	E	*SR*	GW	77911	63033	77933

320314	**SR**	E	*SR*	GW	77912	63034	77934
320315	**SR**	E	*SR*	GW	77913	63035	77935
320316	**SR**	E	*SR*	GW	77914	63036	77936
320317	**SR**	E	*SR*	GW	77915	63037	77937
320318	**SR**	E	*SR*	GW	77916	63038	77938
320319	**SR**	E	*SR*	GW	77917	63039	77939
320320	**SR**	E	*SR*	GW	77918	63040	77940
320321	**SR**	E	*SR*	GW	77919	63041	77941
320322	**SR**	E	*SR*	GW	77920	63042	77942

Class 320/4. Former London Midland Class 321s reduced to 3-car formation and refurbished as Class 320/4s by Wabtec Doncaster or Wabtec Kilmarnock 2015–19.

The original vehicles 71966 and 77960 from 321418 (now 320418) and 78114 and 63082 from 321420 (now 320420) were written off after the Watford Junction accident in 1996. The undamaged vehicles were formed together as 321418 whilst four new vehicles were built in 1997, taking the same numbers as the scrapped vehicles, and these became the second 321420.

DTS(A). Lot No. 31060 1990. –/54(+4) 1TD 2W. 32.0 t.
MS. Lot No. 31062 1990. –/79. 52.2 t.
DTS(B). Lot No. 31061 1990. –/74(+2). 32.0 t.

320401	(321401)	**SR**	E	*SR*	GW	78095	63063	77943
320403	(321403)	**SR**	E	*SR*	GW	78097	63065	77945
320404	(321404)	**SR**	E	*SR*	GW	78098	63066	77946
320411	(321411)	**SR**	E	*SR*	GW	78105	63073	77953
320412	(321412)	**SR**	E	*SR*	GW	78106	63074	77954
320413	(321413)	**SR**	E	*SR*	GW	78107	63075	77955
320414	(321414)	**SR**	E	*SR*	GW	78108	63076	77956
320415	(321415)	**SR**	E	*SR*	GW	78109	63077	77957
320416	(321416)	**SR**	E	*SR*	GW	78110	63078	77958
320417	(321417)	**SR**	E	*SR*	GW	78111	63079	77959
320418	(321418)	**SR**	E	*SR*	GW	78112	63080	77962
320420	(321420)	**SR**	E	*SR*	GW	78114[II]	63082[II]	77960[II]

CLASS 321   BREL YORK

Outer suburban units.

Formation: DTC (DTS on Class 321/9)–MS–TS–DTS.
Construction: Steel.
Traction Motors: Four Brush TM2141C of 268 kW (* Four TSA010163 AC motors of 300 kW).
Wheel Arrangement: 2-2 + Bo-Bo + 2-2 + 2-2.
Braking: Disc (* and regenerative). **Dimensions:** 19.95 x 2.82 m.
Bogies: P7-4 (MS), T3-7 (others). **Couplers:** Tightlock.
Gangways: Within unit.
Control System: Thyristor (* IGBT Inverter).
Doors: Sliding. **Maximum Speed:** 100 mph.
Seating Layout: 1: 2+2 facing, 2: 3+2 facing.
Multiple Working: Within class & with Classes 317, 318, 319, 320, 322 and 323.

Class 321/3.

* "Renatus" rebuilt units with completely new interiors, air conditioning and Quantum seating, still arranged to a 3+2 layout in Standard Class. Fitted with new TSA AC traction motors.

DTC. Lot No. 31053 1988–90. 16/57 (321 347–366 16/56) (* 16/31(+4) 1TD 2W. 29.7 t (* 34.1 t).
MS. Lot No. 31054 1988–90. –/82 (* –/80). 51.5 t (* 53.8 t).
TS. Lot No. 31055 1988–90. –/75 2T (* –/78 1T). 29.1 t (* 31.7 t).
DTS. Lot No. 31056 1988–90. –/78 (* –/76). 29.7 t (* 32.8 t.)

321 301	*	**GR**	E	*GA*	IL	78049	62975	71880	77853
321 302	*	**GR**	E	*GA*	IL	78050	62976	71881	77854
321 303	*	**GR**	E	*GA*	IL	78051	62977	71882	77855
321 304	*	**GR**	E	*GA*	IL	78052	62978	71883	77856
321 305	*	**GR**	E	*GA*	IL	78053	62979	71884	77857
321 306	*	**GR**	E	*GA*	IL	78054	62980	71885	77858
321 307	*	**GR**	E	*GA*	IL	78055	62981	71886	77859
321 308	*	**GR**	E	*GA*	IL	78056	62982	71887	77860
321 309	*	**GR**	E	*GA*	IL	78057	62983	71888	77861
321 310	*	**GR**	E	*GA*	IL	78058	62984	71889	77862
321 311	*	**GR**	E	*GA*	IL	78059	62985	71890	77863
321 312	*	**GR**	E	*GA*	IL	78060	62986	71891	77864
321 313	*	**GR**	E	*GA*	IL	78061	62987	71892	77865
321 314	*	**GR**	E	*GA*	IL	78062	62988	71893	77866
321 315	*	**GR**	E	*GA*	IL	78063	62989	71894	77867
321 316	*	**GR**	E	*GA*	IL	78064	62990	71895	77868
321 317	*	**GR**	E	*GA*	IL	78065	62991	71896	77869
321 318	*	**GR**	E	*GA*	IL	78066	62992	71897	77870
321 319	*	**GR**	E	*GA*	IL	78067	62993	71898	77871
321 320	*	**GR**	E	*GA*	IL	78068	62994	71899	77872
321 321	*	**GR**	E	*GA*	IL	78069	62995	71900	77873
321 322	*	**GR**	E	*GA*	IL	78070	62996	71901	77874
321 323	*	**GR**	E	*GA*	IL	78071	62997	71902	77875
321 324	*	**GR**	E	*GA*	IL	78072	62998	71903	77876
321 325	*	**GR**	E	*GA*	IL	78073	62999	71904	77877
321 326	*	**GR**	E	*GA*	IL	78074	63000	71905	77878
321 327	*	**GR**	E	*GA*	IL	78075	63001	71906	77879
321 328	*	**GR**	E	*GA*	IL	78076	63002	71907	77880
321 329	*	**GR**	E	*GA*	IL	78077	63003	71908	77881
321 330	*	**GR**	E	*GA*	IL	78078	63004	71909	77882
321 331		**NC**	E	*GA*	IL	78079	63005	71910	77883
321 332		**NC**	E	*GA*	IL	78080	63006	71911	77884
321 333		**NC**	E	*GA*	IL	78081	63007	71912	77885
321 334		**NC**	E	*GA*	IL	78082	63008	71913	77886
321 335		**NC**	E	*GA*	IL	78083	63009	71914	77887
321 336		**NC**	E	*GA*	IL	78084	63010	71915	77888
321 337		**NC**	E	*GA*	IL	78085	63011	71916	77889
321 338		**NC**	E	*GA*	IL	78086	63012	71917	77890
321 339		**NC**	E	*GA*	IL	78087	63013	71918	77891
321 340		**NC**	E	*GA*	IL	78088	63014	71919	77892

321 341	**NC**	E	*GA*	IL	78089	63015	71920	77893
321 342	**NC**	E	*GA*	IL	78090	63016	71921	77894
321 343	**NC**	E	*GA*	IL	78091	63017	71922	77895
321 344	**NC**	E	*GA*	IL	78092	63018	71923	77896
321 345	**NC**	E	*GA*	IL	78093	63019	71924	77897
321 346	**NC**	E	*GA*	IL	78094	63020	71925	77898
321 347	**NC**	E	*GA*	IL	78131	63105	71991	78280
321 348	**NC**	E	*GA*	IL	78132	63106	71992	78281
321 349	**NC**	E	*GA*	IL	78133	63107	71993	78282
321 350	**NC**	E	*GA*	IL	78134	63108	71994	78283
321 351	**NC**	E	*GA*	IL	78135	63109	71995	78284
321 352	**NC**	E	*GA*	IL	78136	63110	71996	78285
321 353	**NC**	E	*GA*	IL	78137	63111	71997	78286
321 354	**NC**	E	*GA*	IL	78138	63112	71998	78287
321 355	**NC**	E	*GA*	IL	78139	63113	71999	78288
321 356	**NC**	E	*GA*	IL	78140	63114	72000	78289
321 357	**NC**	E	*GA*	IL	78141	63115	72001	78290
321 358	**NC**	E	*GA*	IL	78142	63116	72002	78291
321 359	**GA**	E	*GA*	IL	78143	63117	72003	78292
321 360	**NC**	E	*GA*	IL	78144	63118	72004	78293
321 361	**GA**	E	*GA*	IL	78145	63119	72005	78294
321 362	**GA**	E	*GA*	IL	78146	63120	72006	78295
321 363	**GA**	E	*GA*	IL	78147	63121	72007	78296
321 364	**GA**	E	*GA*	IL	78148	63122	72008	78297
321 365	**GA**	E	*GA*	IL	78149	63123	72009	78298
321 366	**GA**	E	*GA*	IL	78150	63124	72010	78299

Names (carried on TS):

321 334 Amsterdam
321 336 GEOFFREY FREEMAN ALLEN
321 342 R. Barnes
321 343 RSA RAILWAY STUDY ASSOCIATION
321 351 London Southend Airport
321 361 Phoenix

Class 321/4.

The DTCs of 321 421–437 have had 12 First Class seats declassified.

Units 321 401/403/404/411–418/420 have been refurbished as Class 320/4 3-car units for ScotRail (their TS vehicles are stored or have been scrapped).

† 321 448 received an interior refurbishment as an Eversholt demonstrator unit. Fitted with two different types of interior using seats supplied by Quantum it acted as the pilot unit for the "Renatus" work being carried out on the Class 321/3s. 78130 and 63104 have a "suburban" interior with a 3+2 seating layout and 78279 and 71990 have a "metro" interior with 2+2 seating. It is also fitted with the new TSA AC traction motors.

Non-standard livery: 321 448 Eversholt demonstrator (silver with blue doors and multi-coloured stripes).

DTC. Lot No. 31067 1989–90. 28/40 (321 421–437 16/52, 321 438–447 16/56). 29.8 t. († 16/30(+4) 1TD 2W 33.9 t).
MS. Lot No. 31068 1989–90. –/79 (321 438–447 –/82). 51.6 t († –/82. 54.0 t).
TS. Lot No. 31069 1989–90. –/74 2T (321 438–447 –/75 2T). 29.2 t († –/62 1T. 31.7 t).
DTS. Lot No. 31070 1989–90. –/78. 29.8 t. († –/58. 33.2 t).

321 402	**FB**	E	*GA*	IL	78096	63064	71950	77944
321 405	**FB**	E	*GA*	IL	78099	63067	71953	77947
321 406	**FB**	E	*GA*	IL	78100	63068	71954	77948
321 407	**FB**	E	*GA*	IL	78101	63069	71955	77949
321 408	**FB**	E	*GA*	IL	78102	63070	71956	77950
321 409	**FB**	E	*GA*	IL	78103	63071	71957	77951
321 410	**FB**	E	*GA*	IL	78104	63072	71958	77952
321 419	**FB**	E	*GA*	IL	78113	63081	71967	77961
321 421	**NC**	E	*GA*	IL	78115	63083	71969	77963
321 422	**NC**	E	*GA*	IL	78116	63084	71970	77964
321 423	**NC**	E	*GA*	IL	78117	63085	71971	77965
321 424	**NX**	E	*GA*	IL	78118	63086	71972	77966
321 425	**NC**	E	*GA*	IL	78119	63087	71973	77967
321 426	**NX**	E	*GA*	IL	78120	63088	71974	77968
321 427	**NX**	E	*GA*	IL	78121	63089	71975	77969
321 428	**NX**	E	*GA*	IL	78122	63090	71976	77970
321 429	**NX**	E	*GA*	IL	78123	63091	71977	77971
321 430	**NX**	E	*GA*	IL	78124	63092	71978	77972
321 431	**NX**	E	*GA*	IL	78151	63125	72011	78300
321 432	**NC**	E	*GA*	IL	78152	63126	72012	78301
321 433	**NC**	E	*GA*	IL	78153	63127	72013	78302
321 434	**NC**	E	*GA*	IL	78154	63128	72014	78303
321 435	**NC**	E	*GA*	IL	78155	63129	72015	78304
321 436	**NC**	E	*GA*	IL	78156	63130	72016	78305
321 437	**NC**	E	*GA*	IL	78157	63131	72017	78306
321 438	**GA**	E	*GA*	IL	78158	63132	72018	78307
321 439	**GA**	E	*GA*	IL	78159	63133	72019	78308
321 440	**GA**	E	*GA*	IL	78160	63134	72020	78309
321 441	**GA**	E	*GA*	IL	78161	63135	72021	78310
321 442	**GA**	E	*GA*	IL	78162	63136	72022	78311
321 443	**GA**	E	*GA*	IL	78125	63099	71985	78274
321 444	**NC**	E	*GA*	IL	78126	63100	71986	78275
321 445	**NC**	E	*GA*	IL	78127	63101	71987	78276
321 446	**NC**	E	*GA*	IL	78128	63102	71988	78277
321 447	**GA**	E	*GA*	IL	78129	63103	71989	78278
321 448 †	**0**	E	*GA*	IL	78130	63104	71990	78279
Spare	**FB**	E		ZK (S)	71951	71968		
Spare	**LM**	E		ZB (S)	71959			
Spare	**LM**	E		LM (S)	71963			

Names (carried on TS):

321 409 Dame Alice Owen's School 400 Years of Learning
321 428 The Essex Commuter
321 442 Crouch Valley 1889–2014
321 444 Essex Lifeboats
321 446 George Mullings

Class 321/9. DTS(A)–MS–TS–DTS(B). Refurbished 2015 with a universal access toilet to comply with the 2020 accessibility regulations.

DTS(A). Lot No. 31108 1991. –/45(+6) 1TD 2W. 31.7 t.
MS. Lot No. 31109 1991. –/79. 52.1 t.
TS. Lot No. 31110 1991. –/78. 30.6 t.
DTS(B). Lot No. 31111 1991. –/79. 30.6 t.

321901	**NB**	E		HT	77990	63153	72128	77993
321902	**NB**	E	*NO*	NL	77991	63154	72129	77994
321903	**NB**	E	*NO*	NL	77992	63155	72130	77995

CLASS 322   BREL YORK

Units built for use on Stansted Airport services, used for a number of years with ScotRail before transfer to Northern. Refurbished 2014–15 with a universal access toilet to comply with the 2020 accessibility regulations.

Formation: DTS–MS–TS–DTS.
Construction: Steel.
Traction Motors: Four Brush TM2141C of 268 kW.
Wheel Arrangement: 2-2 + Bo-Bo + 2-2 + 2-2.
Braking: Disc.   **Dimensions:** 19.95/19.92 x 2.82 m.
Bogies: P7-4 (MS), T3-7 (others).   **Couplers:** Tightlock.
Gangways: Within unit.   **Control System:** Thyristor.
Doors: Sliding.   **Maximum Speed:** 100 mph.
Seating Layout: 3+2 facing.
Multiple Working: Within class & with Classes 317, 318, 319, 320, 321 and 323.

DTS(A). Lot No. 31094 1990. –/54(+4) 1TD 2W. 31.7 t.
MS. Lot No. 31092 1990. –/83. 52.1 t.
TS. Lot No. 31093 1990. –/80 1T. 30.6 t.
DTS(B). Lot No. 31091 1990. –/79. 30.6 t.

322481	**NB**	E	*NO*	NL	78163	63137	72023	77985
322482	**NB**	E	*NO*	NL	78164	63138	72024	77986
322483	**NB**	E	*NO*	NL	78165	63139	72025	77987
322484	**NB**	E	*NO*	NL	78166	63140	72026	77988
322485	**NB**	E	*NO*	NL	78167	63141	72027	77989

CLASS 323   HUNSLET TRANSPORTATION PROJECTS

Suburban units.

Formation: DMS–PTS–DMS.
Construction: Welded aluminium alloy.
Traction Motors: Four Holec DMKT 52/24 asynchronous of 146 kW.
Wheel Arrangement: Bo-Bo + 2-2 + Bo-Bo.
Braking: Disc & regenerative.   **Dimensions:** 23.37/23.44 x 2.80 m.
Bogies: SRP BP62 (DMS), BT52 (PTS). **Couplers:** Tightlock.
Gangways: Within unit.   **Control System:** IGBT Inverter.
Doors: Sliding plug.   **Maximum Speed:** 90 mph.
Seating Layout: 3+2 facing/unidirectional.
Multiple Working: Within class & with Classes 317, 318, 319, 320, 321 and 322.

DMS(B) vehicles 65003 and 65005 in 323 203/205 and 65019 and 65021 in 323 219/221 switched between units following accident damage and were not returned to their original sets, instead swapping numbers.

* Fitted with a universal access toilet to comply with the 2020 accessibility regulations.

DMS(A). Lot No. 31112 Hunslet 1992–93. –/98 († –/82, * –/97). 41.0 t.
TS. Lot No. 31113 Hunslet 1992–93. –/88(+5) 1T 2W. († –/80(+5) 1T 2W, * –/81(+3) 1TD 2W). 39.4t.
DMS(B). Lot No. 31114 Hunslet 1992–93. –/98 († –/82, * –/97). 41.0 t.

323 201	*	**WI**	P	*WM*	SO	64001	72201	65001
323 202	*	**WI**	P	*WM*	SO	64002	72202	65002
323 203	*	**WI**	P	*WM*	SO	64003	72203	65003
323 204		**WI**	P	*WM*	SO	64004	72204	65004
323 205		**WI**	P	*WM*	SO	64005	72205	65005
323 206		**WI**	P	*WM*	SO	64006	72206	65006
323 207		**WI**	P	*WM*	SO	64007	72207	65007
323 208		**WI**	P	*WM*	SO	64008	72208	65008
323 209	*	**WI**	P	*WM*	SO	64009	72209	65009
323 210		**WI**	P	*WM*	SO	64010	72210	65010
323 211		**WI**	P	*WM*	SO	64011	72211	65011
323 212		**WI**	P	*WM*	SO	64012	72212	65012
323 213		**WI**	P	*WM*	SO	64013	72213	65013
323 214		**WI**	P	*WM*	SO	64014	72214	65014
323 215		**WI**	P	*WM*	SO	64015	72215	65015
323 216	*	**WI**	P	*WM*	SO	64016	72216	65016
323 217	*	**WI**	P	*WM*	SO	64017	72217	65017
323 218	*	**WI**	P	*WM*	SO	64018	72218	65018
323 219	*	**WI**	P	*WM*	SO	64019	72219	65019
323 220		**WI**	P	*WM*	SO	64020	72220	65020
323 221		**WI**	P	*WM*	SO	64021	72221	65021
323 222		**WI**	P	*WM*	SO	64022	72222	65022
323 223	†	**NO**	P	*NO*	AN	64023	72223	65023
323 224	†	**NO**	P	*NO*	AN	64024	72224	65024
323 225	†	**NO**	P	*NO*	AN	64025	72225	65025
323 226		**NO**	P	*NO*	AN	64026	72226	65026
323 227		**NO**	P	*NO*	AN	64027	72227	65027
323 228		**NO**	P	*NO*	AN	64028	72228	65028
323 229		**NO**	P	*NO*	AN	64029	72229	65029
323 230		**NO**	P	*NO*	AN	64030	72230	65030
323 231		**NO**	P	*NO*	AN	64031	72231	65031
323 232		**NO**	P	*NO*	AN	64032	72232	65032
323 233		**NO**	P	*NO*	AN	64033	72233	65033
323 234		**NO**	P	*NO*	AN	64034	72234	65034
323 235		**NO**	P	*NO*	AN	64035	72235	65035
323 236		**NO**	P	*NO*	AN	64036	72236	65036
323 237		**NO**	P	*NO*	AN	64037	72237	65037
323 238		**NO**	P	*NO*	AN	64038	72238	65038
323 239		**NO**	P	*NO*	AN	64039	72239	65039
323 240		**WI**	P	*WM*	SO	64040	72340	65040
323 241		**WI**	P	*WM*	SO	64041	72341	65041

| 323 242 | **WI** | P | *WM* | SO | 64042 | 72342 | 65042 |
| 323 243 | **WI** | P | *WM* | SO | 64043 | 72343 | 65043 |

CLASS 325   ABB DERBY

Postal units based on Class 319s. Compatible with diesel or electric locomotive haulage. Built for dual voltage use, but 750 V DC third rail shoe gear has been removed as it is not required on current duties.

Formation: DTPMV–MPMV–TPMV–DTPMV.
System: 25 kV AC overhead.
Construction: Steel.
Traction Motors: Four GEC G315BZ of 268 kW.
Wheel Arrangement: 2-2 + Bo-Bo + 2-2 + 2-2.
Braking: Disc.   **Dimensions:** 19.33 x 2.82 m.
Bogies: P7-4 (MPMV), T3-7 (others).   **Couplers:** Drop-head buckeye.
Gangways: None.   **Control System:** GTO Chopper.
Doors: Roller shutter.   **Maximum Speed:** 100 mph.
Multiple Working: Within class.

DTPMV. Lot No. 31144 1995. 29.1 t.
MPMV. Lot No. 31145 1995. 49.5 t.
TPMV. Lot No. 31146 1995. 30.7 t.

325 001	**RM**	RM	*DB*	CE	68300	68340	68360	68301
325 002	**RM**	RM	*DB*	CE	68302	68341	68361	68303
325 003	**RM**	RM	*DB*	CE	68304	68342	68362	68305
325 004	**RM**	RM	*DB*	CE	68306	68343	68363	68307
325 005	**RM**	RM	*DB*	CE	68308	68344	68364	68309
325 006	**RM**	RM	*DB*	CE	68310	68345	68365	68311
325 007	**RM**	RM	*DB*	CE	68312	68346	68366	68313
325 008	**RM**	RM	*DB*	CE	68314	68347	68367	68315
325 009	**RM**	RM	*DB*	CE	68316	68349	68368	68317
325 011	**RM**	RM	*DB*	CE	68320	68350	68370	68321
325 012	**RM**	RM	*DB*	CE	68322	68351	68371	68323
325 013	**RM**	RM	*DB*	CE	68324	68352	68372	68325
325 014	**RM**	RM	*DB*	CE	68326	68353	68373	68327
325 015	**RM**	RM	*DB*	CE	68328	68354	68374	68329
325 016	**RM**	RM	*DB*	CE	68330	68355	68375	68331

Name (carried on one side of each DTPMV):

325 008   Peter Howarth CBE

CLASS 331   CIVITY   CAF

New units being delivered to Northern, to enter traffic from spring 2019. Full details awaited.

Formation: DMS–PTS–DMS or DMS–PTS–TS–DMS.
Construction: Aluminium.
Traction Motors: Four TSA asynchronous of 220 kW.
Wheel Arrangement: Bo-Bo + 2-2 + Bo-Bo or Bo-Bo + 2-2 + 2-2 + Bo-Bo.

Braking: Disc & regenerative.   **Dimensions:** 24.03/23.35 x 2.55 m.
Bogies: CAF.   **Couplers:** Dellner.
Gangways: Within unit.   **Control System:** IGBT Inverter.
Doors: Sliding plug.   **Maximum Speed:** 100 mph.
Heating & ventilation: Air conditioning.
Seating: 2+2 facing/unidirectional.   **Multiple Working:** Within class.

Class 331/0. DMS–PTS–DMS. 3-car units.

DMS. CAF Zaragoza/Newport 2017–20. –/45(+8) 1TD 2W. 40.8 t.
PTS. CAF Zaragoza/Newport 2017–20. –/76(+4). 34.9 t.
DMS. CAF Zaragoza/Newport 2017–20. –/63(+7). 39.8 t.

331001	**NR**	E	*NO*	AN	463001	464001	466001
331002	**NR**	E			463002	464002	466002
331003	**NR**	E			463003	464003	466003
331004	**NR**	E			463004	464004	466004
331005	**NR**	E	*NO*	AN	463005	464005	466005
331006	**NR**	E	*NO*	AN	463006	464006	466006
331007	**NR**	E	*NO*	AN	463007	464007	466007
331008	**NR**	E	*NO*	AN	463008	464008	466008
331009	**NR**	E			463009	464009	466009
331010	**NR**	E			463010	464010	466010
331011	**NR**	E			463011	464011	466011
331012	**NR**	E			463012	464012	466012
331013	**NR**	E			463013	464013	466013
331014	**NR**	E			463014	464014	466014
331015	**NR**	E			463015	464015	466015
331016	**NR**	E			463016	464016	466016
331017	**NR**	E			463017	464017	466017
331018	**NR**	E			463018	464018	466018
331019	**NR**	E			463019	464019	466019
331020	**NR**	E			463020	464020	466020
331021	**NR**	E			463021	464021	466021
331022	**NR**	E			463022	464022	466022
331023	**NR**	E			463023	464023	466023
331024	**NR**	E			463024	464024	466024
331025	**NR**	E			463025	464025	466025
331026	**NR**	E			463026	464026	466026
331027	**NR**	E			463027	464027	466027
331028	**NR**	E			463028	464028	466028
331029	**NR**	E			463029	464029	466029
331030	**NR**	E			463030	464030	466030
331031	**NR**	E			463031	464031	466031

Class 331/1. DMS–PTS–TS–DMS. 4-car units.

DMS. CAF Zaragoza/Newport 2017–19. –/45(+8) 1TD 2W. 40.8 t.
PTS. CAF Zaragoza/Newport 2017–19. –/76(+4). 34.9 t.
TS. CAF Zaragoza/Newport 2017–19. –/76(+4). 30.1 t.
DMS. CAF Zaragoza/Newport 2017–19. –/63(+7). 39.8 t.

331101	**NR**	E	*NO*	AN	463101	464101	465101	466101
331102	**NR**	E			463102	464102	465102	466102

331 103	**NR**	E	*NO*	AN	463103	464103	465103	466103
331 104	**NR**	E	*NO*	AN	463104	464104	465104	466104
331 105	**NR**	E			463105	464105	465105	466105
331 106	**NR**	E	*NO*	AN	463106	464106	465106	466106
331 107	**NR**	E			463107	464107	465107	466107
331 108	**NR**	E	*NO*	AN	463108	464108	465108	466108
331 109	**NR**	E	*NO*	AN	463109	464109	465109	466109
331 110	**NR**	E	*NO*	AN	463110	464110	465110	466110
331 111	**NR**	E			463111	464111	465111	466111
331 112	**NR**	E			463112	464112	465112	466112

Names (carried on driving cars):

331 106   Proud to be Northern | 331 110   Proud to be Northern

CLASS 332   HEATHROW EXPRESS CAF/SIEMENS

Dedicated Heathrow Express units. Five units were increased from 4-car to 5-car in 2002. Operate in coupled pairs at peak times. This class is unique in not being fitted with TPWS equipment (as the route operated is ATP only).

Formation: DMS–TS–PTS–(TS)–DMF.
Construction: Steel.
Traction Motors: Two Siemens monomotors asynchronous of 350 kW.
Wheel Arrangement: B-B + 2-2 + 2-2(+ 2-2) + B-B.
Braking: Disc.   **Dimensions:** 23.74/23.35/23.14 x 2.75 m.
Bogies: CAF.   **Couplers:** Scharfenberg 10L.
Gangways: Within unit.   **Control System:** IGBT Inverter.
Doors: Sliding plug.   **Maximum Speed:** 100 mph.
Heating & ventilation: Air conditioning.
Seating: 1: 1+1 facing/unidirectional, 2: 2+2 mainly unidirectional.
Multiple Working: Within class.

Advertising livery: Tata Communications (various colours).

DMS. CAF 1997–98. –/43(+8). 49.9 t.
72400–413. TS. CAF 1997–98. –/64(+11). 38.4 t.
PTS. CAF 1997–98. –/39(+11) 1TD 2W. 47.6 t.
72414–418. TS. CAF 2002. –/56 35.8 t.
DMF. CAF 1997–98. 20/–. 49.5 t.

332 001	**AL**	HE	*HE*	OH	78400	72412	63400		78401
332 002	**AL**	HE	*HE*	OH	78402	72409	63406		78403
332 003	**AL**	HE	*HE*	OH	78404	72407	63402		78405
332 004	**AL**	HE	*HE*	OH	78406	72405	63403		78407
332 005	**AL**	HE	*HE*	OH	78408	72411	63404	72417	78409
332 006	**AL**	HE	*HE*	OH	78410	72410	63405	72415	78411
332 007	**AL**	HE	*HE*	OH	78412	72401	63401	72414	78413
332 008	**AL**	HE	*HE*	OH	78414	72413	63407		78415
332 009	**AL**	HE	*HE*	OH	78416	72400	63408	72416	78417
332 010	**AL**	HE	*HE*	OH	78418	72402	63409		78419

332011	**AL**	HE	*HE*	OH	78420 72403 63410	78421
332012	**AL**	HE	*HE*	OH	78422 72404 63411	78423
332013	**AL**	HE	*HE*	OH	78424 72408 63412	78425
332014	**AL**	HE		OH	78426 72406 63413	78427

CLASS 333   CAF/SIEMENS

West Yorkshire area suburban units.

Formation: DMS–PTS–TS–DMS.
Construction: Steel.
Traction Motors: Two Siemens monomotors asynchronous of 350 kW.
Wheel Arrangement: B-B + 2-2 + 2-2 + B-B.
Braking: Disc.   **Dimensions:** 23.74/23.35 × 2.75 m.
Bogies: CAF.   **Couplers:** Dellner 10L.
Gangways: Within unit.   **Control System:** IGBT Inverter.
Doors: Sliding plug.   **Maximum Speed:** 100 mph.
Heating & ventilation: Air conditioning. **Multiple Working:** Within class.
Seating Layout: 3+2 facing/unidirectional.

333001–008 were made up to 4-car units from 3-car units in 2002.

333009–016 were made up to 4-car units from 3-car units in 2003.

DMS(A). (odd Nos.) CAF Zaragoza 2001. –/90. 50.0 t.
PTS. CAF Zaragoza 2001. –/73(+7) 1TD 2W. 46.0 t.
TS. CAF Zaragoza 2002–03. –/100. 38.5 t.
DMS(B). (even Nos.) CAF Zaragoza 2001. –/90. 50.0 t.

333001	**NR**	A	*NO*	NL	78451 74461 74477 78452
333002	**YR**	A	*NO*	NL	78453 74462 74478 78454
333003	**NR**	A	*NO*	NL	78455 74463 74479 78456
333004	**YR**	A	*NO*	NL	78457 74464 74480 78458
333005	**YR**	A	*NO*	NL	78459 74465 74481 78460
333006	**YR**	A	*NO*	NL	78461 74466 74482 78462
333007	**YR**	A	*NO*	NL	78463 74467 74483 78464
333008	**NR**	A	*NO*	NL	78465 74468 74484 78466
333009	**NR**	A	*NO*	NL	78467 74469 74485 78468
333010	**NR**	A	*NO*	NL	78469 74470 74486 78470
333011	**NR**	A	*NO*	NL	78471 74471 74487 78472
333012	**NR**	A	*NO*	NL	78473 74472 74488 78474
333013	**NR**	A	*NO*	NL	78475 74473 74489 78476
333014	**NR**	A	*NO*	NL	78477 74474 74490 78478
333015	**NR**	A	*NO*	NL	78479 74475 74491 78480
333016	**YR**	A	*NO*	NL	78481 74476 74492 78482

Name (carried on end cars):

333007 Alderman J Arthur Godwin First Lord Mayor of Bradford 1907

CLASS 334   JUNIPER   ALSTOM BIRMINGHAM

Outer suburban units.

Formation: DMS–PTS–DMS.
Construction: Steel.
Traction Motors: Two Alstom ONIX 800 asynchronous of 270 kW.
Wheel Arrangement: 2-Bo + 2-2 + Bo-2.

Braking: Disc.	**Dimensions:** 21.01/19.94 x 2.80 m.
Bogies: Alstom LTB3/TBP3.	**Couplers:** Dellner.
Gangways: Within unit.	**Control System:** IGBT Inverter.
Doors: Sliding plug.	**Maximum Speed:** 90 mph.

Heating & ventilation: Air conditioning.
Seating Layout: 2+2 facing/unidirectional (3+2 in PTS).
Multiple Working: Within class.

DMS(A). Alstom Birmingham 1999–2001. –/64. 42.6 t.
PTS. Alstom Birmingham 1999–2001. –/55 1TD 1W. 39.4 t.
DMS(B). Alstom Birmingham 1999–2001. –/59(+3). 42.6 t.

334001	**SR**	E	*SR*	GW	64101	74301	65101
334002	**SR**	E	*SR*	GW	64102	74302	65102
334003	**SR**	E	*SR*	GW	64103	74303	65103
334004	**SR**	E	*SR*	GW	64104	74304	65104
334005	**SR**	E	*SR*	GW	64105	74305	65105
334006	**SR**	E	*SR*	GW	64106	74306	65106
334007	**SR**	E	*SR*	GW	64107	74307	65107
334008	**SR**	E	*SR*	GW	64108	74308	65108
334009	**SR**	E	*SR*	GW	64109	74309	65109
334010	**SR**	E	*SR*	GW	64110	74310	65110
334011	**SR**	E	*SR*	GW	64111	74311	65111
334012	**SR**	E	*SR*	GW	64112	74312	65112
334013	**SR**	E	*SR*	GW	64113	74313	65113
334014	**SR**	E	*SR*	GW	64114	74314	65114
334015	**SR**	E	*SR*	GW	64115	74315	65115
334016	**SR**	E	*SR*	GW	64116	74316	65116
334017	**SR**	E	*SR*	GW	64117	74317	65117
334018	**SR**	E	*SR*	GW	64118	74318	65118
334019	**SR**	E	*SR*	GW	64119	74319	65119
334020	**SR**	E	*SR*	GW	64120	74320	65120
334021	**SR**	E	*SR*	GW	64121	74321	65121
334022	**SR**	E	*SR*	GW	64122	74322	65122
334023	**SR**	E	*SR*	GW	64123	74323	65123
334024	**SR**	E	*SR*	GW	64124	74324	65124
334025	**SR**	E	*SR*	GW	64125	74325	65125
334026	**SR**	E	*SR*	GW	64126	74326	65126
334027	**SR**	E	*SR*	GW	64127	74327	65127
334028	**SR**	E	*SR*	GW	64128	74328	65128
334029	**SR**	E	*SR*	GW	64129	74329	65129
334030	**SR**	E	*SR*	GW	64130	74330	65130
334031	**SR**	E	*SR*	GW	64131	74331	65131
334032	**SR**	E	*SR*	GW	64132	74332	65132

334 033	**SR**	E	*SR*	GW	64133	74333	65133
334 034	**SR**	E	*SR*	GW	64134	74334	65134
334 035	**SR**	E	*SR*	GW	64135	74335	65135
334 036	**SR**	E	*SR*	GW	64136	74336	65136
334 037	**SR**	E	*SR*	GW	64137	74337	65137
334 038	**SR**	E	*SR*	GW	64138	74338	65138
334 039	**SR**	E	*SR*	GW	64139	74339	65139
334 040	**SR**	E	*SR*	GW	64140	74340	65140

CLASS 345   AVENTRA   BOMBARDIER DERBY

These 9-car units are being delivered for London's Crossrail/Elizabeth Line. Some units are in service as 7-car units on services between Liverpool Street and Shenfield whilst others are in use between Paddington and Hayes & Harlington (and from December 2019 to Reading) ahead of the opening of the full Elizabeth Line, expected in 2020–21. By autumn 2019 the whole fleet had been built, but with many units stored at Old Oak Common, Old Dalby, Worksop or Derby.

The design is marketed as "Aventra" by Bombardier and is a development on the successful Electrostar design. There is an option for a further 14 9-car units.

Formation: DMS–PMS–MS–MS*–TS–MS*–MS–PMS–DMS.
* Initially these MS vehicles are missing from certain units. For units in traffic that are missing these vehicles, the missing vehicles are shown in *italics*.
System: 25 kV AC overhead.
Construction: Aluminium.
Traction Motors: Two Bombardier asynchronous of 265 kW.
Wheel Arrangement: 2-Bo + Bo-2 + Bo-Bo (+ Bo-2) + 2-2 (+ 2-Bo) + Bo-Bo + 2-Bo + Bo-2.
Braking: Disc & regenerative.   **Dimensions:** 23.62/22.50 m x 2.78 m.
Bogies: FLEXX B5000 inside-frame. **Couplers:** Dellner.
Gangways: Within unit.   **Control System:** IGBT Inverter.
Doors: Sliding plug (three per vehicle). **Maximum Speed:** 90 mph.
Heating & ventilation: Air conditioning.
Seating Layout: Mostly longitudinal, with some 2+2 facing.
Multiple Working: Within class.

DMS(A). Bombardier Derby 2015–19. –/46. 39.0 t.
PMS(A). Bombardier Derby 2015–19. –/46(+6). 37.1 t.
MS(A). Bombardier Derby 2015–19. –/46(+6). 36.5 t.
MS(B). Bombardier Derby 2015–19. –/49(+3). 31.4 t.
TS. Bombardier Derby 2015–19. –/38(+12). 29.7 t.
MS(C). Bombardier Derby 2015–19. –/49(+3). 31.4 t.
MS(D). Bombardier Derby 2015–19. –/46(+6). 37.2 t.
PMS(B). Bombardier Derby 2015–19. –/46(+6). 37.1 t.
DMS(B). Bombardier Derby 2015–19. –/46. 39.0 t.

345 001	**XR**	XR			340101	340201	340301	340401	340501
					340601	340701	340801	340901	
345 002	**XR**	XR			340102	340202	340302	340402	340502
					340602	340702	340802	340902	
345 003	**XR**	XR	*XR*	OC	340103	340203	340303	*340403*	340503
					340603	340703	340803	340903	
345 004	**XR**	XR			340104	340204	340304	340404	340504
					340604	340704	340804	340904	
345 005	**XR**	XR	*XR*	OC	340105	340205	340305	*340405*	340505
					340605	340705	340805	340905	
345 006	**XR**	XR	*XR*	OC	340106	340206	340306	*340406*	340506
					340606	340706	340806	340906	
345 007	**XR**	XR	*XR*	OC	340107	340207	340307	*340407*	340507
					340607	340707	340807	340907	
345 008	**XR**	XR	*XR*	OC	340108	340208	340308	340408	340508
					340608	340708	340808	340908	
345 009	**XR**	XR	*XR*	OC	340109	340209	340309	*340409*	340509
					340609	340709	340809	340909	
345 010	**XR**	XR	*XR*	OC	340110	340210	340310	*340410*	340510
					340610	340710	340810	340910	
345 011	**XR**	XR	*XR*	OC	340111	340211	340311	*340411*	340511
					340611	340711	340811	340911	
345 012	**XR**	XR	*XR*	OC	340112	340212	340312	*340412*	340512
					340612	340712	340812	340912	
345 013	**XR**	XR	*XR*	OC	340113	340213	340313	*340413*	340513
					340613	340713	340813	340913	
345 014	**XR**	XR	*XR*	OC	340114	340214	340314	340414	340514
					340614	340714	340814	340914	
345 015	**XR**	XR	*XR*	OC	340115	340215	340315	*340415*	340515
					340615	340715	340815	340915	
345 016	**XR**	XR	*XR*	OC	340116	340216	340316	*340416*	340516
					340616	340716	340816	340916	
345 017	**XR**	XR	*XR*	OC	340117	340217	340317	*340417*	340517
					340617	340717	340817	340917	
345 018	**XR**	XR			340118	340218	340318	340418	340518
					340618	340718	340818	340918	
345 019	**XR**	XR			340119	340219	340319	340419	340519
					340619	340719	340819	340919	
345 020	**XR**	XR			340120	340220	340320	340420	340520
					340620	340720	340820	340920	
345 021	**XR**	XR			340121	340221	340321	340421	340521
					340621	340721	340821	340921	
345 022	**XR**	XR	*XR*	OC	340122	340222	340322	*340422*	340522
					340622	340722	340822	340922	
345 023	**XR**	XR		WS(S)	340123	340223	340323	340423	340523
					340623	340723	340823	340923	
345 024	**XR**	XR			340124	340224	340324	340424	340524
					340624	340724	340824	340924	
345 025	**XR**	XR			340125	340225	340325	340425	340525
					340625	340725	340825	340925	

345 026	**XR**	XR			340126	340226	340326	340426	340526
					340626	340726	340826	340926	
345 027	**XR**	XR	*XR*	OC	340127	340227	340327	340427	340527
					340627	340727	340827	340927	
345 028	**XR**	XR	*XR*	OC	340128	340228	340328	340428	340528
					340628	340728	340828	340928	
345 029	**XR**	XR	*XR*	OC	340129	340229	340329	*340429*	340529
					340629	340729	340829	340929	
345 030	**XR**	XR	*XR*	OC	340130	340230	340330	340430	340530
					340630	340730	340830	340930	
345 031	**XR**	XR			340131	340231	340331	340431	340531
					340631	340731	340831	340931	
345 032	**XR**	XR			340132	340232	340332	340432	340532
					340632	340732	340832	340932	
345 033	**XR**	XR			340133	340233	340333	340433	340533
					340633	340733	340833	340933	
345 034	**XR**	XR	*XR*	OC	340134	340234	340334	340434	340534
					340634	340734	340834	340934	
345 035	**XR**	XR	*XR*	OC	340135	340235	340335	340435	340535
					340635	340735	340835	340935	
345 036	**XR**	XR			340136	340236	340336	340436	340536
					340636	340736	340836	340936	
345 037	**XR**	XR	*XR*	OC	340137	340237	340337	340437	340537
					340637	340737	340837	340937	
345 038	**XR**	XR	*XR*	OC	340138	340238	340338	*340438*	340538
					340638	340738	340838	340938	
345 039	**XR**	XR	*XR*	OC	340139	340239	340339	*340439*	340539
					340639	340739	340839	340939	
345 040	**XR**	XR	*XR*	OC	340140	340240	340340	*340440*	340540
					340640	340740	340840	340940	
345 041	**XR**	XR			340141	340241	340341	340441	340541
					340641	340741	340841	340941	
345 042	**XR**	XR	*XR*	OC	340142	340242	340342	*340442*	340542
					340642	340742	340842	340942	
345 043	**XR**	XR			340143	340243	340343	340443	340543
					340643	340743	340843	340943	
345 044	**XR**	XR	*XR*	OC	340144	340244	340344	*340444*	340544
					340644	340744	340844	340944	
345 045	**XR**	XR			340145	340245	340345	340445	340545
					340645	340745	340845	340945	
345 046	**XR**	XR			340146	340246	340346	340446	340546
					340646	340746	340846	340946	
345 047	**XR**	XR	*XR*	OC	340147	340247	340347	*340447*	340547
					340647	340747	340847	340947	
345 048	**XR**	XR			340148	340248	340348	340448	340548
					340648	340748	340848	340948	
345 049	**XR**	XR	*XR*	OC	340149	340249	340349	*340449*	340549
					340649	340749	340849	340949	
345 050	**XR**	XR			340150	340250	340350	340450	340550
					340650	340750	340850	340950	

345 051	**XR**	XR		340151	340251	340351	340451	340551
				340651	340751	340851	340951	
345 052	**XR**	XR		340152	340252	340352	340452	340552
				340652	340752	340852	340952	
345 053	**XR**	XR		340153	340253	340353	340453	340553
				340653	340753	340853	340953	
345 054	**XR**	XR		340154	340254	340354	340454	340554
				340654	340754	340854	340954	
345 055	**XR**	XR		340155	340255	340355	340455	340555
				340655	340755	340855	340955	
345 056	**XR**	XR		340156	340256	340356	340456	340556
				340656	340756	340856	340956	
345 057	**XR**	XR		340157	340257	340357	340457	340557
				340657	340757	340857	340957	
345 058	**XR**	XR		340158	340258	340358	340458	340558
				340658	340758	340858	340958	
345 059	**XR**	XR		340159	340259	340359	340459	340559
				340659	340759	340859	340959	
345 060	**XR**	XR	WS(S)	340160	340260	340360	340460	340560
				340660	340760	340860	340960	
345 061	**XR**	XR	WS(S)	340161	340261	340361	340461	340561
				340661	340761	340861	340961	
345 062	**XR**	XR	WS(S)	340162	340262	340362	340462	340562
				340662	340762	340862	340962	
345 063	**XR**	XR	WS(S)	340163	340263	340363	340463	340563
				340663	340763	340863	340963	
345 064	**XR**	XR		340164	340264	340364	340464	340564
				340664	340764	340864	340964	
345 065	**XR**	XR		340165	340265	340365	340465	340565
				340665	340765	340865	340965	
345 066	**XR**	XR		340166	340266	340366	340466	340566
				340666	340766	340866	340966	
345 067	**XR**	XR		340167	340267	340367	340467	340567
				340667	340767	340867	340967	
345 068	**XR**	XR		340168	340268	340368	340468	340568
				340668	340768	340868	340968	
345 069	**XR**	XR		340169	340269	340369	340469	340569
				340669	340769	340869	340969	
345 070	**XR**	XR		340170	340270	340370	340470	340570
				340670	340770	340870	340970	

CLASS 350   DESIRO UK   SIEMENS

Outer suburban and long distance units.

Formation: DMC–TC–PTS–DMC.
Systems: 25 kV AC overhead (350/1s built with 750 V DC, but equipment currently decommissioned).
Construction: Welded aluminium.
Traction Motors: 4 Siemens 1TB2016-0GB02 asynchronous of 250 kW.
Wheel Arrangement: Bo-Bo + 2-2 + 2-2 + Bo-Bo.

Braking: Disc & regenerative.
Bogies: SGP SF5000.
Gangways: Throughout.
Doors: Sliding plug.
Heating & ventilation: Air conditioning.
Seating Layout: Various, see sub-class headings.
Multiple Working: Within class.

Dimensions: 20.34 x 2.79 m.
Couplers: Dellner 12.
Control System: IGBT Inverter.
Maximum Speed: 110 mph.

Class 350/1. Original-build units owned by Angel Trains. Formerly part of an aborted South West Trains 5-car Class 450/2 order. 2+2 seating.

Seating Layout: 1: 2+2 facing, 2: 2+2 facing/unidirectional.

Non-standard and advertising liveries:

350 104/106/115/116/123 Grey with green doors.
350 110 Project 110 (silver centre cars).

* Refurbished. Guard's office removed in TC vehicle with extra luggage racks in its place.

DMS(A). Siemens Krefeld 2004–05. –/60. 48.7 t.
TC. Siemens Krefeld/Prague 2004–05. 24/32 1T. 36.2 t.
PTS. Siemens Krefeld/Prague 2004–05. –/50(+9) 1TD 2W. 45.2 t.
DMS(B). Siemens Krefeld 2004–05. –/60. 49.2 t.

350 101		**LM**	A	*WM*	NN	63761	66811	66861	63711
350 102		**LM**	A	*WM*	NN	63762	66812	66862	63712
350 103		**LM**	A	*WM*	NN	63765	66813	66863	63713
350 104		**0**	A	*WM*	NN	63764	66814	66864	63714
350 105		**LM**	A	*WM*	NN	63763	66815	66868	63715
350 106	*	**0**	A	*WM*	NN	63766	66816	66866	63716
350 107		**LM**	A	*WM*	NN	63767	66817	66867	63717
350 108		**LM**	A	*WM*	NN	63768	66818	66865	63718
350 109		**LM**	A	*WM*	NN	63769	66819	66869	63719
350 110		**AL**	A	*WM*	NN	63770	66820	66870	63720
350 111		**LM**	A	*WM*	NN	63771	66821	66871	63721
350 112		**LM**	A	*WM*	NN	63772	66822	66872	63722
350 113		**LM**	A	*WM*	NN	63773	66823	66873	63723
350 114		**LM**	A	*WM*	NN	63774	66824	66874	63724
350 115	*	**0**	A	*WM*	NN	63775	66825	66875	63725
350 116		**0**	A	*WM*	NN	63776	66826	66876	63726
350 117		**LM**	A	*WM*	NN	63777	66827	66877	63727
350 118		**LM**	A	*WM*	NN	63778	66828	66878	63728
350 119		**LM**	A	*WM*	NN	63779	66829	66879	63729
350 120		**LM**	A	*WM*	NN	63780	66830	66880	63730
350 121		**LM**	A	*WM*	NN	63781	66831	66881	63731
350 122		**LM**	A	*WM*	NN	63782	66832	66882	63732
350 123		**0**	A	*WM*	NN	63783	66833	66883	63733
350 124		**LM**	A	*WM*	NN	63784	66834	66884	63734
350 125		**LM**	A	*WM*	NN	63785	66835	66885	63735
350 126		**LM**	A	*WM*	NN	63786	66836	66886	63736
350 127		**LM**	A	*WM*	NN	63787	66837	66887	63737
350 128		**LM**	A	*WM*	NN	63788	66838	66888	63738

| 350 129 | **LM** | A | *WM* | NN | 63789 | 66839 | 66889 | 63739 |
| 350 130 | **LM** | A | *WM* | NN | 63790 | 66840 | 66890 | 63740 |

Class 350/2. Owned by Porterbrook Leasing.

Seating Layout: 1: 2+2 facing, 2: 3+2 facing/unidirectional.

At the time of writing sets 350233/246/264 are running with misformed formations, as shown.

DMS(A). Siemens Krefeld 2008–09. –/70. 43.7 t.
TC. Siemens Prague 2008–09. 24/42 1T. 35.3 t.
PTS. Siemens Prague 2008–09. –/61(+9) 1TD 2W. 42.9 t.
DMS(B). Siemens Krefeld 2008–09. –/70. 44.2 t.

350 231	**LI**	P	*WM*	NN	61431	65231	67531	61531
350 232	**LI**	P	*WM*	NN	61432	65232	67532	61532
350 233	**LM**	P	*WM*	NN	61433	65233	67533	61546
350 234	**LI**	P	*WM*	NN	61434	65234	67534	61534
350 235	**LM**	P	*WM*	NN	61435	65235	67535	61535
350 236	**LM**	P	*WM*	NN	61436	65236	67536	61536
350 237	**LM**	P	*WM*	NN	61437	65237	67537	61537
350 238	**LM**	P	*WM*	NN	61438	65238	67538	61538
350 239	**LI**	P	*WM*	NN	61439	65239	67539	61539
350 240	**LI**	P	*WM*	NN	61440	65240	67540	61540
350 241	**LM**	P	*WM*	NN	61441	65241	67541	61541
350 242	**LM**	P	*WM*	NN	61442	65242	67542	61542
350 243	**LM**	P	*WM*	NN	61443	65243	67543	61543
350 244	**LI**	P	*WM*	NN	61444	65244	67544	61544
350 245	**LI**	P	*WM*	NN	61445	65245	67545	61545
350 246	**LM**	P	*WM*	NN	61446	65246	67546	61564
350 247	**LM**	P	*WM*	NN	61447	65247	67547	61547
350 248	**LM**	P	*WM*	NN	61448	65248	67548	61548
350 249	**LM**	P	*WM*	NN	61449	65249	67549	61549
350 250	**LM**	P	*WM*	NN	61450	65250	67550	61550
350 251	**LM**	P	*WM*	NN	61451	65251	67551	61551
350 252	**LI**	P	*WM*	NN	61452	65252	67552	61552
350 253	**LI**	P	*WM*	NN	61453	65253	67553	61553
350 254	**LI**	P	*WM*	NN	61454	65254	67554	61554
350 255	**LM**	P	*WM*	NN	61455	65255	67555	61555
350 256	**LM**	P	*WM*	NN	61456	65256	67556	61556
350 257	**LI**	P	*WM*	NN	61457	65257	67557	61557
350 258	**LI**	P	*WM*	NN	61458	65258	67558	61558
350 259	**LI**	P	*WM*	NN	61459	65259	67559	61559
350 260	**LM**	P	*WM*	NN	61460	65260	67560	61560
350 261	**LM**	P	*WM*	NN	61461	65261	67561	61561
350 262	**LI**	P	*WM*	NN	61462	65262	67562	61562
350 263	**LI**	P	*WM*	NN	61463	65263	67563	61563
350 264	**LM**	P	*WM*	NN	61464	65264	67564	61533
350 265	**LM**	P	*WM*	NN	61465	65265	67565	61565
350 266	**LM**	P	*WM*	NN	61466	65266	67566	61566
350 267	**LI**	P	*WM*	NN	61467	65267	67567	61567

Class 350/3. Owned by Angel Trains.

Seating Layout: 1: 2+2 facing, 2: 2+2 facing/unidirectional.

DMS(A). Siemens Krefeld 2014. –/60. 44.2 t.
TC. Siemens Krefeld 2014. 24/36 1T. 36.3 t.
PTS. Siemens Krefeld 2014. –/50(+9) 1TD 2W. 44.0 t.
DMS(B). Siemens Krefeld 2014. –/60. 45.0 t.

350 368	**LN**	A	*WM*	NN	60141	60511	60651	60151
350 369	**LN**	A	*WM*	NN	60142	60512	60652	60152
350 370	**LN**	A	*WM*	NN	60143	60513	60653	60153
350 371	**LN**	A	*WM*	NN	60144	60514	60654	60154
350 372	**LN**	A	*WM*	NN	60145	60515	60655	60155
350 373	**LN**	A	*WM*	NN	60146	60516	60656	60156
350 374	**LN**	A	*WM*	NN	60147	60517	60657	60157
350 375	**LN**	A	*WM*	NN	60148	60518	60658	60158
350 376	**LN**	A	*WM*	NN	60149	60519	60659	60159
350 377	**LN**	A	*WM*	NN	60150	60520	60660	60160

Names (carried on one side of PTS):

350 375	Vic Hall
350 377	Graham Taylor OBE

Class 350/4. Owned by Angel Trains. TransPennine Express units used on the Manchester Airport–Edinburgh/Glasgow route. To transfer to West Midlands Trains in late 2019.

Seating Layout: 1: 2+1 facing, 2: 2+2 facing/unidirectional.

DMS(A). Siemens Krefeld 2013–14. –/56. 44.2 t.
TC. Siemens Krefeld 2013–14. 19/24 1T. 36.2 t.
PTS. Siemens Krefeld 2013–14. –/42 1TD 1T. 44.6 t.
DMS(B). Siemens Krefeld 2013–14. –/56. 45.0 t.

350 401	**LN**	A	*WM*	NN	60691	60901	60941	60671
350 402	**TP**	A	*TP*	AK	60692	60902	60942	60672
350 403	**U**	A	*TP*	AK	60693	60903	60943	60673
350 404	**TP**	A	*TP*	AK	60694	60904	60944	60674
350 405	**TP**	A	*TP*	AK	60695	60905	60945	60675
350 406	**TP**	A	*TP*	AK	60696	60906	60946	60676
350 407	**TP**	A	*TP*	AK	60697	60907	60947	60677
350 408	**TP**	A	*TP*	AK	60698	60908	60948	60678
350 409	**TP**	A	*TP*	AK	60699	60909	60949	60679
350 410	**TP**	A	*TP*	AK	60700	60910	60950	60680

CLASS 357 ELECTROSTAR
ADTRANZ/BOMBARDIER DERBY

Provision for 750 V DC supply if required.

Formation: DMS–MS–PTS–DMS.
Construction: Welded aluminium alloy underframe, sides and roof with steel ends. All sections bolted together.
Traction Motors: Two Adtranz asynchronous of 250 kW.
Wheel Arrangement: 2-Bo + 2-Bo + 2-2 + Bo-2.
Braking: Disc & regenerative.   **Dimensions:** 20.40/19.99 x 2.80 m.
Bogies: Adtranz P3-25/T3-25.   **Couplers:** Tightlock.
Gangways: Within unit.   **Control System:** IGBT Inverter.
Doors: Sliding plug.   **Maximum Speed:** 100 mph.
Heating & ventilation: Air conditioning.
Seating Layout: 3+2 facing/unidirectional.
Multiple Working: Within class.

Class 357/0. Owned by Porterbrook Leasing.

DMS(A). Adtranz Derby 1999–2001. –/71. 40.7 t.
MS. Adtranz Derby 1999–2001. –/78. 36.7 t.
PTS. Adtranz Derby 1999–2001. –/58(+4) 1TD 2W. 39.5 t.
DMS(B). Adtranz Derby 1999–2001. –/71. 40.7 t.

357001	**C2**	P	*C2*	EM	67651	74151	74051	67751
357002	**C2**	P	*C2*	EM	67652	74152	74052	67752
357003	**C2**	P	*C2*	EM	67653	74153	74053	67753
357004	**C2**	P	*C2*	EM	67654	74154	74054	67754
357005	**C2**	P	*C2*	EM	67655	74155	74055	67755
357006	**C2**	P	*C2*	EM	67656	74156	74056	67756
357007	**C2**	P	*C2*	EM	67657	74157	74057	67757
357008	**C2**	P	*C2*	EM	67658	74158	74058	67758
357009	**C2**	P	*C2*	EM	67659	74159	74059	67759
357010	**C2**	P	*C2*	EM	67660	74160	74060	67760
357011	**C2**	P	*C2*	EM	67661	74161	74061	67761
357012	**C2**	P	*C2*	EM	67662	74162	74062	67762
357013	**C2**	P	*C2*	EM	67663	74163	74063	67763
357014	**C2**	P	*C2*	EM	67664	74164	74064	67764
357015	**C2**	P	*C2*	EM	67665	74165	74065	67765
357016	**C2**	P	*C2*	EM	67666	74166	74066	67766
357017	**C2**	P	*C2*	EM	67667	74167	74067	67767
357018	**C2**	P	*C2*	EM	67668	74168	74068	67768
357019	**C2**	P	*C2*	EM	67669	74169	74069	67769
357020	**C2**	P	*C2*	EM	67670	74170	74070	67770
357021	**C2**	P	*C2*	EM	67671	74171	74071	67771
357022	**C2**	P	*C2*	EM	67672	74172	74072	67772
357023	**C2**	P	*C2*	EM	67673	74173	74073	67773
357024	**C2**	P	*C2*	EM	67674	74174	74074	67774
357025	**C2**	P	*C2*	EM	67675	74175	74075	67775
357026	**C2**	P	*C2*	EM	67676	74176	74076	67776

357 027	C2	P	C2	EM	67677	74177	74077	67777
357 028	C2	P	C2	EM	67678	74178	74078	67778
357 029	C2	P	C2	EM	67679	74179	74079	67779
357 030	C2	P	C2	EM	67680	74180	74080	67780
357 031	C2	P	C2	EM	67681	74181	74081	67781
357 032	C2	P	C2	EM	67682	74182	74082	67782
357 033	C2	P	C2	EM	67683	74183	74083	67783
357 034	C2	P	C2	EM	67684	74184	74084	67784
357 035	C2	P	C2	EM	67685	74185	74085	67785
357 036	C2	P	C2	EM	67686	74186	74086	67786
357 037	C2	P	C2	EM	67687	74187	74087	67787
357 038	C2	P	C2	EM	67688	74188	74088	67788
357 039	C2	P	C2	EM	67689	74189	74089	67789
357 040	C2	P	C2	EM	67690	74190	74090	67790
357 041	C2	P	C2	EM	67691	74191	74091	67791
357 042	C2	P	C2	EM	67692	74192	74092	67792
357 043	C2	P	C2	EM	67693	74193	74093	67793
357 044	C2	P	C2	EM	67694	74194	74094	67794
357 045	C2	P	C2	EM	67695	74195	74095	67795
357 046	C2	P	C2	EM	67696	74196	74096	67796

Names (carried on DMS(A) and DMS(B) (one plate on each)):

357 001 BARRY FLAXMAN
357 002 ARTHUR LEWIS STRIDE 1841–1922
357 003 SOUTHEND city.on.sea
357 004 TONY AMOS
357 005 SOUTHEND: 2017 Alternative City of Culture
357 006 DIAMOND JUBILEE 1952–2012
357 007 Sir Andrew Foster
357 011 JOHN LOWING
357 018 Remembering our Fallen 88 1914–1918
357 028 London, Tilbury & Southend Railway 1854–2004
357 029 THOMAS WHITELEGG 1840–1922
357 030 ROBERT HARBEN WHITELEGG 1871–1957

Class 357/2. Owned by Angel Trains.

DMS(A). Bombardier Derby 2001–02. –/71. 40.7 t.
MS. Bombardier Derby 2001–02. –/78. 36.7 t.
PTS. Bombardier Derby 2001–02. –/58(+4) 1TD 2W. 39.5 t.
DMS(B). Bombardier Derby 2001–02. –/71. 40.7 t.

357 201	C2	A	C2	EM	68601	74701	74601	68701
357 202	C2	A	C2	EM	68602	74702	74602	68702
357 203	C2	A	C2	EM	68603	74703	74603	68703
357 204	C2	A	C2	EM	68604	74704	74604	68704
357 205	C2	A	C2	EM	68605	74705	74605	68705
357 206	C2	A	C2	EM	68606	74706	74606	68706
357 207	C2	A	C2	EM	68607	74707	74607	68707
357 208	C2	A	C2	EM	68608	74708	74608	68708
357 209	C2	A	C2	EM	68609	74709	74609	68709
357 210	C2	A	C2	EM	68610	74710	74610	68710

| 357 211 | **C2** | A | *C2* | EM | 68611 | 74711 | 74611 | 68711 |

Names (carried on DMS(A) and DMS(B) (one plate on each)):

357 201	KEN BIRD	357 206	MARTIN AUNGIER
357 202	KENNY MITCHELL	357 207	JOHN PAGE
357 203	HENRY PUMFRETT	357 208	DAVE DAVIS
357 204	DEREK FOWERS	357 209	JAMES SNELLING
357 205	JOHN D'SILVA		

Class 357/3. Owned by Angel Trains. In 2015–16 17 Class 357/2s (357 212–228) were reconfigured as "high density" units 357 312–328 with fewer seats and more standing room for shorter distance workings.

Seating Layout: 2+2 facing/unidirectional.

DMS(A). Bombardier Derby 2001–02. –/56. 40.7 t.
MS. Bombardier Derby 2001–02. –/60. 36.7 t.
PTS. Bombardier Derby 2001–02. –/50 1TD 2W. 39.5 t.
DMS(B). Bombardier Derby 2001–02. –/56. 40.7 t.

357 312	(357 212)	**C2**	A	*C2*	EM	68612	74712	74612	68712
357 313	(357 213)	**C2**	A	*C2*	EM	68613	74713	74613	68713
357 314	(357 214)	**C2**	A	*C2*	EM	68614	74714	74614	68714
357 315	(357 215)	**C2**	A	*C2*	EM	68615	74715	74615	68715
357 316	(357 216)	**C2**	A	*C2*	EM	68616	74716	74616	68716
357 317	(357 217)	**C2**	A	*C2*	EM	68617	74717	74617	68717
357 318	(357 218)	**C2**	A	*C2*	EM	68618	74718	74618	68718
357 319	(357 219)	**C2**	A	*C2*	EM	68619	74719	74619	68719
357 320	(357 220)	**C2**	A	*C2*	EM	68620	74720	74620	68720
357 321	(357 221)	**C2**	A	*C2*	EM	68621	74721	74621	68721
357 322	(357 222)	**C2**	A	*C2*	EM	68622	74722	74622	68722
357 323	(357 223)	**C2**	A	*C2*	EM	68623	74723	74623	68723
357 324	(357 224)	**C2**	A	*C2*	EM	68624	74724	74624	68724
357 325	(357 225)	**C2**	A	*C2*	EM	68625	74725	74625	68725
357 326	(357 226)	**C2**	A	*C2*	EM	68626	74726	74626	68726
357 327	(357 227)	**C2**	A	*C2*	EM	68627	74727	74627	68727
357 328	(357 228)	**C2**	A	*C2*	EM	68628	74728	74628	68728

Names (carried on DMS(A) and DMS(B) (one plate on each)):

357 313   UPMINSTER I.E.C.C.
357 317   ALLAN BURNELL
357 327   SOUTHEND UNITED

CLASS 360/0   DESIRO UK   SIEMENS

Outer suburban/express units.

Formation: DMC–PTS–TS–DMC.
Construction: Welded aluminium.
Traction Motors: Four Siemens 1TB2016-0GB02 asynchronous of 250 kW.
Wheel Arrangement: Bo-Bo + 2-2 + 2-2 + Bo-Bo.
Braking: Disc & regenerative.   **Dimensions:** 20.34 x 2.80 m.

Bogies: SGP SF5000.   **Couplers:** Dellner 12.
Gangways: Within unit.   **Control System:** IGBT Inverter.
Doors: Sliding plug.   **Maximum Speed:** 100 mph.
Heating & ventilation: Air conditioning.
Seating Layout: 1: 2+2 facing, 2: 3+2 facing/unidirectional.
Multiple Working: Within class.

DMC(A). Siemens Krefeld 2002–03. 8/59. 45.0 t.
PTS. Siemens Vienna 2002–03. –/60(+9) 1TD 2W. 43.6 t.
TS. Siemens Vienna 2002–03. –/78. 34.3 t.
DMC(B). Siemens Krefeld 2002–03. 8/59. 44.1 t.

360 101	FB	A	*GA*	IL	65551	72551	74551	68551
360 102	FB	A	*GA*	IL	65552	72552	74552	68552
360 103	FB	A	*GA*	IL	65553	72553	74553	68553
360 104	FB	A	*GA*	IL	65554	72554	74554	68554
360 105	FB	A	*GA*	IL	65555	72555	74555	68555
360 106	FB	A	*GA*	IL	65556	72556	74556	68556
360 107	FB	A	*GA*	IL	65557	72557	74557	68557
360 108	FB	A	*GA*	IL	65558	72558	74558	68558
360 109	FB	A	*GA*	IL	65559	72559	74559	68559
360 110	FB	A	*GA*	IL	65560	72560	74560	68560
360 111	FB	A	*GA*	IL	65561	72561	74561	68561
360 112	FB	A	*GA*	IL	65562	72562	74562	68562
360 113	FB	A	*GA*	IL	65563	72563	74563	68563
360 114	FB	A	*GA*	IL	65564	72564	74564	68564
360 115	FB	A	*GA*	IL	65565	72565	74565	68565
360 116	FB	A	*GA*	IL	65566	72566	74566	68566
360 117	FB	A	*GA*	IL	65567	72567	74567	68567
360 118	FB	A	*GA*	IL	65568	72568	74568	68568
360 119	FB	A	*GA*	IL	65569	72569	74569	68569
360 120	FB	A	*GA*	IL	65570	72570	74570	68570
360 121	FB	A	*GA*	IL	65571	72571	74571	68571

CLASS 360/2   DESIRO UK   SIEMENS

4-car Class 350 testbed units rebuilt for use by Heathrow Express on Paddington–Heathrow Airport stopping services ("Heathrow Connect").

Original 4-car sets 360 201–204 were made up to 5-cars during 2007 using additional TSs. A fifth unit (360 205) was delivered in late 2005 as a 5-car set. In 2018 TfL Rail took over the operation of the Heathrow stopping service, as the first stage of the new Elizabeth Line service.

Formation: DMS–PTS–TS–TS–DMS.
Construction: Welded aluminium.
Traction Motors: Four Siemens 1TB2016-0GB02 asynchronous of 250 kW.
Wheel Arrangement: Bo-Bo + 2-2 + 2-2 + 2-2 + Bo-Bo.
Braking: Disc & regenerative.   **Dimensions:** 20.34 x 2.80 m.
Bogies: SGP SF5000.   **Couplers:** Dellner 12.
Gangways: Within unit.   **Control System:** IGBT Inverter.
Doors: Sliding plug.   **Maximum Speed:** 100 mph.
Heating & ventilation: Air conditioning.

Seating Layout: 3+2 (* 2+2) facing/unidirectional.
Multiple Working: Within class.

DMS(A). Siemens Krefeld 2002–06. –/63 (* –/54). 44.8 t.
PTS. Siemens Krefeld 2002–06. –/57(+9) 1TD 2W (* –/48(+9) 2W). 44.2 t.
TS(A). Siemens Krefeld 2005–06. –/74 (* –/62). 35.3 t.
TS(B). Siemens Krefeld 2002–06. –/74 (* –/62). 34.1 t.
DMS(B). Siemens Krefeld 2002–06. –/63 (* –/54). 44.4 t.

360 201		**HC**	HE	*XR*	OH	78431	63421	72431	72421	78441
360 202		**HC**	HE	*XR*	OH	78432	63422	72432	72422	78442
360 203		**HC**	HE	*XR*	OH	78433	63423	72433	72423	78443
360 204		**HC**	HE	*XR*	OH	78434	63424	72434	72424	78444
360 205	*	**HE**	HE	*XR*	OH	78435	63425	72435	72425	78445

CLASS 365   NETWORKER EXPRESS   ABB YORK

Outer suburban units. Fitted with a universal access toilet to comply with the 2020 accessibility regulations.

Formation: DMC–TS–PTS–DMC.
Systems: 25 kV AC overhead but with 750 V DC third rail capability (units 365 501–516 were formerly used on DC lines in the South-East).
Construction: Welded aluminium alloy.
Traction Motors: Four GEC-Alsthom G354CX asynchronous of 157 kW.
Wheel Arrangement: Bo-Bo + 2-2 + 2-2 + Bo-Bo.
Braking: Disc & rheostatic.   **Dimensions:** 20.89/20.06 x 2.81 m.
Bogies: ABB P3-16/T3-16.   **Couplers:** Tightlock.
Gangways: Within unit.   **Control System:** GTO Inverter.
Doors: Sliding plug.   **Maximum Speed:** 100 mph.
Seating Layout: 1: 2+2 facing, 2: 2+2 facing.
Multiple Working: Within class only.

DMC(A). Lot No. 31133 1994–95. 12/56. 41.7 t.
TS. Lot No. 31134 1994–95. –/58 1TD 2W 32.9 t.
PTS. Lot No. 31135 1994–95. –/70 1T. 35.2 t.
DMC(B). Lot No. 31136 1994–95. 12/56. 41.7 t.

365 501	**TL**	TF		CY	65894	72241	72240	65935
365 502	**TL**	TF	*GN*	HE	65895	72243	72242	65936
365 503	**TL**	TF		CY	65896	72245	72244	65937
365 504	**TL**	TF	*GN*	HE	65897	72247	72246	65938
365 505	**TL**	TF		CY	65898	72249	72248	65939
365 506	**TL**	TF	*GN*	HE	65899	72251	72250	65940
365 507	**TL**	TF		CY	65900	72253	72252	65941
365 508	**TL**	TF	*GN*	HE	65901	72255	72254	65942
365 509	**TL**	TF		CY	65902	72257	72256	65943
365 510	**TL**	TF	*GN*	HE	65903	72259	72258	65944
365 511	**TL**	TF	*GN*	HE	65904	72261	72260	65945
365 512	**TL**	TF	*GN*	HE	65905	72263	72262	65946
365 513	**TL**	TF		CY	65906	72265	72264	65947
365 514	**TL**	TF	*GN*	HE	65907	72267	72266	65948
365 515	**TL**	TF		CY	65908	72269	72268	65949

365516	**TL**	TF	*GN*	HE	65909	72271	72270	65950
365517	**TL**	TF		CY	65910	72273	72272	65951
365518	**TL**	TF	*GN*	HE	65911	72275	72274	65952
365519	**TL**	TF		CY	65912	72277	72276	65953
365520	**TL**	TF	*GN*	HE	65913	72279	72278	65954
365521	**TL**	TF		CY	65914	72281	72280	65955
365522	**TL**	TF	*GN*	HE	65915	72283	72282	65956
365523	**TL**	TF		CY	65916	72285	72284	65957
365524	**TL**	TF	*GN*	HE	65917	72287	72286	65958
365525	**TL**	TF		CY	65918	72289	72288	65959
365527	**TL**	TF		CY	65920	72293	72292	65961
365528	**TL**	TF	*GN*	HE	65921	72295	72294	65962
365529	**TL**	TF		CY	65922	72297	72296	65963
365530	**TL**	TF	*GN*	HE	65923	72299	72298	65964
365531	**TL**	TF		CY	65924	72301	72300	65965
365532	**TL**	TF	*GN*	HE	65925	72303	72302	65966
365533	**TL**	TF		CY	65926	72305	72304	65967
365534	**TL**	TF	*GN*	HE	65927	72307	72306	65968
365535	**TL**	TF		CY	65928	72309	72308	65969
365536	**TL**	TF	*GN*	HE	65929	72311	72310	65970
365537	**TL**	TF		CY	65930	72313	72312	65971
365538	**TL**	TF	*GN*	HE	65931	72315	72314	65972
365539	**TL**	TF	*GN*	HE	65932	72317	72316	65973
365540	**TL**	TF	*GN*	HE	65933	72319	72318	65974
365541	**TL**	TF		ZI	65934	72321	72320	65975

Name (carried on each DMC):

365537　Daniel Edwards (1974–2010) Cambridge Driver

CLASS 375 ELECTROSTAR
ADTRANZ/BOMBARDIER DERBY

Express and outer suburban units.

Formation: Various, see sub-class headings.
Systems: 25 kV AC overhead/750 V DC third rail (some third rail only with provision for retro-fitting of AC equipment).
Construction: Welded aluminium alloy underframe, sides and roof with steel ends. All sections bolted together.
Traction Motors: Two Adtranz asynchronous of 250 kW.
Wheel Arrangement: 2-Bo (+ 2-Bo) + 2-2 + Bo-2.

Braking: Disc & regenerative.	**Dimensions:** 20.40/19.99 x 2.80 m.
Bogies: Adtranz P3-25/T3-25.	**Couplers:** Dellner 12.
Gangways: Throughout.	**Control System:** IGBT Inverter.
Doors: Sliding plug.	**Maximum Speed:** 100 mph.

Heating & ventilation: Air conditioning.
Seating Layout: 1: 2+2 facing/unidirectional. 2: 2+2 facing/unidirectional (except 375/9 – 3+2 facing/unidirectional).
Multiple Working: Within class and with Classes 376, 377, 378 and 379.

Class 375/3. Express units. 750 V DC only. DMS–TS–DMC.

DMS. Bombardier Derby 2001–02. –/60. 43.8 t.
TS. Bombardier Derby 2001–02. –/56 1TD 2W. 35.5 t.
DMC. Bombardier Derby 2001–02. 12/48. 43.8 t.

375301	**SB**	E	*SE*	RM	67921	74351	67931
375302	**SB**	E	*SE*	RM	67922	74352	67932
375303	**SB**	E	*SE*	RM	67923	74353	67933
375304	**SB**	E	*SE*	RM	67924	74354	67934
375305	**SB**	E	*SE*	RM	67925	74355	67935
375306	**SB**	E	*SE*	RM	67926	74356	67936
375307	**SB**	E	*SE*	RM	67927	74357	67937
375308	**SB**	E	*SE*	RM	67928	74358	67938
375309	**SB**	E	*SE*	RM	67929	74359	67939
375310	**SB**	E	*SE*	RM	67930	74360	67940

Class 375/6. Express units. 25 kV AC/750 V DC. DMS–MC–PTS–DMS.

DMS(A). Adtranz Derby 1999–2001. –/60. 46.2 t.
MC. Adtranz Derby 1999–2001. 16/50 1T. 40.5 t.
PTS. Adtranz Derby 1999–2001. –/56 1TD 2W. 40.7 t.
DMS(B). Adtranz Derby 1999–2001. –/60. 46.2 t.

375601	**SB**	E	*SE*	RM	67801	74251	74201	67851
375602	**SB**	E	*SE*	RM	67802	74252	74202	67852
375603	**SB**	E	*SE*	RM	67803	74253	74203	67853
375604	**SB**	E	*SE*	RM	67804	74254	74204	67854
375605	**SB**	E	*SE*	RM	67805	74255	74205	67855
375606	**SB**	E	*SE*	RM	67806	74256	74206	67856
375607	**SB**	E	*SE*	RM	67807	74257	74207	67857
375608	**SB**	E	*SE*	RM	67808	74258	74208	67858
375609	**SB**	E	*SE*	RM	67809	74259	74209	67859
375610	**SB**	E	*SE*	RM	67810	74260	74210	67860
375611	**SB**	E	*SE*	RM	67811	74261	74211	67861
375612	**SB**	E	*SE*	RM	67812	74262	74212	67862
375613	**SB**	E	*SE*	RM	67813	74263	74213	67863
375614	**SB**	E	*SE*	RM	67814	74264	74214	67864
375615	**SB**	E	*SE*	RM	67815	74265	74215	67865
375616	**SB**	E	*SE*	RM	67816	74266	74216	67866
375617	**SB**	E	*SE*	RM	67817	74267	74217	67867
375618	**SB**	E	*SE*	RM	67818	74268	74218	67868
375619	**SB**	E	*SE*	RM	67819	74269	74219	67869
375620	**SB**	E	*SE*	RM	67820	74270	74220	67870
375621	**SB**	E	*SE*	RM	67821	74271	74221	67871
375622	**SB**	E	*SE*	RM	67822	74272	74222	67872
375623	**SB**	E	*SE*	RM	67823	74273	74223	67873
375624	**SB**	E	*SE*	RM	67824	74274	74224	67874
375625	**SB**	E	*SE*	RM	67825	74275	74225	67875
375626	**SB**	E	*SE*	RM	67826	74276	74226	67876
375627	**SB**	E	*SE*	RM	67827	74277	74227	67877
375628	**SB**	E	*SE*	RM	67828	74278	74228	67878
375629	**SB**	E	*SE*	RM	67829	74279	74229	67879

| 375630 | **SB** | E | *SE* | RM | 67830 | 74280 | 74230 | 67880 |

Names (carried on one side of each MC or TS):

375619 Driver John Neve | 375623 Hospice in the Weald

Class 375/7. Express units. 750 V DC only. DMS–MC–TS–DMS.

DMS(A). Bombardier Derby 2001–02. –/60. 43.8 t.
MC. Bombardier Derby 2001–02. 16/50 1T. 36.4 t.
TS. Bombardier Derby 2001–02. –/56 1TD 2W. 34.1 t.
DMS(B). Bombardier Derby 2001–02. –/60. 43.8 t.

375701	**SB**	E	*SE*	RM	67831	74281	74231	67881
375702	**SB**	E	*SE*	RM	67832	74282	74232	67882
375703	**SB**	E	*SE*	RM	67833	74283	74233	67883
375704	**SB**	E	*SE*	RM	67834	74284	74234	67884
375705	**SB**	E	*SE*	RM	67835	74285	74235	67885
375706	**SB**	E	*SE*	RM	67836	74286	74236	67886
375707	**SB**	E	*SE*	RM	67837	74287	74237	67887
375708	**SB**	E	*SE*	RM	67838	74288	74238	67888
375709	**SB**	E	*SE*	RM	67839	74289	74239	67889
375710	**SB**	E	*SE*	RM	67840	74290	74240	67890
375711	**SB**	E	*SE*	RM	67841	74291	74241	67891
375712	**SB**	E	*SE*	RM	67842	74292	74242	67892
375713	**SB**	E	*SE*	RM	67843	74293	74243	67893
375714	**SB**	E	*SE*	RM	67844	74294	74244	67894
375715	**SB**	E	*SE*	RM	67845	74295	74245	67895

Names (carried on one side of each MC or TS):

375701 Kent Air Ambulance Explorer | 375714   Rochester Cathedral
375710 Rochester Castle

Class 375/8. Express units. 750 V DC only. DMS–MC–TS–DMS.

375 801–820 are fitted with de-icing equipment. TS weighs 36.5 t.

DMS(A). Bombardier Derby 2004. –/60. 43.3 t.
MC. Bombardier Derby 2004. 16/50 1T. 39.8 t.
TS. Bombardier Derby 2004. –/52 1TD 2W. 35.9 t.
DMS(B). Bombardier Derby 2004. –/64. 43.3 t.

375801	**SB**	E	*SE*	RM	73301	79001	78201	73701
375802	**SB**	E	*SE*	RM	73302	79002	78202	73702
375803	**SB**	E	*SE*	RM	73303	79003	78203	73703
375804	**SB**	E	*SE*	RM	73304	79004	78204	73704
375805	**SB**	E	*SE*	RM	73305	79005	78205	73705
375806	**SB**	E	*SE*	RM	73306	79006	78206	73706
375807	**SB**	E	*SE*	RM	73307	79007	78207	73707
375808	**SB**	E	*SE*	RM	73308	79008	78208	73708
375809	**SB**	E	*SE*	RM	73309	79009	78209	73709
375810	**SB**	E	*SE*	RM	73310	79010	78210	73710
375811	**SB**	E	*SE*	RM	73311	79011	78211	73711
375812	**SB**	E	*SE*	RM	73312	79012	78212	73712
375813	**SB**	E	*SE*	RM	73313	79013	78213	73713

375814	**SB**	E	*SE*	RM	73314	79014	78214	73714
375815	**SB**	E	*SE*	RM	73315	79015	78215	73715
375816	**SB**	E	*SE*	RM	73316	79016	78216	73716
375817	**SB**	E	*SE*	RM	73317	79017	78217	73717
375818	**SB**	E	*SE*	RM	73318	79018	78218	73718
375819	**SB**	E	*SE*	RM	73319	79019	78219	73719
375820	**SB**	E	*SE*	RM	73320	79020	78220	73720
375821	**SB**	E	*SE*	RM	73321	79021	78221	73721
375822	**SB**	E	*SE*	RM	73322	79022	78222	73722
375823	**SB**	E	*SE*	RM	73323	79023	78223	73723
375824	**SB**	E	*SE*	RM	73324	79024	78224	73724
375825	**SB**	E	*SE*	RM	73325	79025	78225	73725
375826	**SB**	E	*SE*	RM	73326	79026	78226	73726
375827	**SB**	E	*SE*	RM	73327	79027	78227	73727
375828	**SB**	E	*SE*	RM	73328	79028	78228	73728
375829	**SB**	E	*SE*	RM	73329	79029	78229	73729
375830	**SB**	E	*SE*	RM	73330	79030	78230	73730

Names (carried on one side of each MS or TS):

375823 Ashford Proudly Served by Rail for 175 years

Class 375/9. Outer suburban units. 750 V DC only. DMC–MS–TS–DMC.

DMC(A). Bombardier Derby 2003–04. 12/59. 43.4 t.
MS. Bombardier Derby 2003–04. –/73 1T. 39.3 t.
TS. Bombardier Derby 2003–04. –/62 1TD 2W. 35.6 t.
DMC(B). Bombardier Derby 2003–04. 12/59. 43.4 t.

375901	**SB**	E	*SE*	RM	73331	79031	79061	73731
375902	**SB**	E	*SE*	RM	73332	79032	79062	73732
375903	**SB**	E	*SE*	RM	73333	79033	79063	73733
375904	**SB**	E	*SE*	RM	73334	79034	79064	73734
375905	**SB**	E	*SE*	RM	73335	79035	79065	73735
375906	**SB**	E	*SE*	RM	73336	79036	79066	73736
375907	**SB**	E	*SE*	RM	73337	79037	79067	73737
375908	**SB**	E	*SE*	RM	73338	79038	79068	73738
375909	**SB**	E	*SE*	RM	73339	79039	79069	73739
375910	**SB**	E	*SE*	RM	73340	79040	79070	73740
375911	**SB**	E	*SE*	RM	73341	79041	79071	73741
375912	**SB**	E	*SE*	RM	73342	79042	79072	73742
375913	**SB**	E	*SE*	RM	73343	79043	79073	73743
375914	**SB**	E	*SE*	RM	73344	79044	79074	73744
375915	**SB**	E	*SE*	RM	73345	79045	79075	73745
375916	**SB**	E	*SE*	RM	73346	79046	79076	73746
375917	**SB**	E	*SE*	RM	73347	79047	79077	73747
375918	**SB**	E	*SE*	RM	73348	79048	79078	73748
375919	**SB**	E	*SE*	RM	73349	79049	79079	73749
375920	**SB**	E	*SE*	RM	73350	79050	79080	73750
375921	**SB**	E	*SE*	RM	73351	79051	79081	73751
375922	**SB**	E	*SE*	RM	73352	79052	79082	73752
375923	**SB**	E	*SE*	RM	73353	79053	79083	73753
375924	**SB**	E	*SE*	RM	73354	79054	79084	73754

375925	**SB**	E	*SE*	RM	73355	79055	79085	73755
375926	**SB**	E	*SE*	RM	73356	79056	79086	73756
375927	**SB**	E	*SE*	RM	73357	79057	79087	73757

CLASS 376 ELECTROSTAR BOMBARDIER DERBY

Inner suburban units.

Formation: DMS–MS–TS–MS–DMS.
System: 750 V DC third rail.
Construction: Welded aluminium alloy underframe, sides and roof with steel ends. All sections bolted together.
Traction Motors: Two Bombardier asynchronous of 200 kW.
Wheel Arrangement: 2-Bo + 2-Bo + 2-2 + Bo-2 + Bo-2.
Braking: Disc & regenerative.   **Dimensions:** 20.40/19.99 x 2.80 m.
Bogies: Bombardier P3-25/T3-25.   **Couplers:** Dellner 12.
Gangways: Within unit.   **Control System:** IGBT Inverter.
Doors: Sliding.   **Maximum Speed:** 75 mph.
Heating & ventilation: Pressure heating and ventilation.
Seating Layout: 2+2 low density facing.
Multiple Working: Within class and with Classes 375, 377, 378 and 379.

DMS(A). Bombardier Derby 2004–05. –/36(+6) 1W. 42.1 t.
MS. Bombardier Derby 2004–05. –/48. 36.2 t.
TS. Bombardier Derby 2004–05. –/48. 36.3 t.
DMS(B). Bombardier Derby 2004–05. –/36(+6) 1W. 42.1 t.

376001	**CN**	E	*SE*	SG	61101	63301	64301	63501	61601
376002	**CN**	E	*SE*	SG	61102	63302	64302	63502	61602
376003	**CN**	E	*SE*	SG	61103	63303	64303	63503	61603
376004	**CN**	E	*SE*	SG	61104	63304	64304	63504	61604
376005	**CN**	E	*SE*	SG	61105	63305	64305	63505	61605
376006	**CN**	E	*SE*	SG	61106	63306	64306	63506	61606
376007	**CN**	E	*SE*	SG	61107	63307	64307	63507	61607
376008	**CN**	E	*SE*	SG	61108	63308	64308	63508	61608
376009	**CN**	E	*SE*	SG	61109	63309	64309	63509	61609
376010	**CN**	E	*SE*	SG	61110	63310	64310	63510	61610
376011	**CN**	E	*SE*	SG	61111	63311	64311	63511	61611
376012	**CN**	E	*SE*	SG	61112	63312	64312	63512	61612
376013	**CN**	E	*SE*	SG	61113	63313	64313	63513	61613
376014	**CN**	E	*SE*	SG	61114	63314	64314	63514	61614
376015	**CN**	E	*SE*	SG	61115	63315	64315	63515	61615
376016	**CN**	E	*SE*	SG	61116	63316	64316	63516	61616
376017	**CN**	E	*SE*	SG	61117	63317	64317	63517	61617
376018	**CN**	E	*SE*	SG	61118	63318	64318	63518	61618
376019	**CN**	E	*SE*	SG	61119	63319	64319	63519	61619
376020	**CN**	E	*SE*	SG	61120	63320	64320	63520	61620
376021	**CN**	E	*SE*	SG	61121	63321	64321	63521	61621
376022	**CN**	E	*SE*	SG	61122	63322	64322	63522	61622
376023	**CN**	E	*SE*	SG	61123	63323	64323	63523	61623
376024	**CN**	E	*SE*	SG	61124	63324	64324	63524	61624
376025	**CN**	E	*SE*	SG	61125	63325	64325	63525	61625

376026	CN	E	SE	SG	61126 63326 64326 63526 61626
376027	CN	E	SE	SG	61127 63327 64327 63527 61627
376028	CN	E	SE	SG	61128 63328 64328 63528 61628
376029	CN	E	SE	SG	61129 63329 64329 63529 61629
376030	CN	E	SE	SG	61130 63330 64330 63530 61630
376031	CN	E	SE	SG	61131 63331 64331 63531 61631
376032	CN	E	SE	SG	61132 63332 64332 63532 61632
376033	CN	E	SE	SG	61133 63333 64333 63533 61633
376034	CN	E	SE	SG	61134 63334 64334 63534 61634
376035	CN	E	SE	SG	61135 63335 64335 63535 61635
376036	CN	E	SE	SG	61136 63336 64336 63536 61636

Name (carried on TSO): 376001   Alan Doggett

CLASS 377   ELECTROSTAR   BOMBARDIER DERBY

Express and outer suburban units.

Formation: Various, see sub-class headings.
Systems: 25 kV AC overhead/750 V DC third rail or third rail only with provision for retro-fitting of AC equipment.
Construction: Welded aluminium alloy underframe, sides and roof with steel ends. All sections bolted together.
Traction Motors: Two Bombardier asynchronous of 250 kW.
Wheel Arrangement: 2-Bo + 2-2 + Bo-2 or 2-Bo + 2-Bo + 2-2 + Bo-2 or 2-Bo + 2-Bo + 2-2 + Bo-2 + Bo-2.
Braking: Disc & regenerative.   **Dimensions:** 20.39/20.00 x 2.80 m.
Bogies: Bombardier P3-25/T3-25.   **Couplers:** Dellner 12.
Gangways: Throughout.   **Control System:** IGBT Inverter.
Doors: Sliding plug.   **Maximum Speed:** 100 mph.
Heating & ventilation: Air conditioning.
Seating Layout: Various, see sub-class headings.
Multiple Working: Within class and with Classes 375, 376, 378, 379 and 387.

Class 377/1. 750 V DC only. DMC–MS–TS–DMC.
Seating layout: 1: 2+2 facing/unidirectional, 2: 2+2 facing/unidirectional (377 101–119), 3+2/2+2 facing/unidirectional (377 120–139), 3+2 (middle cars and 2+2 (end cars) facing/unidirectional (377 140–164).

DMC(A). Bombardier Derby 2002–03. 12/48 (s 12/56). 44.8 t.
MS. Bombardier Derby 2002–03. –/62 (s –/70, t –/69). 1T. 39.0 t.
TS. Bombardier Derby 2002–03. –/52 (s –/60, t –/57). 1TD 2W. 35.4 t.
DMC(B). Bombardier Derby 2002–03. 12/48 (s 12/56). 43.4 t.

377101	SN	P	SN	SU	78501 77101 78901 78701
377102	SN	P	SN	SU	78502 77102 78902 78702
377103	SN	P	SN	SU	78503 77103 78903 78703
377104	SN	P	SN	SU	78504 77104 78904 78704
377105	SN	P	SN	SU	78505 77105 78905 78705
377106	SN	P	SN	SU	78506 77106 78906 78706
377107	SN	P	SN	SU	78507 77107 78907 78707
377108	SN	P	SN	SU	78508 77108 78908 78708
377109	SN	P	SN	SU	78509 77109 78909 78709

377 110		**SN**	P	*SN*	SU	78510	77110	78910	78710
377 111		**SN**	P	*SN*	SU	78511	77111	78911	78711
377 112		**SN**	P	*SN*	SU	78512	77112	78912	78712
377 113		**SN**	P	*SN*	SU	78513	77113	78913	78713
377 114		**SN**	P	*SN*	SU	78514	77114	78914	78714
377 115		**SN**	P	*SN*	SU	78515	77115	78915	78715
377 116		**SN**	P	*SN*	SU	78516	77116	78916	78716
377 117		**SN**	P	*SN*	SU	78517	77117	78917	78717
377 118		**SN**	P	*SN*	SU	78518	77118	78918	78718
377 119		**SN**	P	*SN*	SU	78519	77119	78919	78719
377 120	s	**SN**	P	*SN*	SU	78520	77120	78920	78720
377 121	s	**SN**	P	*SN*	SU	78521	77121	78921	78721
377 122	s	**SN**	P	*SN*	SU	78522	77122	78922	78722
377 123	s	**SN**	P	*SN*	SU	78523	77123	78923	78723
377 124	s	**SN**	P	*SN*	SU	78524	77124	78924	78724
377 125	s	**SN**	P	*SN*	SU	78525	77125	78925	78725
377 126	s	**SN**	P	*SN*	SU	78526	77126	78926	78726
377 127	s	**SN**	P	*SN*	SU	78527	77127	78927	78727
377 128	s	**SN**	P	*SN*	SU	78528	77128	78928	78728
377 129	s	**SN**	P	*SN*	SU	78529	77129	78929	78729
377 130	s	**SN**	P	*SN*	SU	78530	77130	78930	78730
377 131	s	**SN**	P	*SN*	SU	78531	77131	78931	78731
377 132	s	**SN**	P	*SN*	SU	78532	77132	78932	78732
377 133	s	**SN**	P	*SN*	SU	78533	77133	78933	78733
377 134	s	**SN**	P	*SN*	SU	78534	77134	78934	78734
377 135	s	**SN**	P	*SN*	SU	78535	77135	78935	78735
377 136	s	**SN**	P	*SN*	SU	78536	77136	78936	78736
377 137	s	**SN**	P	*SN*	SU	78537	77137	78937	78737
377 138	s	**SN**	P	*SN*	SU	78538	77138	78938	78738
377 139	s	**SN**	P	*SN*	SU	78539	77139	78939	78739
377 140	t	**SN**	P	*SN*	SU	78540	77140	78940	78740
377 141	t	**SN**	P	*SN*	SU	78541	77141	78941	78741
377 142	t	**SN**	P	*SN*	SU	78542	77142	78942	78742
377 143	t	**SN**	P	*SN*	SU	78543	77143	78943	78743
377 144	t	**SN**	P	*SN*	SU	78544	77144	78944	78744
377 145	t	**SN**	P	*SN*	SU	78545	77145	78945	78745
377 146	t	**SN**	P	*SN*	SU	78546	77146	78946	78746
377 147	t	**SN**	P	*SN*	SU	78547	77147	78947	78747
377 148	t	**SN**	P	*SN*	SU	78548	77148	78948	78748
377 149	t	**SN**	P	*SN*	SU	78549	77149	78949	78749
377 150	t	**SN**	P	*SN*	SU	78550	77150	78950	78750
377 151	t	**SN**	P	*SN*	SU	78551	77151	78951	78751
377 152	t	**SN**	P	*SN*	SU	78552	77152	78952	78752
377 153	t	**SN**	P	*SN*	SU	78553	77153	78953	78753
377 154	t	**SN**	P	*SN*	SU	78554	77154	78954	78754
377 155	t	**SN**	P	*SN*	SU	78555	77155	78955	78755
377 156	t	**SN**	P	*SN*	SU	78556	77156	78956	78756
377 157	t	**SN**	P	*SN*	SU	78557	77157	78957	78757
377 158	t	**SN**	P	*SN*	SU	78558	77158	78958	78758
377 159	t	**SN**	P	*SN*	SU	78559	77159	78959	78759
377 160	t	**SN**	P	*SN*	SU	78560	77160	78960	78760

377 161	t	**SN**	P	*SN*	SU	78561	77161	78961	78761
377 162	t	**SN**	P	*SN*	SU	78562	77162	78962	78762
377 163	t	**SN**	P	*SE*	RM	78563	77163	78963	78763
377 164	t	**SN**	P	*SE*	RM	78564	77164	78964	78764

Class 377/2. 25 kV AC/750 V DC. DMC–MS–PTS–DMC. Dual-voltage units.
Seating layout: 1: 2+2 facing/unidirectional, 2: 2+2 and 3+2 facing/unidirectional (3+2 seating in middle cars only).

DMC(A). Bombardier Derby 2003–04. 12/48. 44.2 t.
MS. Bombardier Derby 2003–04. –/69 1T. 39.8 t.
PTS. Bombardier Derby 2003–04. –/57 1TD 2W. 40.1 t.
DMC(B). Bombardier Derby 2003–04. 12/48. 44.2 t.

377 201	**SN**	P	*SN*	SU	78571	77171	78971	78771
377 202	**SN**	P	*SN*	SU	78572	77172	78972	78772
377 203	**SN**	P	*SN*	SU	78573	77173	78973	78773
377 204	**SN**	P	*SN*	SU	78574	77174	78974	78774
377 205	**SN**	P	*SN*	SU	78575	77175	78975	78775
377 206	**SN**	P	*SN*	SU	78576	77176	78976	78776
377 207	**SN**	P	*SN*	SU	78577	77177	78977	78777
377 208	**SN**	P	*SN*	SU	78578	77178	78978	78778
377 209	**SN**	P	*SN*	SU	78579	77179	78979	78779
377 210	**SN**	P	*SN*	SU	78580	77180	78980	78780
377 211	**SN**	P	*SN*	SU	78581	77181	78981	78781
377 212	**SN**	P	*SN*	SU	78582	77182	78982	78782
377 213	**SN**	P	*SN*	SU	78583	77183	78983	78783
377 214	**SN**	P	*SN*	SU	78584	77184	78984	78784
377 215	**SN**	P	*SN*	SU	78585	77185	78985	78785

Class 377/3. 750 V DC only. DMC–TS–DMC.
Seating Layout: 1: 2+2 facing/unidirectional, 2: 2+2 facing/unidirectional.

Units built as Class 375, but renumbered in the Class 377/3 range when fitted with Dellner couplers.

377 342 was formerly 377 442. It had been reformed as a 3-car unit owing to fire damage to MS vehicle 78842 in 2016.

DMC(A). Bombardier Derby 2001–02. 12/48. 43.5 t.
TS. Bombardier Derby 2001–02. –/56 1TD 2W. 35.4 t.
DMC(B). Bombardier Derby 2001–02. 12/48. 43.5 t.

377 301	(375 311)	**SN**	P	*SN*	SU	68201	74801	68401
377 302	(375 312)	**SN**	P	*SN*	SU	68202	74802	68402
377 303	(375 313)	**SN**	P	*SN*	SU	68203	74803	68403
377 304	(375 314)	**SN**	P	*SN*	SU	68204	74804	68404
377 305	(375 315)	**SN**	P	*SN*	SU	68205	74805	68405
377 306	(375 316)	**SN**	P	*SN*	SU	68206	74806	68406
377 307	(375 317)	**SN**	P	*SN*	SU	68207	74807	68407
377 308	(375 318)	**SN**	P	*SN*	SU	68208	74808	68408
377 309	(375 319)	**SN**	P	*SN*	SU	68209	74809	68409
377 310	(375 320)	**SN**	P	*SN*	SU	68210	74810	68410
377 311	(375 321)	**SN**	P	*SN*	SU	68211	74811	68411
377 312	(375 322)	**SN**	P	*SN*	SU	68212	74812	68412

377313	(375323)	**SN**	P	*SN*	SU	68213	74813	68413
377314	(375324)	**SN**	P	*SN*	SU	68214	74814	68414
377315	(375325)	**SN**	P	*SN*	SU	68215	74815	68415
377316	(375326)	**SN**	P	*SN*	SU	68216	74816	68416
377317	(375327)	**SN**	P	*SN*	SU	68217	74817	68417
377318	(375328)	**SN**	P	*SN*	SU	68218	74818	68418
377319	(375329)	**SN**	P	*SN*	SU	68219	74819	68419
377320	(375330)	**SN**	P	*SN*	SU	68220	74820	68420
377321	(375331)	**SN**	P	*SN*	SU	68221	74821	68421
377322	(375332)	**SN**	P	*SN*	SU	68222	74822	68422
377323	(375333)	**SN**	P	*SN*	SU	68223	74823	68423
377324	(375334)	**SN**	P	*SN*	SU	68224	74824	68424
377325	(375335)	**SN**	P	*SN*	SU	68225	74825	68425
377326	(375336)	**SN**	P	*SN*	SU	68226	74826	68426
377327	(375337)	**SN**	P	*SN*	SU	68227	74827	68427
377328	(375338)	**SN**	P	*SN*	SU	68228	74828	68428
377342	(377442)	**SN**	P	*SN*	SU	73442	78642	73842

Class 377/4. 750 V DC only. DMC–MS–TS–DMC.
Seating Layout: 1: 2+2 facing/two seats longitudinal, 2: 2+2 and 3+2 facing/unidirectional (3+2 seating in middle cars only).

DMC(A). Bombardier Derby 2004–05. 10/48. 43.1 t.
MS. Bombardier Derby 2004–05. –/69 1T. 39.3 t.
TS. Bombardier Derby 2004–05. –/56 1TD 2W. 35.3 t.
DMC(B). Bombardier Derby 2004–05. 10/48. 43.2 t.

377401	**SN**	P	*SN*	SU	73401	78801	78601	73801
377402	**SN**	P	*SN*	SU	73402	78802	78602	73802
377403	**SN**	P	*SN*	SU	73403	78803	78603	73803
377404	**SN**	P	*SN*	SU	73404	78804	78604	73804
377405	**SN**	P	*SN*	SU	73405	78805	78605	73805
377406	**SN**	P	*SN*	SU	73406	78806	78606	73806
377407	**SN**	P	*SN*	SU	73407	78807	78607	73807
377408	**SN**	P	*SN*	SU	73408	78808	78608	73808
377409	**SN**	P	*SN*	SU	73409	78809	78609	73809
377410	**SN**	P	*SN*	SU	73410	78810	78610	73810
377411	**SN**	P	*SN*	SU	73411	78811	78611	73811
377412	**SN**	P	*SN*	SU	73412	78812	78612	73812
377413	**SN**	P	*SN*	SU	73413	78813	78613	73813
377414	**SN**	P	*SN*	SU	73414	78814	78614	73814
377415	**SN**	P	*SN*	SU	73415	78815	78615	73815
377416	**SN**	P	*SN*	SU	73416	78816	78616	73816
377417	**SN**	P	*SN*	SU	73417	78817	78617	73817
377418	**SN**	P	*SN*	SU	73418	78818	78618	73818
377419	**SN**	P	*SN*	SU	73419	78819	78619	73819
377420	**SN**	P	*SN*	SU	73420	78820	78620	73820
377421	**SN**	P	*SN*	SU	73421	78821	78621	73821
377422	**SN**	P	*SN*	SU	73422	78822	78622	73822
377423	**SN**	P	*SN*	SU	73423	78823	78623	73823
377424	**SN**	P	*SN*	SU	73424	78824	78624	73824
377425	**SN**	P	*SN*	SU	73425	78825	78625	73825

377 426	**SN**	P	*SN*	SU	73426	78826	78626	73826
377 427	**SN**	P	*SN*	SU	73427	78827	78627	73827
377 428	**SN**	P	*SN*	SU	73428	78828	78628	73828
377 429	**SN**	P	*SN*	SU	73429	78829	78629	73829
377 430	**SN**	P	*SN*	SU	73430	78830	78630	73830
377 431	**SN**	P	*SN*	SU	73431	78831	78631	73831
377 432	**SN**	P	*SN*	SU	73432	78832	78632	73832
377 433	**SN**	P	*SN*	SU	73433	78833	78633	73833
377 434	**SN**	P	*SN*	SU	73434	78834	78634	73834
377 435	**SN**	P	*SN*	SU	73435	78835	78635	73835
377 436	**SN**	P	*SN*	SU	73436	78836	78636	73836
377 437	**SN**	P	*SN*	SU	73437	78837	78637	73837
377 438	**SN**	P	*SN*	SU	73438	78838	78638	73838
377 439	**SN**	P	*SN*	SU	73439	78839	78639	73839
377 440	**SN**	P	*SN*	SU	73440	78840	78640	73840
377 441	**SN**	P	*SN*	SU	73441	78841	78641	73841
377 443	**SN**	P	*SN*	SU	73443	78843	78643	73843
377 444	**SN**	P	*SN*	SU	73444	78844	78644	73844
377 445	**SN**	P	*SN*	SU	73445	78845	78645	73845
377 446	**SN**	P	*SN*	SU	73446	78846	78646	73846
377 447	**SN**	P	*SN*	SU	73447	78847	78647	73847
377 448	**SN**	P	*SN*	SU	73448	78848	78648	73848
377 449	**SN**	P	*SN*	SU	73449	78849	78649	73849
377 450	**SN**	P	*SN*	SU	73450	78850	78650	73850
377 451	**SN**	P	*SN*	SU	73451	78851	78651	73851
377 452	**SN**	P	*SN*	SU	73452	78852	78652	73852
377 453	**SN**	P	*SN*	SU	73453	78853	78653	73853
377 454	**SN**	P	*SN*	SU	73454	78854	78654	73854
377 455	**SN**	P	*SN*	SU	73455	78855	78655	73855
377 456	**SN**	P	*SN*	SU	73456	78856	78656	73856
377 457	**SN**	P	*SN*	SU	73457	78857	78657	73857
377 458	**SN**	P	*SN*	SU	73458	78858	78658	73858
377 459	**SN**	P	*SN*	SU	73459	78859	78659	73859
377 460	**SN**	P	*SN*	SU	73460	78860	78660	73860
377 461	**SN**	P	*SN*	SU	73461	78861	78661	73861
377 462	**SN**	P	*SN*	SU	73462	78862	78662	73862
377 463	**SN**	P	*SN*	SU	73463	78863	78663	73863
377 464	**SN**	P	*SN*	SU	73464	78864	78664	73864
377 465	**SN**	P	*SN*	SU	73465	78865	78665	73865
377 466	**SN**	P	*SN*	SU	73466	78866	78666	73866
377 467	**SN**	P	*SN*	SU	73467	78867	78667	73867
377 468	**SN**	P	*SN*	SU	73468	78868	78668	73868
377 469	**SN**	P	*SN*	SU	73469	78869	78669	73869
377 470	**SN**	P	*SN*	SU	73470	78870	78670	73870
377 471	**SN**	P	*SN*	SU	73471	78871	78671	73871
377 472	**SN**	P	*SN*	SU	73472	78872	78672	73872
377 473	**SN**	P	*SN*	SU	73473	78873	78673	73873
377 474	**SN**	P	*SN*	SU	73474	78874	78674	73874
377 475	**SN**	P	*SN*	SU	73475	78875	78675	73875
Spare	**SN**	P		ZN		78842		

Class 377/5. 25 kV AC/750 V DC. DMC–MS–PTS–DMS. Dual-voltage units. Details as Class 377/2 unless stated.

DMC. Bombardier Derby 2008–09. 10/48. 43.1 t.
MS. Bombardier Derby 2008–09. –/69 1T. 40.3 t.
PTS. Bombardier Derby 2008–09. –/56 1TD 2W. 40.6 t.
DMS. Bombardier Derby 2008–09. –/58. 44.9 t.

377 501	**FB**	P	*SE*	RM	73501	75901	74901	73601
377 502	**FB**	P	*SE*	RM	73502	75902	74902	73602
377 503	**FB**	P	*SE*	RM	73503	75903	74903	73603
377 504	**FB**	P	*SE*	RM	73504	75904	74904	73604
377 505	**FB**	P	*SE*	RM	73505	75905	74905	73605
377 506	**FB**	P	*SE*	RM	73506	75906	74906	73606
377 507	**FB**	P	*SE*	RM	73507	75907	74907	73607
377 508	**FB**	P	*SE*	RM	73508	75908	74908	73608
377 509	**FB**	P	*SE*	RM	73509	75909	74909	73609
377 510	**FB**	P	*SE*	RM	73510	75910	74910	73610
377 511	**FB**	P	*SE*	RM	73511	75911	74911	73611
377 512	**FB**	P	*SE*	RM	73512	75912	74912	73612
377 513	**FB**	P	*SE*	RM	73513	75913	74913	73613
377 514	**FB**	P	*SE*	RM	73514	75914	74914	73614
377 515	**FB**	P	*SE*	RM	73515	75915	74915	73615
377 516	**FB**	P	*SE*	RM	73516	75916	74916	73616
377 517	**FB**	P	*SE*	RM	73517	75917	74917	73617
377 518	**FB**	P	*SE*	RM	73518	75918	74918	73618
377 519	**FB**	P	*SE*	RM	73519	75919	74919	73619
377 520	**FB**	P	*SE*	RM	73520	75920	74920	73620
377 521	**FB**	P	*SE*	RM	73521	75921	74921	73621
377 522	**FB**	P	*SE*	RM	73522	75922	74922	73622
377 523	**FB**	P	*SE*	RM	73523	75923	74923	73623

Class 377/6. 750 V DC. DMS–MS–TS–MS–DMS. 5-car suburban units fitted with Fainsa seating. Technically the same as the 377/5s but using the slightly modified Class 379-style bodyshell.

Seating Layout: 2+2 facing/unidirectional.

DMS. Bombardier Derby 2012–13. 24/36. 44.7 t.
MS. Bombardier Derby 2012–13. –/64 1T. 38.8 t.
TS. Bombardier Derby 2012–13. –/46(+2) 1TD 2W. 37.8 t.
MS. Bombardier Derby 2012–13. –/66. 38.3 t.
DMS. Bombardier Derby 2012–13. –/62. 44.7 t.

377 601	**SN**	P	*SN*	SU	70101	70201	70301	70401	70501
377 602	**SN**	P	*SN*	SU	70102	70202	70302	70402	70502
377 603	**SN**	P	*SN*	SU	70103	70203	70303	70403	70503
377 604	**SN**	P	*SN*	SU	70104	70204	70304	70404	70504
377 605	**SN**	P	*SN*	SU	70105	70205	70305	70405	70505
377 606	**SN**	P	*SN*	SU	70106	70206	70306	70406	70506
377 607	**SN**	P	*SN*	SU	70107	70207	70307	70407	70507
377 608	**SN**	P	*SN*	SU	70108	70208	70308	70408	70508
377 609	**SN**	P	*SN*	SU	70109	70209	70309	70409	70509
377 610	**SN**	P	*SN*	SU	70110	70210	70310	70410	70510

377611	**SN**	P	*SN*	SU	70111	70211	70311	70411	70511
377612	**SN**	P	*SN*	SU	70112	70212	70312	70412	70512
377613	**SN**	P	*SN*	SU	70113	70213	70313	70413	70513
377614	**SN**	P	*SN*	SU	70114	70214	70314	70414	70514
377615	**SN**	P	*SN*	SU	70115	70215	70315	70415	70515
377616	**SN**	P	*SN*	SU	70116	70216	70316	70416	70516
377617	**SN**	P	*SN*	SU	70117	70217	70317	70417	70517
377618	**SN**	P	*SN*	SU	70118	70218	70318	70418	70518
377619	**SN**	P	*SN*	SU	70119	70219	70319	70419	70519
377620	**SN**	P	*SN*	SU	70120	70220	70320	70420	70520
377621	**SN**	P	*SN*	SU	70121	70221	70321	70421	70521
377622	**SN**	P	*SN*	SU	70122	70222	70322	70422	70522
377623	**SN**	P	*SN*	SU	70123	70223	70323	70423	70523
377624	**SN**	P	*SN*	SU	70124	70224	70324	70424	70524
377625	**SN**	P	*SN*	SU	70125	70225	70325	70425	70525
377626	**SN**	P	*SN*	SU	70126	70226	70326	70426	70526

Class 377/7. 25kV AC/750V DC. DMS–MS–TS–MS–DMS. Dual-voltage units, used on both the South Croydon–Milton Keynes cross-London services and on suburban services alongside the Class 377/6s.

DMS. Bombardier Derby 2013–14. 24/36. 45.6 t.
MS. Bombardier Derby 2013–14. –/64 1T. 41.0 t.
PTS. Bombardier Derby 2013–14. –/46(+2) 1TD 2W. 40.9 t.
MS. Bombardier Derby 2013–14. –/66. 39.6 t.
DMS. Bombardier Derby 2013–14. –/62. 45.2 t.

377701	**SN**	P	*SN*	SU	65201	70601	65601	70701	65401
377702	**SN**	P	*SN*	SU	65202	70602	65602	70702	65402
377703	**SN**	P	*SN*	SU	65203	70603	65603	70703	65403
377704	**SN**	P	*SN*	SU	65204	70604	65604	70704	65404
377705	**SN**	P	*SN*	SU	65205	70605	65605	70705	65405
377706	**SN**	P	*SN*	SU	65206	70606	65606	70706	65406
377707	**SN**	P	*SN*	SU	65207	70607	65607	70707	65407
377708	**SN**	P	*SN*	SU	65208	70608	65608	70708	65408

CLASS 378   CAPITALSTAR   BOMBARDIER DERBY

These suburban Electrostars are designated "Capitalstars" by TfL.

Formation: DMS–MS–TS–MS–DMS or DMS–MS–PTS–MS–DMS.
System: Class 378/1 750 V DC third rail only. Class 378/2 25 kV AC overhead and 750 V DC third rail.
Construction: Welded aluminium alloy underframe, sides and roof with steel ends. All sections bolted together.
Traction Motors: Three Bombardier asynchronous of 200 kW.
Wheel Arrangement: 1A-Bo + 1A-Bo + 2-2 + Bo-1A + Bo-1A.
Braking: Disc & regenerative.   **Dimensions:** 20.46/20.14 x 2.80 m.
Bogies: Bombardier P3-25/T3-25.   **Couplers:** Dellner 12.
Gangways: Within unit + end doors. **Control System:** IGBT Inverter.
Doors: Sliding.   **Maximum Speed:** 75 mph.
Heating & ventilation: Air conditioning.
Seating Layout: Longitudinal ("tube style") low density.

Multiple Working: Within class and with Classes 375, 376, 377 and 379.

57 extra MSs (in the 384xx number series) were delivered 2014–15 to make all units up to 5-cars.

Class 378/1. 750 V DC. DMS–MS–TS–MS–DMS. Third rail only units used on the East London Line. Provision for retro-fitting as dual voltage.

378 150–154 are fitted with de-icing equipment.

DMS(A). Bombardier Derby 2009–10. –/36. 43.1 t.
MS(A). Bombardier Derby 2009–10. –/40. 39.3 t.
TS. Bombardier Derby 2009–10. –/34(+6) 2W. 34.3t.
MS(B). Bombardier Derby 2014–15. –/40. 40.2 t.
DMS(B). Bombardier Derby 2009–10. –/36. 42.7 t.

378 135	LD	QW	LO	NG	38035	38235	38335	38435	38135
378 136	LD	QW	LO	NG	38036	38236	38336	38436	38136
378 137	LO	QW	LO	NG	38037	38237	38337	38437	38137
378 138	LO	QW	LO	NG	38038	38238	38338	38438	38138
378 139	LO	QW	LO	NG	38039	38239	38339	38439	38139
378 140	LO	QW	LO	NG	38040	38240	38340	38440	38140
378 141	LO	QW	LO	NG	38041	38241	38341	38441	38141
378 142	LO	QW	LO	NG	38042	38242	38342	38442	38142
378 143	LO	QW	LO	NG	38043	38243	38343	38443	38143
378 144	LO	QW	LO	NG	38044	38244	38344	38444	38144
378 145	LO	QW	LO	NG	38045	38245	38345	38445	38145
378 146	LO	QW	LO	NG	38046	38246	38346	38446	38146
378 147	LD	QW	LO	NG	38047	38247	38347	38447	38147
378 148	LO	QW	LO	NG	38048	38248	38348	38448	38148
378 149	LO	QW	LO	NG	38049	38249	38349	38449	38149
378 150	LD	QW	LO	NG	38050	38250	38350	38450	38150
378 151	LO	QW	LO	NG	38051	38251	38351	38451	38151
378 152	LO	QW	LO	NG	38052	38252	38352	38452	38152
378 153	LO	QW	LO	NG	38053	38253	38353	38453	38153
378 154	LO	QW	LO	NG	38054	38254	38354	38454	38154

Name (carried on DMS(A)): 378 135   Daks Hamilton

Class 378/2. 25 kV AC/750 V DC. DMS–MS–PTS–MS–DMS or DMS–MS–PTS–DMS. Dual-voltage units mainly used on North London Railway services. 378 201–224 were built as 3-car units 378 001–024 and extended to 4-car units in 2010.

Fitted with tripcocks for operation on the tracks shared with London Underground between Queens Park and Harrow & Wealdstone.

378 216–220 are fitted with de-icing equipment.

378 206/209/232 have been temporarily reduced back to 4-car formations.

DMS(A). Bombardier Derby 2008–11. –/36. 43.4 t.
MS(A). Bombardier Derby 2008–11. –/40. 39.6 t.
PTS. Bombardier Derby 2008–11. –/34(+6) 2W. 39.2t.
MS(B). Bombardier Derby 2014–15. –/40. 40.4 t.
DMS(B). Bombardier Derby 2008–11. –/36. 43.1 t.

378 201	**LO**	QW	*LO*	NG	38001	38201	38301	38401	38101
378 202	**LO**	QW	*LO*	NG	38002	38202	38302	38402	38102
378 203	**LO**	QW	*LO*	NG	38003	38203	38303	38403	38103
378 204	**LO**	QW	*LO*	NG	38004	38204	38304	38404	38104
378 205	**LO**	QW	*LO*	NG	38005	38205	38305	38405	38105
378 206	**LO**	QW	*LO*	NG	38006	38206	38306		38106
378 207	**LO**	QW	*LO*	NG	38007	38207	38307	38407	38107
378 208	**LO**	QW	*LO*	NG	38008	38208	38308	38408	38108
378 209	**LO**	QW	*LO*	NG	38009	38209	38309		38109
378 210	**LO**	QW	*LO*	NG	38010	38210	38310	38410	38110
378 211	**LO**	QW	*LO*	NG	38011	38211	38311	38411	38111
378 212	**LO**	QW	*LO*	NG	38012	38212	38312	38412	38112
378 213	**LO**	QW	*LO*	NG	38013	38213	38313	38413	38113
378 214	**LO**	QW	*LO*	NG	38014	38214	38314	38414	38114
378 215	**LO**	QW	*LO*	NG	38015	38215	38315	38415	38115
378 216	**LO**	QW	*LO*	NG	38016	38216	38316	38416	38116
378 217	**LO**	QW	*LO*	NG	38017	38217	38317	38417	38117
378 218	**LO**	QW	*LO*	NG	38018	38218	38318	38418	38118
378 219	**LO**	QW	*LO*	NG	38019	38219	38319	38419	38119
378 220	**LO**	QW	*LO*	NG	38020	38220	38320	38420	38120
378 221	**LO**	QW	*LO*	NG	38021	38221	38321	38421	38121
378 222	**LO**	QW	*LO*	NG	38022	38222	38322	38422	38122
378 223	**LO**	QW	*LO*	NG	38023	38223	38323	38423	38123
378 224	**LO**	QW	*LO*	NG	38024	38224	38324	38424	38124
378 225	**LO**	QW	*LO*	NG	38025	38225	38325	38425	38125
378 226	**LO**	QW	*LO*	NG	38026	38226	38326	38426	38126
378 227	**LO**	QW	*LO*	NG	38027	38227	38327	38427	38127
378 228	**LO**	QW	*LO*	NG	38028	38228	38328	38428	38128
378 229	**LO**	QW	*LO*	NG	38029	38229	38329	38429	38129
378 230	**LO**	QW	*LO*	NG	38030	38230	38330	38430	38130
378 231	**LO**	QW	*LO*	NG	38031	38231	38331	38431	38131
378 232	**LO**	QW	*LO*	NG	38032	38232	38332		38132
378 233	**LO**	QW	*LO*	NG	38033	38233	38333	38433	38133
378 234	**LO**	QW	*LO*	NG	38034	38234	38334	38434	38134
378 255	**LO**	QW	*LO*	NG	38055	38255	38355	38455	38155
378 256	**LO**	QW	*LO*	NG	38056	38256	38356	38456	38156
378 257	**LO**	QW	*LO*	NG	38057	38257	38357	38457	38157
Spares	**LO**	QW		WN		38406	38409	38432	

Names (carried on DMS(A)):

| 378 204 | Professor Sir Peter Hall | 378 233 | Ian Brown CBE |

CLASS 379   ELECTROSTAR   BOMBARDIER DERBY

Express Electrostars used on Liverpool Street–Stansted Airport and Liverpool Street–Cambridge services.

Formation: DMS–MS–PTS–DMC.
System: 25 kV AC overhead.

Construction: Welded aluminium alloy underframe, sides and roof with steel ends. All sections bolted together.
Traction Motors: Two Bombardier asynchronous of 200 kW.
Wheel Arrangement: 2-Bo + 2-Bo + 2-2 + Bo-2.
Braking: Disc & regenerative.   **Dimensions:** 20.00 x 2.80 m.
Bogies: Bombardier P3-25/T3-25.   **Couplers:** Dellner 12.
Gangways: Throughout.   **Control System:** IGBT Inverter.
Doors: Sliding plug.   **Maximum Speed:** 100 mph.
Heating & ventilation: Air conditioning.
Seating Layout: 1: 2+1 facing. 2: 2+2 facing/unidirectional.
Multiple Working: Within class and with Classes 375, 376, 377 and 378.

DMS. Bombardier Derby 2010–11. –/60. 42.1 t.
MS. Bombardier Derby 2010–11. –/62 1T. 38.6 t.
PTS. Bombardier Derby 2010–11. –/43(+2) 1TD 2W. 40.9 t.
DMC. Bombardier Derby 2010–11. 20/24. 42.3 t.

379001	**NC**	MQ	*GA*	IL	61201	61701	61901	62101
379002	**NC**	MQ	*GA*	IL	61202	61702	61902	62102
379003	**NC**	MQ	*GA*	IL	61203	61703	61903	62103
379004	**NC**	MQ	*GA*	IL	61204	61704	61904	62104
379005	**NC**	MQ	*GA*	IL	61205	61705	61905	62105
379006	**NC**	MQ	*GA*	IL	61206	61706	61906	62106
379007	**NC**	MQ	*GA*	IL	61207	61707	61907	62107
379008	**NC**	MQ	*GA*	IL	61208	61708	61908	62108
379009	**NC**	MQ	*GA*	IL	61209	61709	61909	62109
379010	**NC**	MQ	*GA*	IL	61210	61710	61910	62110
379011	**NC**	MQ	*GA*	IL	61211	61711	61911	62111
379012	**NC**	MQ	*GA*	IL	61212	61712	61912	62112
379013	**NC**	MQ	*GA*	IL	61213	61713	61913	62113
379014	**NC**	MQ	*GA*	IL	61214	61714	61914	62114
379015	**NC**	MQ	*GA*	IL	61215	61715	61915	62115
379016	**NC**	MQ	*GA*	IL	61216	61716	61916	62116
379017	**NC**	MQ	*GA*	IL	61217	61717	61917	62117
379018	**NC**	MQ	*GA*	IL	61218	61718	61918	62118
379019	**NC**	MQ	*GA*	IL	61219	61719	61919	62119
379020	**NC**	MQ	*GA*	IL	61220	61720	61920	62120
379021	**NC**	MQ	*GA*	IL	61221	61721	61921	62121
379022	**NC**	MQ	*GA*	IL	61222	61722	61922	62122
379023	**NC**	MQ	*GA*	IL	61223	61723	61923	62123
379024	**NC**	MQ	*GA*	IL	61224	61724	61924	62124
379025	**NC**	MQ	*GA*	IL	61225	61725	61925	62125
379026	**NC**	MQ	*GA*	IL	61226	61726	61926	62126
379027	**NC**	MQ	*GA*	IL	61227	61727	61927	62127
379028	**NC**	MQ	*GA*	IL	61228	61728	61928	62128
379029	**NC**	MQ	*GA*	IL	61229	61729	61929	62129
379030	**NC**	MQ	*GA*	IL	61230	61730	61930	62130

Names (carried on end cars):

379005	Stansted Express	379015	City of Cambridge
379011	Ely Cathedral	379025	Go Discover
379012	The West Anglian		

CLASS 380   DESIRO UK   SIEMENS

ScotRail units mainly used on Strathclyde area services.

Formation: DMS–PTS–DMS or DMS–PTS–TS–DMS.
System: 25 kV AC overhead.
Construction: Welded aluminium with steel ends.
Traction Motors: Four Siemens ITB2016-0GB02 asynchronous of 250 kW.
Wheel Arrangement: Bo-Bo + 2-2 (+2-2) + Bo-Bo

Braking: Disc & regenerative.	**Dimensions:** 23.78/23.57 x 2.80 m.
Bogies: SGP SF5000.	**Couplers:** Voith.
Gangways: Throughout.	**Control System:** IGBT Inverter.
Doors: Sliding plug.	**Maximum Speed:** 100 mph.
Heating & ventilation: Air conditioning.	**Seating Layout:** 2+2 facing/unidirectional.

Multiple Working: Within class.

DMS(A). Siemens Krefeld 2009–10. –/70. 45.0 t.
PTS. Siemens Krefeld 2009–10. –/57(+12) 1TD 2W. 42.7 t.
TS. Siemens Krefeld 2009–10. –/74 1T. 34.8 t.
DMS(B). Siemens Krefeld 2009–10. –/64(+5). 44.9 t.

Class 380/0. 3-car units. **Formation:** DMS–PTS–DMS.

380 001	**SR**	E	*SR*	GW	38501	38601	38701
380 002	**SR**	E	*SR*	GW	38502	38602	38702
380 003	**SR**	E	*SR*	GW	38503	38603	38703
380 004	**SR**	E	*SR*	GW	38504	38604	38704
380 005	**SR**	E	*SR*	GW	38505	38605	38705
380 006	**SR**	E	*SR*	GW	38506	38606	38706
380 007	**SR**	E	*SR*	GW	38507	38607	38707
380 008	**SR**	E	*SR*	GW	38508	38608	38708
380 009	**SR**	E	*SR*	GW	38509	38609	38709
380 010	**SR**	E	*SR*	GW	38510	38610	38710
380 011	**SR**	E	*SR*	GW	38511	38611	38711
380 012	**SR**	E	*SR*	GW	38512	38612	38712
380 013	**SR**	E	*SR*	GW	38513	38613	38713
380 014	**SR**	E	*SR*	GW	38514	38614	38714
380 015	**SR**	E	*SR*	GW	38515	38615	38715
380 016	**SR**	E	*SR*	GW	38516	38616	38716
380 017	**SR**	E	*SR*	GW	38517	38617	38717
380 018	**SR**	E	*SR*	GW	38518	38618	38718
380 019	**SR**	E	*SR*	GW	38519	38619	38719
380 020	**SR**	E	*SR*	GW	38520	38620	38720
380 021	**SR**	E	*SR*	GW	38521	38621	38721
380 022	**SR**	E	*SR*	GW	38522	38622	38722

Class 380/1. 4-car units. **Formation:** DMS–PTS–TS–DMS.

380 101	**SR**	E	*SR*	GW	38551	38651	38851	38751
380 102	**SR**	E	*SR*	GW	38552	38652	38852	38752
380 103	**SR**	E	*SR*	GW	38553	38653	38853	38753
380 104	**SR**	E	*SR*	GW	38554	38654	38854	38754
380 105	**SR**	E	*SR*	GW	38555	38655	38855	38755
380 106	**SR**	E	*SR*	GW	38556	38656	38856	38756

380 107	**SR**	E	*SR*	GW	38557	38657	38857	38757
380 108	**SR**	E	*SR*	GW	38558	38658	38858	38758
380 109	**SR**	E	*SR*	GW	38559	38659	38859	38759
380 110	**SR**	E	*SR*	GW	38560	38660	38860	38760
380 111	**SR**	E	*SR*	GW	38561	38661	38861	38761
380 112	**SR**	E	*SR*	GW	38562	38662	38862	38762
380 113	**SR**	E	*SR*	GW	38563	38663	38863	38763
380 114	**SR**	E	*SR*	GW	38564	38664	38864	38764
380 115	**SR**	E	*SR*	GW	38565	38665	38865	38765
380 116	**SR**	E	*SR*	GW	38566	38666	38866	38766

CLASS 385   AT200   HITACHI

New 3- and 4-car ScotRail units, financed by Caledonian Rail Leasing. There is an option for a further ten 3-car units.

Formation: DMS–PTS–DMS or DMC–PTS–TS–DMS.
System: 25 kV AC overhead.
Construction: Aluminium.
Traction Motors: Four Hitachi asynchronous of 250 kW.
Wheel Arrangement: Bo-Bo + 2-2 + Bo-2 or Bo-Bo + 2-2 + 2-2 + Bo-Bo.
Braking: Disc & regenerative.
Dimensions: 23.18/22.08 x 2.74 m.   **Couplers:** Dellner.
Bogies: Hitachi.   **Control System:** IGBT Inverter.
Gangways: Throughout.   **Maximum Speed:** 100 mph.
Doors: Sliding plug.   **Multiple Working:** Within class only.
Heating & ventilation: Air conditioning.
Seating Layout: 1: 2+1 facing. 2: 2+2 facing/unidirectional.

Class 385/0. 3-car units. Standard Class only. **Formation:** DMS–PTS–DMS.

DMS(A): Hitachi Newton Aycliffe/Kasado 2016–18. –/48(+9) 1TD 2W. 44.6 t.
PTS: Hitachi Newton Aycliffe/Kasado 2016–18. –/80. 38.4 t.
DMS(B): Hitachi Newton Aycliffe/Kasado 2016–18. –62(+5) 1T. 42.0 t.

385 001	**SR**	CL	*SR*	EC	441001	442001	444001
385 002	**SR**	CL	*SR*	EC	441002	442002	444002
385 003	**SR**	CL	*SR*	EC	441003	442003	444003
385 004	**SR**	CL	*SR*	EC	441004	442004	444004
385 005	**SR**	CL	*SR*	EC	441005	442005	444005
385 006	**SR**	CL	*SR*	EC	441006	442006	444006
385 007	**SR**	CL	*SR*	EC	441007	442007	444007
385 008	**SR**	CL	*SR*	EC	441008	442008	444008
385 009	**SR**	CL	*SR*	EC	441009	442009	444009
385 010	**SR**	CL	*SR*	EC	441010	442010	444010
385 011	**SR**	CL	*SR*	EC	441011	442011	444011
385 012	**SR**	CL	*SR*	EC	441012	442012	444012
385 013	**SR**	CL	*SR*	EC	441013	442013	444013
385 014	**SR**	CL	*SR*	EC	441014	442014	444014
385 015	**SR**	CL	*SR*	EC	441015	442015	444015
385 016	**SR**	CL	*SR*	EC	441016	442016	444016
385 017	**SR**	CL	*SR*	EC	441017	442017	444017
385 018	**SR**	CL	*SR*	EC	441018	442018	444018

385 019	**SR**	CL	*SR*	EC	441019	442019	444019
385 020	**SR**	CL	*SR*	EC	441020	442020	444020
385 021	**SR**	CL	*SR*	EC	441021	442021	444021
385 022	**SR**	CL	*SR*	EC	441022	442022	444022
385 023	**SR**	CL	*SR*	EC	441023	442023	444023
385 024	**SR**	CL	*SR*	EC	441024	442024	444024
385 025	**SR**	CL	*SR*	EC	441025	442025	444025
385 026	**SR**	CL	*SR*	EC	441026	442026	444026
385 027	**SR**	CL	*SR*	EC	441027	442027	444027
385 028	**SR**	CL	*SR*	EC	441028	442028	444028
385 029	**SR**	CL	*SR*	EC	441029	442029	444029
385 030	**SR**	CL	*SR*	EC	441030	442030	444030
385 031	**SR**	CL	*SR*	EC	441031	442031	444031
385 032	**SR**	CL	*SR*	EC	441032	442032	444032
385 033	**SR**	CL	*SR*	EC	441033	442033	444033
385 034	**SR**	CL	*SR*	EC	441034	442034	444034
385 035	**SR**	CL	*SR*	EC	441035	442035	444035
385 036	**SR**	CL	*SR*	EC	441036	442036	444036
385 037	**SR**	CL	*SR*	EC	441037	442037	444037
385 038	**SR**	CL	*SR*	EC	441038	442038	444038
385 039	**SR**	CL	*SR*	EC	441039	442039	444039
385 040	**SR**	CL	*SR*	EC	441040	442040	444040
385 041	**SR**	CL	*SR*	EC	441041	442041	444041
385 042	**SR**	CL	*SR*	EC	441042	442042	444042
385 043	**SR**	CL	*SR*	EC	441043	442043	444043
385 044	**SR**	CL	*SR*	EC	441044	442044	444044
385 045	**SR**	CL	*SR*	EC	441045	442045	444045
385 046	**SR**	CL	*SR*	EC	441046	442046	444046

Class 385/1. 4-car units. Standard Class and First Class seating.
Formation: DMC–PTS–TS–DMS.

DMC: Hitachi Newton Aycliffe/Kasado 2016–18. 20/15(+9) 1TD 2W. 44.7 t.
PTS: Hitachi Newton Aycliffe/Kasado 2016–18. –/80. 38.4 t.
TS: Hitachi Newton Aycliffe/Kasado 2016–18. –/80. 31.5 t.
DMS: Hitachi Newton Aycliffe/Kasado 2016–18. –62(+5) 1T. 44.5 t.

385 101	**SR**	CL	*SR*	EC	441101	442101	443101	444101
385 102	**SR**	CL	*SR*	EC	441102	442102	443102	444102
385 103	**SR**	CL	*SR*	EC	441103	442103	443103	444103
385 104	**SR**	CL	*SR*	EC	441104	442104	443104	444104
385 105	**SR**	CL	*SR*	EC	441105	442105	443105	444105
385 106	**SR**	CL	*SR*	EC	441106	442106	443106	444106
385 107	**SR**	CL	*SR*	EC	441107	442107	443107	444107
385 108	**SR**	CL	*SR*	EC	441108	442108	443108	444108
385 109	**SR**	CL	*SR*	EC	441109	442109	443109	444109
385 110	**SR**	CL	*SR*	EC	441110	442110	443110	444110
385 111	**SR**	CL	*SR*	EC	441111	442111	443111	444111
385 112	**SR**	CL	*SR*	EC	441112	442112	443112	444112
385 113	**SR**	CL	*SR*	EC	441113	442113	443113	444113
385 114	**SR**	CL	*SR*	EC	441114	442114	443114	444114
385 115	**SR**	CL	*SR*	EC	441115	442115	443115	444115
385 116	**SR**	CL	*SR*	EC	441116	442116	443116	444116

385 117	**SR**	CL	*SR*	EC	441117	442117	443117	444117
385 118	**SR**	CL	*SR*	EC	441118	442118	443118	444118
385 119	**SR**	CL	*SR*	EC	441119	442119	443119	444119
385 120	**SR**	CL	*SR*	EC	441120	442120	443120	444120
385 121	**SR**	CL	*SR*	EC	441121	442121	443121	444121
385 122	**SR**	CL	*SR*	EC	441122	442122	443122	444122
385 123	**SR**	CL	*SR*	EC	441123	442123	443123	444123
385 124	**SR**	CL	*SR*	EC	441124	442124	443124	444124

CLASS 387   ELECTROSTAR   BOMBARDIER DERBY

The first 29 110 mph Class 387/1s were delivered in 2014–15 for Thameslink. In 2016–17 these transferred to Great Northern for services from King's Cross to Cambridge/King's Lynn and Peterborough.

A further 27 Class 387/2 units were delivered to Southern for Gatwick Express services in 2016.

Great Western Railway has taken delivery of 45 Class 387/1s for services between London Paddington and Reading, Didcot Parkway and Newbury and these now reach Swindon for stabling. 387 130–141 are currently being fitted with ETCS for use on the Heathrow Express service.

Part of a speculative order by Porterbrook Leasing, c2c has six Class 387/3s on lease for 5 years from late 2016. Porterbrook had originally placed an order for 20 speculative units but the other 14 from this order were later incorporated into the GWR fleet.

Formation: DMC–MS–PTS–DMS.
System: 25 kV AC overhead and 750 V DC third rail.
Construction: Welded aluminium alloy underframe, sides and roof with steel ends. All sections bolted together.
Traction Motors: Two Bombardier asynchronous of 250 kW.
Wheel Arrangement: 2-Bo + 2-Bo + 2-2 + Bo-2.
Braking: Disc & regenerative.   **Dimensions:** 20.39/20.00 x 2.80 m.
Bogies: Bombardier P3-25/T3-25.   **Couplers:** Dellner 12.
Gangways: Throughout.   **Control System:** IGBT Inverter.
Doors: Sliding plug.   **Maximum Speed:** 110 mph.
Heating & ventilation: Air conditioning.
Seating Layout: 2+2 facing/unidirectional.
Multiple Working: Within class and with Class 377.

Class 387/1. Units built for Thameslink, but now used by Great Northern.

DMC. Bombardier Derby 2014–15. 22/34. 46.0 t.
MS. Bombardier Derby 2014–15. –/62 1T. 41.3 t.
PTS. Bombardier Derby 2014–15. –/45(+2) 1TD 2W. 41.6 t.
DMS. Bombardier Derby 2014–15. –/60. 45.9 t.

387 101	**TG**	P	*GN*	HE	421101	422101	423101	424101
387 102	**TG**	P	*GN*	HE	421102	422102	423102	424102
387 103	**TG**	P	*GN*	HE	421103	422103	423103	424103
387 104	**TG**	P	*GN*	HE	421104	422104	423104	424104
387 105	**TG**	P	*SN*	SL	421105	422105	423105	424105

387 106	**TG**	P	*GN*	HE	421106	422106	423106	424106
387 107	**TG**	P	*GN*	HE	421107	422107	423107	424107
387 108	**TG**	P	*GN*	HE	421108	422108	423108	424108
387 109	**TG**	P	*GN*	HE	421109	422109	423109	424109
387 110	**TG**	P	*GN*	HE	421110	422110	423110	424110
387 111	**TG**	P	*GN*	HE	421111	422111	423111	424111
387 112	**TG**	P	*GN*	HE	421112	422112	423112	424112
387 113	**TG**	P	*GN*	HE	421113	422113	423113	424113
387 114	**TG**	P	*GN*	HE	421114	422114	423114	424114
387 115	**TG**	P	*GN*	HE	421115	422115	423115	424115
387 116	**TG**	P	*GN*	HE	421116	422116	423116	424116
387 117	**TG**	P	*GN*	HE	421117	422117	423117	424117
387 118	**TG**	P	*GN*	HE	421118	422118	423118	424118
387 119	**TG**	P	*GN*	HE	421119	422119	423119	424119
387 120	**TG**	P	*GN*	HE	421120	422120	423120	424120
387 121	**TG**	P	*GN*	HE	421121	422121	423121	424121
387 122	**TG**	P	*GN*	HE	421122	422122	423122	424122
387 123	**TG**	P	*GN*	HE	421123	422123	423123	424123
387 124	**TG**	P	*GN*	HE	421124	422124	423124	424124
387 125	**TG**	P	*GN*	HE	421125	422125	423125	424125
387 126	**TG**	P	*GN*	HE	421126	422126	423126	424126
387 127	**TG**	P	*GN*	HE	421127	422127	423127	424127
387 128	**TG**	P	*GN*	HE	421128	422128	423128	424128
387 129	**TG**	P	*GN*	HE	421129	422129	423129	424129

Name (carried on DMC): 387 124   Paul McCann

Class 387/1. Great Western Railway units.

DMC. Bombardier Derby 2016–17. –/56. 46.0 t.
MS. Bombardier Derby 2016–17. –/62 1T. 41.3 t.
PTS. Bombardier Derby 2016–17. –/45(+2) 1TD 2W. 41.6 t.
DMS. Bombardier Derby 2016–17. –/60. 45.9 t.

387 130	**HX**	P	*GW*	RG	421130	422130	423130	424130
387 131	**HX**	P	*GW*	RG	421131	422131	423131	424131
387 132	**HX**	P	*GW*	RG	421132	422132	423132	424132
387 133	**HX**	P	*GW*	RG	421133	422133	423133	424133
387 134	**HX**	P	*GW*	RG	421134	422134	423134	424134
387 135	**HX**	P	*GW*	RG	421135	422135	423135	424135
387 136	**GW**	P	*GW*	RG	421136	422136	423136	424136
387 137	**GW**	P	*GW*	RG	421137	422137	423137	424137
387 138	**GW**	P	*GW*	RG	421138	422138	423138	424138
387 139	**GW**	P	*GW*	RG	421139	422139	423139	424139
387 140	**HX**	P	*GW*	RG	421140	422140	423140	424140
387 141	**GW**	P	*GW*	RG	421141	422141	423141	424141
387 142	**GW**	P	*GW*	RG	421142	422142	423142	424142
387 143	**GW**	P	*GW*	RG	421143	422143	423143	424143
387 144	**GW**	P	*GW*	RG	421144	422144	423144	424144
387 145	**GW**	P	*GW*	RG	421145	422145	423145	424145
387 146	**GW**	P	*GW*	RG	421146	422146	423146	424146
387 147	**GW**	P	*GW*	RG	421147	422147	423147	424147
387 148	**GW**	P	*GW*	RG	421148	422148	423148	424148

▲ Southern operates the oldest EMUs on the mainland in the form of the 313s on the Brighton Coastway routes. On 21/07/19 313 213 leaves Seaford with the 15.29 Seaford–Brighton. **Jamie Squibbs**

▼ ScotRail Saltire-liveried 318 256 and 320 315 pass Craigenhill with the 09.28 Glasgow Central–Lanark on 23/09/18. **Robin Ralston**

▲ New Greater Anglia-liveried "Renatus" 321 317 leads 321 426 into Chelmsford with the 17.44 Braintree–London Liverpool Street on 06/08/19. **Robert Pritchard**

▼ Royal Mail-liveried 325 002+325 013+325 012 pass Crawford with 1M44 16.20 Shieldmuir–Warrington RMT postal on 10/10/18. **Robin Ralston**

▲ New Northern-liveried 331 009 passes Longport with a driver training run from Stoke-on-Trent to Macclesfield on 19/09/19. **Cliff Beeton**

▼ New Northern-liveried 333 001 leaves Cononley with the 13.47 Skipton–Leeds on 14/03/19. **Paul Biggs**

▲ ScotRail Saltire-liveried 334 027+334 023 pass Hillend Reservoir with the 09.24 Milngavie–Edinburgh on 24/09/18. **Robin Ralston**

▼ Elizabeth Line unit 345 008, running as a 7-car set, stands at Shenfield with the 09.14 to London Liverpool Street on 20/06/19. **Andy Chard**

▲ London Northwestern Railway-liveried 350 372 passes Ansty with the 16.07 London Euston–Liverpool Lime Street on 29/07/19. **Dave Gommersall**

▼ c2c-liveried 357 009 passes Shadwell with the 12.24 London Fenchurch Street–Southend Central on 13/10/18. **Alex Dasi-Sutton**

▲ Southeastern blue-liveried 375 622 brings up the rear of the 17.10 London Charing Cross–Ramsgate led by 375 630 at St Johns on 05/08/18. **Robert Pritchard**

▼ ScotRail Saltire-liveried 380 103 passes Breich with the 11.16 Glasgow Central–Edinburgh Waverley on 17/09/19. **Ian Lothian**

▲ ScotRail Saltire-liveried 385 015 has just left Lanark with the 08.53 to Glasgow Central on 22/05/19. **Robin Ralston**

▼ Great Western Railway-liveried 387 158 and 387 141 pass Acton Main Line with the 17.42 London Paddington–Reading on 31/05/19. **Robert Pritchard**

▲ New Virgin Trains-liveried 390 045, with "Pride" vinyls, passes Lamington with the 16.38 Glasgow Central–London Euston on 12/05/19.　　**Robin Ralston**

▼ Southeastern blue-liveried 395 017 passes Rainham on HS1 with 15.37 St Pancras–Ramsgate on 22/10/17.　　**Robert Pritchard**

▲ One of the new CAF-built TransPennine Express Class 397s, 397 005, is seen near Lanark Junction with the 12.05 Glasgow Central–Liverpool Lime Street crew training run on 02/10/19. **Robin Ralston**

▼ South Western Railway-liveried 442 420 and 442 410 are seen on a gauging run at London Waterloo before leaving to Bournemouth on 19/06/19. **Chris Wilson**

▲ In South West Trains blue livery, with South Western Railway branding, 450 017 leaves Weymouth with the 15.20 to London Waterloo on 26/06/19. **Stephen Ginn**

▼ South West Trains red-liveried 456 016, with Class 455s 5702 and 5704, pass Raynes Park with the 09.37 Guildford–London Waterloo on 12/07/19.
Alex Dasi-Sutton

▲ South West Trains blue-liveried 458 535 and 458 503 leave Wimbledon with the diverted 10.09 London Waterloo–Reading on 17/08/19. **Robin Ralston**

▼ Southeastern suburban-liveried 465 191+465 019 approach Slade Green with the 13.12 London Charing Cross–Dartford on 05/04/19. **Robert Pritchard**

▲ London Transport maroon-liveried 483 008 arrives at Smallbrook Junction with a Ryde Pier Head–Shanklin service on 26/08/19. **Tony Christie**

▼ Merseyrail-liveried 508 139 arrives at Birkenhead Central with a Liverpool Central–Chester service on 07/09/19. **Paul Senior**

▲ Thameslink-liveried 700 138 passes Stoats Nest Junction (Coulsdon) with the 07.59 Brighton–Bedford on 07/08/18. **Robert Pritchard**

▼ Revised London Overground-liveried 710 261 arrives at Leyton Midland Road with a Gospel Oak–Barking service on 23/09/19. **Stuart Hicks**

▲ New Great Northern unit 717 014 passes Enfield Chase with the 15.27 Gordon Hill–Hornsey depot empty stock on 14/02/19. **Robert Pritchard**

▼ Greater Anglia 745 005, one of ten new 12-car sets for the Norwich route, passes Brantham on test from Norwich to London Liverpool Street on 02/10/19. **Paul Biggs**

▲ New Greater Anglia bi-mode unit 755 413 is seen at Lowestoft with a 15.27 press special to Norwich on 04/09/19. **Robert Pritchard**

▼ LNER bi-mode Azuma 800 107 passes Eaton Lane crossing near Retford with the 18.03 London King's Cross–Skipton on 22/07/19. **Robert Pritchard**

▲ TransPennine Express-liveried 802 201 is seen near Burnmouth on the ECML with the 11.33 Edinburgh–Newcastle test run on 17/09/19. **Robin Ralston**

▼ Siemens e320 Eurostar 4022/21 passes Westenhanger with the 13.40 Paris–London St Pancras on 05/08/18. **Robert Pritchard**

387 149	**GW**	P	*GW*	RG	421149	422149	423149	424149
387 150	**GW**	P	*GW*	RG	421150	422150	423150	424150
387 151	**GW**	P	*GW*	RG	421151	422151	423151	424151
387 152	**GW**	P	*GW*	RG	421152	422152	423152	424152
387 153	**GW**	P	*GW*	RG	421153	422153	423153	424153
387 154	**GW**	P	*GW*	RG	421154	422154	423154	424154
387 155	**GW**	P	*GW*	RG	421155	422155	423155	424155
387 156	**GW**	P	*GW*	RG	421156	422156	423156	424156
387 157	**GW**	P	*GW*	RG	421157	422157	423157	424157
387 158	**GW**	P	*GW*	RG	421158	422158	423158	424158
387 159	**GW**	P	*GW*	RG	421159	422159	423159	424159
387 160	**GW**	P	*GW*	RG	421160	422160	423160	424160
387 161	**GW**	P	*GW*	RG	421161	422161	423161	424161
387 162	**GW**	P	*GW*	RG	421162	422162	423162	424162
387 163	**GW**	P	*GW*	RG	421163	422163	423163	424163
387 164	**GW**	P	*GW*	RG	421164	422164	423164	424164
387 165	**GW**	P	*GW*	RG	421165	422165	423165	424165
387 166	**GW**	P	*GW*	RG	421166	422166	423166	424166
387 167	**GW**	P	*GW*	RG	421167	422167	423167	424167
387 168	**GW**	P	*GW*	RG	421168	422168	423168	424168
387 169	**GW**	P	*GW*	RG	421169	422169	423169	424169
387 170	**GW**	P	*GW*	RG	421170	422170	423170	424170
387 171	**GW**	P	*GW*	RG	421171	422171	423171	424171
387 172	**GW**	P	*GW*	RG	421172	422172	423172	424172
387 173	**GW**	P	*GW*	RG	421173	422173	423173	424173
387 174	**GW**	P	*GW*	RG	421174	422174	423174	424174

Class 387/2. Southern units used on Gatwick Express-branded services on the London Victoria–Gatwick Airport–Brighton route.

DMC. Bombardier Derby 2015–16. 22/34. 46.0 t.
MS. Bombardier Derby 2015–16. –/60 1T. 41.3 t.
PTS. Bombardier Derby 2015–16. –/45(+2) 1TD 2W. 41.6 t.
DMS. Bombardier Derby 2015–16. –/60. 45.9 t.

387 201	**GX**	P	*SN*	SL	421201	422201	423201	424201
387 202	**GX**	P	*SN*	SL	421202	422202	423202	424202
387 203	**GX**	P	*SN*	SL	421203	422203	423203	424203
387 204	**GX**	P	*SN*	SL	421204	422204	423204	424204
387 205	**GX**	P	*SN*	SL	421205	422205	423205	424205
387 206	**GX**	P	*SN*	SL	421206	422206	423206	424206
387 207	**GX**	P	*SN*	SL	421207	422207	423207	424207
387 208	**GX**	P	*SN*	SL	421208	422208	423208	424208
387 209	**GX**	P	*SN*	SL	421209	422209	423209	424209
387 210	**GX**	P	*SN*	SL	421210	422210	423210	424210
387 211	**GX**	P	*SN*	SL	421211	422211	423211	424211
387 212	**GX**	P	*SN*	SL	421212	422212	423212	424212
387 213	**GX**	P	*SN*	SL	421213	422213	423213	424213
387 214	**GX**	P	*SN*	SL	421214	422214	423214	424214
387 215	**GX**	P	*SN*	SL	421215	422215	423215	424215
387 216	**GX**	P	*SN*	SL	421216	422216	423216	424216
387 217	**GX**	P	*SN*	SL	421217	422217	423217	424217

387 218	**GX**	P	*SN*	SL	421218	422218	423218	424218
387 219	**GX**	P	*SN*	SL	421219	422219	423219	424219
387 220	**GX**	P	*SN*	SL	421220	422220	423220	424220
387 221	**GX**	P	*SN*	SL	421221	422221	423221	424221
387 222	**GX**	P	*SN*	SL	421222	422222	423222	424222
387 223	**GX**	P	*SN*	SL	421223	422223	423223	424223
387 224	**GX**	P	*SN*	SL	421224	422224	423224	424224
387 225	**GX**	P	*SN*	SL	421225	422225	423225	424225
387 226	**GX**	P	*SN*	SL	421226	422226	423226	424226
387 227	**GX**	P	*SN*	SL	421227	422227	423227	424227

Class 387/3. c2c units, originally ordered speculatively by Porterbrook Leasing.

DMS(A). Bombardier Derby 2016. –/56. 46.0 t.
MS. Bombardier Derby 2016. –/62 1T. 41.3 t.
PTS. Bombardier Derby 2016. –/45(+2) 1TD 2W. 41.6 t.
DMS(B). Bombardier Derby 2016. –/60. 45.9 t.

387 301	**C2**	P	*C2*	EM	421301	422301	423301	424301
387 302	**C2**	P	*C2*	EM	421302	422302	423302	424302
387 303	**C2**	P	*C2*	EM	421303	422303	423303	424303
387 304	**C2**	P	*C2*	EM	421304	422304	423304	424304
387 305	**C2**	P	*C2*	EM	421305	422305	423305	424305
387 306	**C2**	P	*C2*	EM	421306	422306	423306	424306

CLASS 390   PENDOLINO   ALSTOM

Tilting units used on the West Coast Main Line.

Formation: As listed below.
Construction: Welded aluminium alloy.
Traction Motors: Two Alstom ONIX 800 of 425 kW.
Wheel Arrangement: 1A-A1 + 1A-A1 + 2-2 + 1A-A1 (+ 2-2 + 1A-A1) + 2-2 + 1A-A1 + 2-2 + 1A-A1 + 1A-A1.
Braking: Disc, rheostatic & regenerative.
Dimensions: 24.80/23.90 x 2.73 m.
Couplers: Dellner 12.
Bogies: Fiat-SIG.
Control System: IGBT Inverter.
Gangways: Within unit.
Maximum Speed: 125 mph.
Doors: Sliding plug.
Heating & ventilation: Air conditioning.
Seating Layout: 1: 2+1 facing/unidirectional, 2: 2+2 facing/unidirectional.
Multiple Working: Within class. Can also be controlled from Class 57/3 locos.

Units up to 390034 were delivered as 8-car sets, without the TS (688xx). During 2004–05 these units were increased to 9-cars.

62 extra vehicles were built 2010–12 to lengthen 31 sets to 11-cars. On renumbering units were renumbered by adding 100 to the set number. Four new complete 11-car units were also delivered. All these extra vehicles were built at Savigliano, Italy (all original Pendolino vehicles were built at Birmingham).

The 9-car units had their MF(B) converted to an MS in 2015 to give them a better balance of Standard to First Class seating.

390033 was written off in the Lambrigg accident of February 2007.

DMRBF: Alstom Birmingham/Savigliano 2001–05/2010–12. 18/–. 56.3 t.
MF(A): Alstom Birmingham/Savigliano 2001–05/2010–12. 37/–(+2) 1TD 1W. 52.3 t.
PTF: Alstom Birmingham/Savigliano 2001–05/2010–12. 44/– 1T. 51.2 t.

MF(B: 11-car): Alstom Birmingham/Savigliano 2001–05/2010–12. 46/– 1T. 52.3 t.
MS(C: 9-car): Alstom Birmingham/Savigliano 2001–05/2010–12. –/76 1T. 52.3 t.
(TS: Alstom Savigliano 2010–12. –/74 1T. 49.2 t.)
(MS: Alstom Savigliano 2010–12. –/76 1T. 52.2 t.)
TS: Alstom Birmingham/Savigliano 2001–05/2010–12. –/76 1T. 45.5 t.
MS(A): Alstom Birmingham/Savigliano 2001–05/2010–12. –/62(+4) 1TD 1W. 52.0 t.
PTSRMB: Alstom Birmingham/Savigliano 2001–05/2010–12. –/48. 53.2 t.
MS(B): Alstom Birmingham/Savigliano 2001–05/2010–12. –/62(+2) 1TD 1W. 52.5 t.
DMS: Alstom Birmingham/Savigliano 2001–05/2010–12. –/46 1T. 54.5 t.

Non-standard liveries:

390 045 "Pride" vinyls on driving cars.
390 122/137/152 White with grey doors.

Class 390/0. Original build 9-car units.

Formation: DMRF–MF–PTF–MS–TS–MS–PTSRMB–MS–DMS.

390 001	**VW**	A	*VW*	MA	69101	69401	69501	69601	68801
					69701	69801	69901	69201	
390 002	**VW**	A	*VW*	MA	69102	69402	69502	69602	68802
					69702	69802	69902	69202	
390 005	**VW**	A	*VW*	MA	69105	69405	69505	69605	68805
					69705	69805	69905	69205	
390 006	**VW**	A	*VW*	MA	69106	69406	69506	69606	68806
					69706	69806	69906	69206	
390 008	**VW**	A	*VW*	MA	69108	69408	69508	69608	68808
					69708	69808	69908	69208	
390 009	**VW**	A	*VW*	MA	69109	69409	69509	69609	68809
					69709	69809	69909	69209	
390 010	**VW**	A	*VW*	MA	69110	69410	69510	69610	68810
					69710	69810	69910	69210	
390 011	**VW**	A	*VW*	MA	69111	69411	69511	69611	68811
					69711	69811	69911	69211	
390 013	**VW**	A	*VW*	MA	69113	69413	69513	69613	68813
					69713	69813	69913	69213	
390 016	**VW**	A	*VW*	MA	69116	69416	69516	69616	68816
					69716	69816	69916	69216	
390 020	**VW**	A	*VW*	MA	69120	69420	69520	69620	68820
					69720	69820	69920	69220	
390 039	**VW**	A	*VW*	MA	69139	69439	69539	69639	68839
					69739	69839	69939	69239	
390 040	**VW**	A	*VW*	MA	69140	69440	69540	69640	68840
					69740	69840	69940	69240	
390 042	**VW**	A	*VW*	MA	69142	69442	69542	69642	68842
					69742	69842	69942	69242	
390 043	**VW**	A	*VW*	MA	69143	69443	69543	69643	68843
					69743	69843	69943	69243	
390 044	**VW**	A	*VW*	MA	69144	69444	69544	69644	68844
					69744	69844	69944	69244	
390 045	**VW**	A	*VW*	MA	69145	69445	69545	69645	68845
					69745	69845	69945	69245	

390 046	**VW**	A	*VW* MA	69146 69446 69546 69646 68846
				69746 69846 69946 69246
390 047	**VW**	A	*VW* MA	69147 69447 69547 69647 68847
				69747 69847 69947 69247
390 049	**VW**	A	*VW* MA	69149 69449 69549 69649 68849
				69749 69849 69949 69249
390 050	**VW**	A	*VW* MA	69150 69450 69550 69650 68850
				69750 69850 69950 69250

Class 390/1. Original build 9-car units later extended to 11-cars, except 390 154–157 which were built new (in Italy) as 11-cars.
Formation: DMRF–MF–PTF–MF–TS–MS–TS–MS–PTSRMB–MS–DMS.

390 103	**VW**	A	*VW* MA	69103 69403 69503 69603 65303 68903
				68803 69703 69803 69903 69203
390 104	**VW**	A	*VW* MA	69104 69404 69504 69604 65304 68904
				68804 69704 69804 69904 69204
390 107	**VW**	A	*VW* MA	69107 69407 69507 69607 65307 68907
				68807 69707 69807 69907 69207
390 112	**VW**	A	*VW* MA	69112 69412 69512 69612 65312 68912
				68812 69712 69812 69912 69212
390 114	**VW**	A	*VW* MA	69114 69414 69514 69614 65314 68914
				68814 69714 69814 69914 69214
390 115	**VW**	A	*VW* MA	69115 69415 69515 69615 65315 68915
				68815 69715 69815 69915 69215
390 117	**VW**	A	*VW* MA	69117 69417 69517 69617 65317 68917
				68817 69717 69817 69917 69217
390 118	**VW**	A	*VW* MA	69118 69418 69518 69618 65318 68918
				68818 69718 69818 69918 69218
390 119	**VW**	A	*VW* MA	69119 69419 69519 69619 65319 68919
				68819 69719 69819 69919 69219
390 121	**VW**	A	*VW* MA	69121 69421 69521 69621 65321 68921
				68821 69721 69821 69921 69221
390 122	**0**	A	*VW* MA	69122 69422 69522 69622 65322 68922
				68822 69722 69822 69922 69222
390 123	**VW**	A	*VW* MA	69123 69423 69523 69623 65323 68923
				68823 69723 69823 69923 69223
390 124	**VW**	A	*VW* MA	69124 69424 69524 69624 65324 68924
				68824 69724 69824 69924 69224
390 125	**VW**	A	*VW* MA	69125 69425 69525 69625 65325 68925
				68825 69725 69825 69925 69225
390 126	**VW**	A	*VW* MA	69126 69426 69526 69626 65326 68926
				68826 69726 69826 69926 69226
390 127	**VW**	A	*VW* MA	69127 69427 69527 69627 65327 68927
				68827 69727 69827 69927 69227
390 128	**VW**	A	*VW* MA	69128 69428 69528 69628 65328 68928
				68828 69728 69828 69928 69228
390 129	**VW**	A	*VW* MA	69129 69429 69529 69629 65329 68929
				68829 69729 69829 69929 69229
390 130	**VW**	A	*VW* MA	69130 69430 69530 69630 65330 68930
				68830 69730 69830 69930 69230

390 131	**VW**	A	*VW*	MA	69131	69431	69531	69631	65331	68931
					68831	69731	69831	69931	69231	
390 132	**VW**	A	*VW*	MA	69132	69432	69532	69632	65332	68932
					68832	69732	69832	69932	69232	
390 134	**VW**	A	*VW*	MA	69134	69434	69534	69634	65334	68934
					68834	69734	69834	69934	69234	
390 135	**VW**	A	*VW*	MA	69135	69435	69535	69635	65335	68935
					68835	69735	69835	69935	69235	
390 136	**VW**	A	*VW*	MA	69136	69436	69536	69636	65336	68936
					68836	69736	69836	69936	69236	
390 137	**0**	A	*VW*	MA	69137	69437	69537	69637	65337	68937
					68837	69737	69837	69937	69237	
390 138	**VW**	A	*VW*	MA	69138	69438	69538	69638	65338	68938
					68838	69738	69838	69938	69238	
390 141	**VW**	A	*VW*	MA	69141	69441	69541	69641	65341	68941
					68841	69741	69841	69941	69241	
390 148	**VW**	A	*VW*	MA	69148	69448	69548	69648	65348	68948
					68848	69748	69848	69948	69248	
390 151	**0**	A	*VW*	MA	69151	69451	69551	69651	65351	68951
					68851	69751	69851	69951	69251	
390 152	**0**	A	*VW*	MA	69152	69452	69552	69652	65352	68952
					68852	69752	69852	69952	69252	
390 153	**VT**	A	*VW*	MA	69153	69453	69553	69653	65353	68953
					68853	69753	69853	69953	69253	
390 154	**VT**	A	*VW*	MA	69154	69454	69554	69654	65354	68954
					68854	69754	69854	69954	69254	
390 155	**VT**	A	*VW*	MA	69155	69455	69555	69655	65355	68955
					68855	69755	69855	69955	69255	
390 156	**VT**	A	*VW*	MA	69156	69456	69556	69656	65356	68956
					68856	69756	69856	69956	69256	
390 157	**VT**	A	*VW*	MA	69157	69457	69557	69657	65357	68957
					68857	69757	69857	69957	69257	

Names (carried on MF No. 696xx):

390 001 Bee Together	390 125 Virgin Stagecoach
390 002 Stephen Sutton	390 128 City of Preston
390 005 City of Wolverhampton	390 129 City of Stoke-on-Trent
390 006 Rethink Mental Illness	390 130 City of Edinburgh
390 008 CHARLES RENNIE MACKINTOSH	390 131 City of Liverpool
390 009 Treaty of Union	390 132 City of Birmingham
390 010 Cumbrian Spirit	390 134 City of Carlisle
390 011 City of Lichfield	390 135 City of Lancaster
390 013 Blackpool Belle	390 136 City of Coventry
390 039 Lady Godiva	390 138 City of London
390 045 Virgin Pride	390 141 City of Chester
390 047 CLIC Sargent	390 148 Flying Scouseman
390 104 Alstom Pendolino	390 153 Mission Accomplished
390 114 City of Manchester	390 154 Matthew Flinders
390 115 Crewe – All Change	390 155 X-MEN Days of Future Past
390 117 Blue Peter	390 156 Stockport 170
390 119 Unknown Soldier	390 157 Chad Varah
390 122 Penny the Pendolino	

CLASS 395   JAVELIN   HITACHI JAPAN

6-car dual-voltage units used on Southeastern High Speed trains from London St Pancras.

Formation: PDTS–MS–MS–MS–MS–PDTS.
Systems: 25 kV AC overhead/750 V DC third rail.
Construction: Aluminium.
Traction Motors: Four Hitachi asynchronous of 210 kW.
Wheel Arrangement: 2-2 + Bo-Bo + Bo-Bo + Bo-Bo + Bo-Bo + 2-2.
Braking: Disc, rheostatic & regenerative.
Dimensions: 20.88/20.0 x 2.81 m.   **Couplers:** Scharfenberg.
Bogies: Hitachi.   **Control System:** IGBT Inverter.
Gangways: Within unit.   **Maximum Speed:** 140 mph.
Doors: Single-leaf sliding.   **Multiple Working:** Within class only.
Heating & ventilation: Air conditioning.
Seating Layout: 2+2 facing/unidirectional (mainly unidirectional).

PDTS(A): Hitachi Kasado, Japan 2006–09. –/28(+12) 1TD 2W. 46.7 t.
MS: Hitachi Kasado, Japan 2006–09. –/66. 45.0t–45.7 t.
PDTS(B): Hitachi Kasado, Japan 2006–09. –/48 1T. 46.7 t.

395 001	**SB**	E	*SE*	AD	39011	39012	39013	39014	39015	39016
395 002	**SB**	E	*SE*	AD	39021	39022	39023	39024	39025	39026
395 003	**SB**	E	*SE*	AD	39031	39032	39033	39034	39035	39036
395 004	**SB**	E	*SE*	AD	39041	39042	39043	39044	39045	39046
395 005	**SB**	E	*SE*	AD	39051	39052	39053	39054	39055	39056
395 006	**SB**	E	*SE*	AD	39061	39062	39063	39064	39065	39066
395 007	**SB**	E	*SE*	AD	39071	39072	39073	39074	39075	39076
395 008	**SB**	E	*SE*	AD	39081	39082	39083	39084	39085	39086
395 009	**SB**	E	*SE*	AD	39091	39092	39093	39094	39095	39096
395 010	**SB**	E	*SE*	AD	39101	39102	39103	39104	39105	39106
395 011	**SB**	E	*SE*	AD	39111	39112	39113	39114	39115	39116
395 012	**SB**	E	*SE*	AD	39121	39122	39123	39124	39125	39126
395 013	**SB**	E	*SE*	AD	39131	39132	39133	39134	39135	39136
395 014	**SB**	E	*SE*	AD	39141	39142	39143	39144	39145	39146
395 015	**SB**	E	*SE*	AD	39151	39152	39153	39154	39155	39156
395 016	**SB**	E	*SE*	AD	39161	39162	39163	39164	39165	39166
395 017	**SB**	E	*SE*	AD	39171	39172	39173	39174	39175	39176
395 018	**SB**	E	*SE*	AD	39181	39182	39183	39184	39185	39186
395 019	**SB**	E	*SE*	AD	39191	39192	39193	39194	39195	39196
395 020	**SB**	E	*SE*	AD	39201	39202	39203	39204	39205	39206
395 021	**SB**	E	*SE*	AD	39211	39212	39213	39214	39215	39216
395 022	**SB**	E	*SE*	AD	39221	39222	39223	39224	39225	39226
395 023	**SB**	E	*SE*	AD	39231	39232	39233	39234	39235	39236
395 024	**SB**	E	*SE*	AD	39241	39242	39243	39244	39245	39246
395 025	**SB**	E	*SE*	AD	39251	39252	39253	39254	39255	39256
395 026	**SB**	E	*SE*	AD	39261	39262	39263	39264	39265	39266
395 027	**SB**	E	*SE*	AD	39271	39272	39273	39274	39275	39276
395 028	**SB**	E	*SE*	AD	39281	39282	39283	39284	39285	39286
395 029	**SB**	E	*SE*	AD	39291	39292	39293	39294	39295	39296

Names (carried on end cars):

395001	Dame Kelly Holmes	395018	THE VICTORY Javelin
395002	Sebastian Coe	395019	Jessica Ennis
395003	Sir Steve Redgrave	395020	Jason Kenny
395004	Sir Chris Hoy	395021	Ed Clancy MBE
395005	Dame Tanni Grey-Thompson	395022	Alistair Brownlee
395006	Daley Thompson	395023	Ellie Simmonds
395007	Steve Backley	395024	Jonnie Peacock
395008	Ben Ainslie	395025	Victoria Pendleton
395009	Rebecca Adlington	395026	Marc Woods
395010	Duncan Goodhew	395027	Hannah Cockcroft
395011	Katherine Grainger	395028	Laura Trott
395013	HORNBY Visitor Centre Margate, Kent	395029	David Weir
395017	PASSCHENDAELE Javelin		

CLASS 397   CIVITY   CAF

New units currently being delivered to TransPennine Express, to enter service from autumn 2019. Full details awaited.

Formation: DMF–PTS–MS–PTS–DMS.
Construction: Aluminium.
Traction Motors:
Wheel Arrangement:
Braking: Disc and regenerative.   **Dimensions:** 24.03/23.35 x 2.71 m.
Bogies: CAF.   **Couplers:** Dellner.
Gangways: Within unit.   **Control System:** IGBT Inverter.
Doors: Sliding plug.   **Maximum Speed:** 125 mph.
Heating & ventilation: Air conditioning.
Seating:
Multiple Working: Within class.

DMF. CAF Beasain 2017–19.
PTS(A). CAF Beasain 2017–19.
MS. CAF Beasain 2017–19.
PTS(B). CAF Beasain 2017–19.
DMS. CAF Beasain 2017–19.

397001	**TP**	E	471001	472001	473001	474001	475001
397002	**TP**	E	471002	472002	473002	474002	475002
397003	**TP**	E	471003	472003	473003	474003	475003
397004	**TP**	E	471004	472004	473004	474004	475004
397005	**TP**	E	471005	472005	473005	474005	475005
397006	**TP**	E	471006	472006	473006	474006	475006
397007	**TP**	E	471007	472007	473007	474007	475007
397008	**TP**	E	471008	472008	473008	474008	475008
397009	**TP**	E	471009	472009	473009	474009	475009
397010	**TP**	E	471010	472010	473010	474010	475010
397011	**TP**	E	471011	472011	473011	474011	475011
397012	**TP**	E	471012	472012	473012	474012	475012

CLASS 399   CITYLINK   VOSSLOH/STADLER

The Class 399s are tram-trains used on the pilot Sheffield–Rotherham Parkgate tram-train service, operated by Stagecoach Supertram. Dual-voltage 750 V DC/25 kV AC (although currently only planned to operate on 750 V DC). For operation on Network Rail lines EMU running numbers 399201–207 are carried (as well as vehicle numbers in the 999xxx series), as well as the Stagecoach Supertram fleet numbers 201–207.

Entered service on the Supertram network in autumn 2017 and on the national railway network as tram-trains from October 2018.

Following two accidents in autumn 2018 unit 399202 is currently operating as a hybrid set, using one end vehicle from 399204. The other three vehicles have been returned to Spain for repairs.

At the time of writing units 399201/202/203/206 have tram-train wheel profiles for operating on the National Rail network to Rotherham Parkgate. 399205/207 can only operate on the tramway network, but could be modified to operate to Rotherham if required.

Formation: DMS–MS–DMS.
Systems: 750 V DC/25 kV AC overhead.
Construction: Steel.
Traction Motors: Six VEM of 145 kW per unit.
Wheel Arrangement: Bo-2-Bo-Bo.
Braking: Disc, regenerative & emergency track.
Dimensions: 37.20 x 2.65 m (full set). **Couplers:** Albert (emergency use).
Bogies: Vossloh.   **Control System:** IGBT Inverter.
Gangways: Within unit.   **Maximum Speed:** 60 mph.
Doors: Sliding plug.   **Multiple Working:** Within class only.
Seating Layout: 2+2 facing/unidirectional.
Weight: 64 t.

DMS(A): Vossloh, Valencia 2014–15. –/22(+4) 1W.
MS: Vossloh, Valencia 2014–15. –/44.
DMS(B): Vossloh, Valencia 2014–15. –/22(+4) 1W.

399 201	**SD**	SY	*SY*	NU	999001	999101	999201
399 202	**SD**	SY	*SY*	NU	999002	999102	999204
399 203	**SD**	SY	*SY*	NU	999003	999103	999203
399 204	**SD**	SY		NU	999004	999104	999202
399 205	**SD**	SY	*SY*	NU	999005	999105	999205
399 206	**SD**	SY	*SY*	NU	999006	999106	999206
399 207	**SD**	SY	*SY*	NU	999007	999107	999207

Name (carried on cars 999002 and 999204):

399 202   Theo – The Children's Hospital Charity

2. 750 V DC THIRD RAIL EMUs

These classes use the third rail system at 750 V DC (unless stated). Outer couplers are buckeyes on units built before 1982 with bar couplers within the units. Newer units generally have Dellner outer couplers.

CLASS 442   WESSEX EXPRESS   BREL DERBY

Units built for Waterloo–Bournemouth–Weymouth services. Previously used by South West Trains, used by Southern until 2017. 18 units are being refurbished and returned to service with South Western Railway during 2019–20. These are also be retractioned with AC motors.

Units 442 401/405/407/412/421/424 are in long-term store and will not be returned to service.

Formation: DTS(A)–TS–MBC–TS(W)–DTS(B).
Construction: Steel.
Traction Motors: Four EE546 of 300 kW recovered from Class 432s.
Wheel Arrangement: 2-2 + 2-2 + Bo-Bo + 2-2 + 2-2.
Braking: Disc.   **Dimensions:** 23.15/23.00 x 2.74 m.
Bogies: Two BREL P7 motor bogies (MBS). T3 bogies (trailer cars).
Couplers: Buckeye.   **Control System:** 1986-type.
Gangways: Throughout.   **Maximum Speed:** 100 mph.
Doors: Sliding plug.   **Heating & Ventilation:** Air conditioning.
Seating Layout: 1: 2+1 facing, 2: 2+2 mainly unidirectional.
Multiple Working: Within class and Class 33/1 & 73 locos in an emergency.

DTS(A). Lot No. 31030 Derby 1988–89. –/74. 38.5 t.
TS. Lot No. 31032 Derby 1988–89. –/76 2T. 37.5 t.
MBC. Lot No. 31034 Derby 1988–89. 24/28. 55.0 t.
TS(W). Lot No. 31033 Derby 1988–89. –/66(+4) 1TD 1T 2W. 37.8 t.
DTS(B). Lot No. 31031 Derby 1988–89. –/74. 37.3 t.

* Refurbished South Western Railway units. Full details awaited.

442401		GV	A		EP	77382	71818	62937	71842	77414
442402		GV	A		ZG	77383	71819	62938	71843	77407
442403	*	SW	A	SW	BM	77384	71820	62941	71844	77408
442404		SW	A		ZG	77385	71821	62939	71845	77409
442405		GV	A		ZG	77386	71822	62944	71846	77410
442406	*	SW	A	SW	BM	77389	71823	62942	71847	77411
442407		GV	A		EP	77388	71824	62943	71848	77412
442408	*	SW	A	SW	BM	77387	71825	62945	71849	77413
442409	*	SW	A		BM	77390	71826	62946	71850	77406
442410	*	SW	A	SW	BM	77391	71827	62948	71851	77415
442411		SW	A		BM	77392	71828	62940	71858	77422
442412		GV	A		EP	77393	71829	62947	71853	77417
442413	*	SW	A	SW	BM	77394	71830	62949	71854	77418
442414	*	SW	A	SW	BM	77395	71831	62950	71855	77419
442415		SW	A		ZG	77396	71832	62951	71856	77420
442416		SW	A		BM	77397	71833	62952	71857	77421

442 417	*	**SW**	A	*SW*	BM	77398	71834	62953	71852	77416
442 418		**SW**	A		BM	77399	71835	62954	71859	77423
442 419		**SW**	A		BM	77400	71836	62955	71860	77424
442 420	*	**SW**	A	*SW*	BM	77401	71837	62956	71861	77425
442 421		**GV**	A		EP	77402	71838	62957	71862	77426
442 422		**SW**	A		ZG	77403	71839	62958	71863	77427
442 423		**SW**	A		BM	77404	71840	62959	71864	77428
442 424		**GV**	A		ZG	77405	71841	62960	71865	77429

CLASS 444   DESIRO UK   SIEMENS

Express units.

Formation: DMS–TS–TS–TS–DMC.
Construction: Aluminium.
Traction Motors: Four Siemens 1TB2016-0GB02 asynchronous of 250 kW.
Wheel Arrangement: Bo-Bo + 2-2 + 2-2 + 2-2 + Bo-Bo.
Braking: Disc, rheostatic & regenerative. **Dimensions:** 23.57 x 2.69 m.
Bogies: SGP SF5000.   **Couplers:** Dellner 12.
Gangways: Throughout.   **Control System:** IGBT Inverter.
Doors: Single-leaf sliding plug.   **Maximum Speed:** 100 mph.
Heating & Ventilation: Air conditioning.
Seating Layout: 1: 2+2 facing/unidirectional, 2: 2+2 facing/unidirectional.
Multiple Working: Within class and with Class 450.

DMS. Siemens Vienna/Krefeld 2003–04. –/76. 51.0t.
TS 67101–145. Siemens Vienna/Krefeld 2003–04. –/76 1T. 40.3t.
TS 67151–195. Siemens Vienna/Krefeld 2003–04. –/76 1T. 36.8t.
TS. Siemens Vienna/Krefeld 2003–04. –59 1TD 1T 2W. 42.1t.
DMC. Siemens Vienna/Krefeld 2003–04. 32/40. 51.3t.

444 001	**ST**	A	*SW*	NT	63801	67101	67151	67201	63851
444 002	**ST**	A	*SW*	NT	63802	67102	67152	67202	63852
444 003	**ST**	A	*SW*	NT	63803	67103	67153	67203	63853
444 004	**ST**	A	*SW*	NT	63804	67104	67154	67204	63854
444 005	**ST**	A	*SW*	NT	63805	67105	67155	67205	63855
444 006	**ST**	A	*SW*	NT	63806	67106	67156	67206	63856
444 007	**ST**	A	*SW*	NT	63807	67107	67157	67207	63857
444 008	**ST**	A	*SW*	NT	63808	67108	67158	67208	63858
444 009	**ST**	A	*SW*	NT	63809	67109	67159	67209	63859
444 010	**ST**	A	*SW*	NT	63810	67110	67160	67210	63860
444 011	**ST**	A	*SW*	NT	63811	67111	67161	67211	63861
444 012	**ST**	A	*SW*	NT	63812	67112	67162	67212	63862
444 013	**ST**	A	*SW*	NT	63813	67113	67163	67213	63863
444 014	**ST**	A	*SW*	NT	63814	67114	67164	67214	63864
444 015	**ST**	A	*SW*	NT	63815	67115	67165	67215	63865
444 016	**ST**	A	*SW*	NT	63816	67116	67166	67216	63866
444 017	**ST**	A	*SW*	NT	63817	67117	67167	67217	63867
444 018	**ST**	A	*SW*	NT	63818	67118	67168	67218	63868
444 019	**ST**	A	*SW*	NT	63819	67119	67169	67219	63869
444 020	**ST**	A	*SW*	NT	63820	67120	67170	67220	63870
444 021	**ST**	A	*SW*	NT	63821	67121	67171	67221	63871

444 022	**ST**	A	*SW*	NT	63822	67122	67172	67222	63872
444 023	**ST**	A	*SW*	NT	63823	67123	67173	67223	63873
444 024	**ST**	A	*SW*	NT	63824	67124	67174	67224	63874
444 025	**ST**	A	*SW*	NT	63825	67125	67175	67225	63875
444 026	**ST**	A	*SW*	NT	63826	67126	67176	67226	63876
444 027	**ST**	A	*SW*	NT	63827	67127	67177	67227	63877
444 028	**ST**	A	*SW*	NT	63828	67128	67178	67228	63878
444 029	**ST**	A	*SW*	NT	63829	67129	67179	67229	63879
444 030	**ST**	A	*SW*	NT	63830	67130	67180	67230	63880
444 031	**ST**	A	*SW*	NT	63831	67131	67181	67231	63881
444 032	**ST**	A	*SW*	NT	63832	67132	67182	67232	63882
444 033	**ST**	A	*SW*	NT	63833	67133	67183	67233	63883
444 034	**ST**	A	*SW*	NT	63834	67134	67184	67234	63884
444 035	**ST**	A	*SW*	NT	63835	67135	67185	67235	63885
444 036	**ST**	A	*SW*	NT	63836	67136	67186	67236	63886
444 037	**ST**	A	*SW*	NT	63837	67137	67187	67237	63887
444 038	**ST**	A	*SW*	NT	63838	67138	67188	67238	63888
444 039	**ST**	A	*SW*	NT	63839	67139	67189	67239	63889
444 040	**SW**	A	*SW*	NT	63840	67140	67190	67240	63890
444 041	**ST**	A	*SW*	NT	63841	67141	67191	67241	63891
444 042	**ST**	A	*SW*	NT	63842	67142	67192	67242	63892
444 043	**ST**	A	*SW*	NT	63843	67143	67193	67243	63893
444 044	**ST**	A	*SW*	NT	63844	67144	67194	67244	63894
444 045	**ST**	A	*SW*	NT	63845	67145	67195	67245	63895

Names (carried on TSRMB):

444 001	NAOMI HOUSE	444 038	SOUTH WESTERN RAILWAY
444 012	DESTINATION WEYMOUTH	444 040	THE D-DAY STORY PORTSMOUTH
444 018	THE FAB 444		

CLASS 450   DESIRO UK   SIEMENS

Outer suburban units.

Formation: DMS–TC–TS–DMS (450 111–127: DMS–TS–TC–DMS). * DMC–TS–TS–DMC.
Construction: Aluminium.
Traction Motors: Four Siemens 1TB2016-0GB02 asynchronous of 250 kW.
Wheel Arrangement: Bo-Bo + 2-2 + 2-2 + Bo-Bo.
Braking: Disc, rheostatic & regenerative. **Dimensions:** 20.34 x 2.79 m.
Bogies: SGP SF5000.   **Couplers:** Dellner 12.
Gangways: Throughout.   **Control System:** IGBT Inverter.
Doors: Sliding plug.   **Maximum Speed:** 100 mph.
Heating & Ventilation: Air conditioning.
Seating Layout: 1: 2+2 facing/unidirectional, 2: 3+2 facing/unidirectional.
Multiple Working: Within class and with Class 444.

Class 450/0. Standard units.

DMC(A). Siemens Krefeld/Vienna 2002–06. –/70 (* 8/62). 48.0 t.
TS(A). Siemens Krefeld/Vienna 2002–06. 24/32(+4) 1T (* –/69(+4) 1T). 35.8 t.
TS(B). Siemens Krefeld/Vienna 2002–06. –/61(+9) 1TD 2W. 39.8 t.
DMC(B). Siemens Krefeld/Vienna 2002–06. –/70 (* 8/62). 48.6 t.

* Units refurbished with First Class moved to the end cars and the guard's office removed in favour of more seats.

450001	*	**SD**	A	*SW*	NT	63201	64201	68101	63601
450002	*	**SD**	A	*SW*	NT	63202	64202	68102	63602
450003	*	**SD**	A	*SW*	NT	63203	64203	68103	63603
450004	*	**SD**	A	*SW*	NT	63204	64204	68104	63604
450005	*	**SD**	A	*SW*	NT	63205	64205	68105	63605
450006	*	**SD**	A	*SW*	NT	63206	64206	68106	63606
450007	*	**SD**	A	*SW*	NT	63207	64207	68107	63607
450008	*	**SD**	A	*SW*	NT	63208	64208	68108	63608
450009	*	**SD**	A	*SW*	NT	63209	64209	68109	63609
450010	*	**SD**	A	*SW*	NT	63210	64210	68110	63610
450011	*	**SD**	A	*SW*	NT	63211	64211	68111	63611
450012	*	**SD**	A	*SW*	NT	63212	64212	68112	63612
450013	*	**SD**	A	*SW*	NT	63213	64213	68113	63613
450014		**SD**	A	*SW*	NT	63214	64214	68114	63614
450015	*	**SD**	A	*SW*	NT	63215	64215	68115	63615
450016	*	**SD**	A	*SW*	NT	63216	64216	68116	63616
450017	*	**SD**	A	*SW*	NT	63217	64217	68117	63617
450018	*	**SD**	A	*SW*	NT	63218	64218	68118	63618
450019	*	**SD**	A	*SW*	NT	63219	64219	68119	63619
450020	*	**SD**	A	*SW*	NT	63220	64220	68120	63620
450021		**SD**	A	*SW*	NT	63221	64221	68121	63621
450022		**SD**	A	*SW*	NT	63222	64222	68122	63622
450023	*	**SD**	A	*SW*	NT	63223	64223	68123	63623
450024		**SD**	A	*SW*	NT	63224	64224	68124	63624
450025	*	**SD**	A	*SW*	NT	63225	64225	68125	63625
450026	*	**SD**	A	*SW*	NT	63226	64226	68126	63626
450027	*	**SD**	A	*SW*	NT	63227	64227	68127	63627
450028		**SD**	A	*SW*	NT	63228	64228	68128	63628
450029		**SD**	A	*SW*	NT	63229	64229	68129	63629
450030	*	**SD**	A	*SW*	NT	63230	64230	68130	63630
450031	*	**SD**	A	*SW*	NT	63231	64231	68131	63631
450032	*	**SD**	A	*SW*	NT	63232	64232	68132	63632
450033	*	**SD**	A	*SW*	NT	63233	64233	68133	63633
450034	*	**SD**	A	*SW*	NT	63234	64234	68134	63634
450035	*	**SD**	A	*SW*	NT	63235	64235	68135	63635
450036	*	**SD**	A	*SW*	NT	63236	64236	68136	63636
450037	*	**SD**	A	*SW*	NT	63237	64237	68137	63637
450038	*	**SD**	A	*SW*	NT	63238	64238	68138	63638
450039	*	**SD**	A	*SW*	NT	63239	64239	68139	63639
450040	*	**SD**	A	*SW*	NT	63240	64240	68140	63640
450041	*	**SD**	A	*SW*	NT	63241	64241	68141	63641
450042	*	**SD**	A	*SW*	NT	63242	64242	68142	63642
450071	*	**SD**	A	*SW*	NT	63271	64271	68171	63671
450072	*	**SD**	A	*SW*	NT	63272	64272	68172	63672
450073	*	**SD**	A	*SW*	NT	63273	64273	68173	63673
450074		**SD**	A	*SW*	NT	63274	64274	68174	63674
450075	*	**SD**	A	*SW*	NT	63275	64275	68175	63675
450076	*	**SD**	A	*SW*	NT	63276	64276	68176	63676

450 077	*	SD	A	SW	NT	63277	64277	68177	63677
450 078	*	SD	A	SW	NT	63278	64278	68178	63678
450 079	*	SD	A	SW	NT	63279	64279	68179	63679
450 080	*	SD	A	SW	NT	63280	64280	68180	63680
450 081	*	SD	A	SW	NT	63281	64281	68181	63681
450 082	*	SD	A	SW	NT	63282	64282	68182	63682
450 083	*	SD	A	SW	NT	63283	64283	68183	63683
450 084	*	SD	A	SW	NT	63284	64284	68184	63684
450 085	*	SD	A	SW	NT	63285	64285	68185	63685
450 086	*	SD	A	SW	NT	63286	64286	68186	63686
450 087	*	SD	A	SW	NT	63287	64287	68187	63687
450 088	*	SD	A	SW	NT	63288	64288	68188	63688
450 089	*	SD	A	SW	NT	63289	64289	68189	63689
450 090	*	SD	A	SW	NT	63290	64290	68190	63690
450 091	*	SD	A	SW	NT	63291	64291	68191	63691
450 092	*	SD	A	SW	NT	63292	64292	68192	63692
450 093	*	SD	A	SW	NT	63293	64293	68193	63693
450 094	*	SD	A	SW	NT	63294	64294	68194	63694
450 095	*	SD	A	SW	NT	63295	64295	68195	63695
450 096	*	SD	A	SW	NT	63296	64296	68196	63696
450 097	*	SD	A	SW	NT	63297	64297	68197	63697
450 098	*	SD	A	SW	NT	63298	64298	68198	63698
450 099		SD	A	SW	NT	63299	64299	68199	63699
450 100	*	SD	A	SW	NT	63300	64300	68200	63700
450 101	*	SD	A	SW	NT	63701	66851	66801	63751
450 102	*	SD	A	SW	NT	63702	66852	66802	63752
450 103	*	SD	A	SW	NT	63703	66853	66803	63753
450 104	*	SD	A	SW	NT	63704	66854	66804	63754
450 105	*	SD	A	SW	NT	63705	66855	66805	63755
450 106	*	SD	A	SW	NT	63706	66856	66806	63756
450 107	*	SD	A	SW	NT	63707	66857	66807	63757
450 108	*	SD	A	SW	NT	63708	66858	66808	63758
450 109		SD	A	SW	NT	63709	66859	66809	63759
450 110	*	SD	A	SW	NT	63710	66860	66810	63760
450 111	*	SW	A	SW	NT	63901	66921	66901	63921
450 112	*	SD	A	SW	NT	63902	66922	66902	63922
450 113	*	SD	A	SW	NT	63903	66923	66903	63923
450 114	*	SD	A	SW	NT	63904	66924	66904	63924
450 115	*	SD	A	SW	NT	63905	66925	66905	63925
450 116	*	SD	A	SW	NT	63906	66926	66906	63926
450 117	*	SD	A	SW	NT	63907	66927	66907	63927
450 118		SD	A	SW	NT	63908	66928	66908	63928
450 119	*	SD	A	SW	NT	63909	66929	66909	63929
450 120	*	SD	A	SW	NT	63910	66930	66910	63930
450 121	*	SD	A	SW	NT	63911	66931	66911	63931
450 122	*	SD	A	SW	NT	63912	66932	66912	63932
450 123	*	SD	A	SW	NT	63913	66933	66913	63933
450 124	*	SD	A	SW	NT	63914	66934	66914	63934
450 125	*	SD	A	SW	NT	63915	66935	66915	63935
450 126	*	SD	A	SW	NT	63916	66936	66916	63936
450 127	*	SD	A	SW	NT	63917	66937	66917	63937

Names (carried on DMSO(B)):

450015 DESIRO	450114 FAIRBRIDGE investing in the future
450042 TRELOAR COLLEGE	450127 DAVE GUNSON

Class 450/5. 28 units converted 2007–08 with First Class removed and a modified seating layout with more standing room (some Standard Class seats were taken out). First Class was refitted in 2013 but the removed Standard Class seats were not refitted so the units have kept their 450 5xx series numbers.

DMS(A). Siemens Krefeld/Vienna 2002–04. –/64. 48.0 t.
TC. Siemens Krefeld/Vienna 2002–04. 24/30(+4) 1T. 35.5 t.
TS. Siemens Krefeld/Vienna 2002–04. –/56(+9) 1TD 2W. 39.8 t.
DMS(B). Siemens Krefeld/Vienna 2002–04. –/64. 48.6 t.

450543	(450043)	**SD**	A	*SW*	NT	63243	64243	68143	63643
450544	(450044)	**SD**	A	*SW*	NT	63244	64244	68144	63644
450545	(450045)	**SD**	A	*SW*	NT	63245	64245	68145	63645
450546	(450046)	**SD**	A	*SW*	NT	63246	64246	68146	63646
450547	(450047)	**SD**	A	*SW*	NT	63247	64247	68147	63647
450548	(450048)	**SD**	A	*SW*	NT	63248	64248	68148	63648
450549	(450049)	**SD**	A	*SW*	NT	63249	64249	68149	63649
450550	(450050)	**SD**	A	*SW*	NT	63250	64250	68150	63650
450551	(450051)	**SD**	A	*SW*	NT	63251	64251	68151	63651
450552	(450052)	**SD**	A	*SW*	NT	63252	64252	68152	63652
450553	(450053)	**SD**	A	*SW*	NT	63253	64253	68153	63653
450554	(450054)	**SD**	A	*SW*	NT	63254	64254	68154	63654
450555	(450055)	**SD**	A	*SW*	NT	63255	64255	68155	63655
450556	(450056)	**SD**	A	*SW*	NT	63256	64256	68156	63656
450557	(450057)	**SD**	A	*SW*	NT	63257	64257	68157	63657
450558	(450058)	**SD**	A	*SW*	NT	63258	64258	68158	63658
450559	(450059)	**SD**	A	*SW*	NT	63259	64259	68159	63659
450560	(450060)	**SD**	A	*SW*	NT	63260	64260	68160	63660
450561	(450061)	**SD**	A	*SW*	NT	63261	64261	68161	63661
450562	(450062)	**SD**	A	*SW*	NT	63262	64262	68162	63662
450563	(450063)	**SD**	A	*SW*	NT	63263	64263	68163	63663
450564	(450064)	**SD**	A	*SW*	NT	63264	64264	68164	63664
450565	(450065)	**SD**	A	*SW*	NT	63265	64265	68165	63665
450566	(450066)	**SD**	A	*SW*	NT	63266	64266	68166	63666
450567	(450067)	**SD**	A	*SW*	NT	63267	64267	68167	63667
450568	(450068)	**SD**	A	*SW*	NT	63268	64268	68168	63668
450569	(450069)	**SD**	A	*SW*	NT	63269	64269	68169	63669
450570	(450070)	**SD**	A	*SW*	NT	63270	64270	68170	63670

CLASS 455   BREL YORK

Inner suburban units. During 2016–17 the South Western Railway fleet was fitted with new AC traction motors by Vossloh Kiepe.

Formation: DTS–MS–TS–DTS.
Construction: Steel. Class 455/7 TS have a steel underframe and an aluminium alloy body and roof.

Traction Motors: Four GEC507-20J of 185 kW, some recovered from Class 405s (* Four TSA010163 AC motors of 240 kW).
Wheel Arrangement: 2-2 + Bo-Bo + 2-2 + 2-2.
Braking: Disc (* and regenerative).   **Dimensions:** 19.92/19.83 x 2.82 m.
Bogies: P7 (motor) and T3 (455/8 & 455/9) BX1 (455/7) trailer.
Gangways: Within unit + end doors (sealed on Southern units).
Couplers: Tightlock.   **Maximum Speed:** 75 mph.
Control System: 1982-type, camshaft (* IGBT Inverter).
Doors: Sliding.   **Heating & Ventilation:** Various.
Seating Layout: All units refurbished. SWR units: 2+2 high-back unidirectional/facing seating. Southern units: 3+2 high back mainly facing seating.
Multiple Working: Within class and with Class 456.

Class 455/7. South Western Railway units. Second series with TSs originally in Class 508s. Pressure heating & ventilation.

DTS. Lot No. 30976 1984–85. –/50(+4) 1W. 30.8t.
MS. Lot No. 30975 1984–85. –/68. 45.7t.
TS. Lot No. 30944 1979–80. –/68. 26.1t.

5701	*	SS	P	SW	WD	77727	62783	71545	77728
5702	*	SS	P	SW	WD	77729	62784	71547	77730
5703	*	SS	P	SW	WD	77731	62785	71540	77732
5704	*	SS	P	SW	WD	77733	62786	71548	77734
5705	*	SS	P	SW	WD	77735	62787	71565	77736
5706	*	SS	P	SW	WD	77737	62788	71534	77738
5707	*	SS	P	SW	WD	77739	62789	71536	77740
5708	*	SS	P	SW	WD	77741	62790	71560	77742
5709	*	SS	P	SW	WD	77743	62791	71532	77744
5710	*	SS	P	SW	WD	77745	62792	71566	77746
5711	*	SS	P	SW	WD	77747	62793	71542	77748
5712	*	SS	P	SW	WD	77749	62794	71546	77750
5713	*	SS	P	SW	WD	77751	62795	71567	77752
5714	*	SS	P	SW	WD	77753	62796	71539	77754
5715	*	SS	P	SW	WD	77755	62797	71535	77756
5716	*	SS	P	SW	WD	77757	62798	71564	77758
5717	*	SS	P	SW	WD	77759	62799	71528	77760
5718	*	SS	P	SW	WD	77761	62800	71557	77762
5719	*	SS	P	SW	WD	77763	62801	71558	77764
5720	*	SS	P	SW	WD	77765	62802	71568	77766
5721	*	SS	P	SW	WD	77767	62803	71553	77768
5722	*	SS	P	SW	WD	77769	62804	71533	77770
5723	*	SS	P	SW	WD	77771	62805	71526	77772
5724	*	SS	P	SW	WD	77773	62806	71561	77774
5725	*	SS	P	SW	WD	77775	62807	71541	77776
5726	*	SS	P	SW	WD	77777	62808	71556	77778
5727	*	SS	P	SW	WD	77779	62809	71562	77780
5728	*	SS	P	SW	WD	77781	62810	71527	77782
5729	*	SS	P	SW	WD	77783	62811	71550	77784
5730	*	SS	P	SW	WD	77785	62812	71551	77786
5731	*	SS	P	SW	WD	77787	62813	71555	77788
5732	*	SS	P	SW	WD	77789	62814	71552	77790

5733	*	SS	P	SW	WD	77791	62815	71549	77792
5734	*	SS	P	SW	WD	77793	62816	71531	77794
5735	*	SS	P	SW	WD	77795	62817	71563	77796
5736	*	SS	P	SW	WD	77797	62818	71554	77798
5737	*	SS	P	SW	WD	77799	62819	71544	77800
5738	*	SS	P	SW	WD	77801	62820	71529	77802
5739	*	SS	P	SW	WD	77803	62821	71537	77804
5740	*	SS	P	SW	WD	77805	62822	71530	77806
5741	*	SS	P	SW	WD	77807	62823	71559	77808
5742	*	SS	P	SW	WD	77809	62824	71543	77810
5750	*	SS	P	SW	WD	77811	62825	71538	77812

Class 455/8. Southern units. First series. Pressure heating & ventilation. Fitted with in-cab air conditioning systems meaning that the end door has been sealed.

DTS. Lot No. 30972 York 1982–84. –/74. 33.6 t.
MS. Lot No. 30973 York 1982–84. –/84. 45.6 t.
TS. Lot No. 30974 York 1982–84. –/75(+3) 2W. 34.0 t.

455801	SN	E	SN	SL	77627	62709	71657	77580
455802	SN	E	SN	SL	77581	62710	71664	77582
455803	SN	E	SN	SL	77583	62711	71639	77584
455804	SN	E	SN	SL	77585	62712	71640	77586
455805	SN	E	SN	SL	77587	62713	71641	77588
455806	SN	E	SN	SL	77589	62714	71642	77590
455807	SN	E	SN	SL	77591	62715	71643	77592
455808	SN	E	SN	SL	77637	62716	71644	77594
455809	SN	E	SN	SL	77623	62717	71648	77602
455810	SN	E	SN	SL	77597	62718	71646	77598
455811	SN	E	SN	SL	77599	62719	71647	77600
455812	SN	E	SN	SL	77595	62720	71645	77626
455813	SN	E	SN	SL	77603	62721	71649	77604
455814	SN	E	SN	SL	77605	62722	71650	77606
455815	SN	E	SN	SL	77607	62723	71651	77608
455816	SN	E	SN	SL	77609	62724	71652	77633
455817	SN	E	SN	SL	77611	62725	71653	77612
455818	SN	E	SN	SL	77613	62726	71654	77632
455819	SN	E	SN	SL	77615	62727	71637	77616
455820	SN	E	SN	SL	77617	62728	71656	77618
455821	SN	E	SN	SL	77619	62729	71655	77620
455822	SN	E	SN	SL	77621	62730	71658	77622
455823	SN	E	SN	SL	77601	62731	71659	77596
455824	SN	E	SN	SL	77593	62732	71660	77624
455825	SN	E	SN	SL	77579	62733	71661	77628
455826	SN	E	SN	SL	77630	62734	71662	77629
455827	SN	E	SN	SL	77610	62735	71663	77614
455828	SN	E	SN	SL	77631	62736	71638	77634
455829	SN	E	SN	SL	77635	62737	71665	77636
455830	SN	E	SN	SL	77625	62743	71666	77638
455831	SN	E	SN	SL	77639	62739	71667	77640
455832	SN	E	SN	SL	77641	62740	71668	77642

455833	**SN**	E	*SN*	SL	77643	62741	71669	77644
455834	**SN**	E	*SN*	SL	77645	62742	71670	77646
455835	**SN**	E	*SN*	SL	77647	62738	71671	77648
455836	**SN**	E	*SN*	SL	77649	62744	71672	77650
455837	**SN**	E	*SN*	SL	77651	62745	71673	77652
455838	**SN**	E	*SN*	SL	77653	62746	71674	77654
455839	**SN**	E	*SN*	SL	77655	62747	71675	77656
455840	**SN**	E	*SN*	SL	77657	62748	71676	77658
455841	**SN**	E	*SN*	SL	77659	62749	71677	77660
455842	**SN**	E	*SN*	SL	77661	62750	71678	77662
455843	**SN**	E	*SN*	SL	77663	62751	71679	77664
455844	**SN**	E	*SN*	SL	77665	62752	71680	77666
455845	**SN**	E	*SN*	SL	77667	62753	71681	77668
455846	**SN**	E	*SN*	SL	77669	62754	71682	77670

Class 455/8. South Western Railway units. First series. Pressure heating & ventilation.

DTS. Lot No. 30972 York 1982–84. −50(+4) 1W. 29.5 t.
MS. Lot No. 30973 York 1982–84. −/68. 45.6 t.
TS. Lot No. 30974 York 1982–84. −/68. 27.1 t.

5847	*	**SS**	P	*SW*	WD	77671	62755	71683	77672
5848	*	**SS**	P	*SW*	WD	77673	62756	71684	77674
5849	*	**SS**	P	*SW*	WD	77675	62757	71685	77676
5850	*	**SS**	P	*SW*	WD	77677	62758	71686	77678
5851	*	**SS**	P	*SW*	WD	77679	62759	71687	77680
5852	*	**SS**	P	*SW*	WD	77681	62760	71688	77682
5853	*	**SS**	P	*SW*	WD	77683	62761	71689	77684
5854	*	**SS**	P	*SW*	WD	77685	62762	71690	77686
5855	*	**SS**	P	*SW*	WD	77687	62763	71691	77688
5856	*	**SS**	P	*SW*	WD	77689	62764	71692	77690
5857	*	**SS**	P	*SW*	WD	77691	62765	71693	77692
5858	*	**SS**	P	*SW*	WD	77693	62766	71694	77694
5859	*	**SS**	P	*SW*	WD	77695	62767	71695	77696
5860	*	**SS**	P	*SW*	WD	77697	62768	71696	77698
5861	*	**SS**	P	*SW*	WD	77699	62769	71697	77700
5862	*	**SS**	P	*SW*	WD	77701	62770	71698	77702
5863	*	**SS**	P	*SW*	WD	77703	62771	71699	77704
5864	*	**SS**	P	*SW*	WD	77705	62772	71700	77706
5865	*	**SS**	P	*SW*	WD	77707	62773	71701	77708
5866	*	**SS**	P	*SW*	WD	77709	62774	71702	77710
5867	*	**SS**	P	*SW*	WD	77711	62775	71703	77712
5868	*	**SS**	P	*SW*	WD	77713	62776	71704	77714
5869	*	**SS**	P	*SW*	WD	77715	62777	71705	77716
5870	*	**SS**	P	*SW*	WD	77717	62778	71706	77718
5871	*	**SS**	P	*SW*	WD	77719	62779	71707	77720
5872	*	**SS**	P	*SW*	WD	77721	62780	71708	77722
5873	*	**SS**	P	*SW*	WD	77723	62781	71709	77724
5874	*	**SS**	P	*SW*	WD	77725	62782	71710	77726

Class 455/9. South Western Railway units. Third series. Convection heating.
Dimensions: 19.96/20.18 x 2.82 m.

67301 and 67400 were converted from Class 210 DEMU vehicles to replace
accident damaged cars.

DTS. Lot No. 30991 York 1985. –/50(+4) 1W. 30.7 t.
MS. Lot No. 30992 York 1985. –/68. 46.3 t.
MS 67301. Lot No. 30932 Derby 1981. –/68.   t.
TS. Lot No. 30993 York 1985. –/68. 28.3 t.
TS 67400. Lot No. 30932 Derby 1981. –/68. 26.5 t.

5901	*	**SS**	P	*SW*	WD	77813	62826	71714	77814
5902	*	**SS**	P	*SW*	WD	77815	62827	71715	77816
5903	*	**SS**	P	*SW*	WD	77817	62828	71716	77818
5904	*	**SS**	P	*SW*	WD	77819	62829	71717	77820
5905	*	**SS**	P	*SW*	WD	77821	62830	71725	77822
5906	*	**SS**	P	*SW*	WD	77823	62831	71719	77824
5907	*	**SS**	P	*SW*	WD	77825	62832	71720	77826
5908	*	**SS**	P	*SW*	WD	77827	62833	71721	77828
5909	*	**SS**	P	*SW*	WD	77829	62834	71722	77830
5910	*	**SS**	P	*SW*	WD	77831	62835	71723	77832
5911	*	**SS**	P	*SW*	WD	77833	62836	71724	77834
5912	*	**SS**	P	*SW*	WD	77835	62837	67400	77836
5913	*	**SS**	P	*SW*	WD	77837	67301	71726	77838
5914	*	**SS**	P	*SW*	WD	77839	62839	71727	77840
5915	*	**SS**	P	*SW*	WD	77841	62840	71728	77842
5916	*	**SS**	P	*SW*	WD	77843	62841	71729	77844
5917	*	**SS**	P	*SW*	WD	77845	62842	71730	77846
5918	*	**SS**	P	*SW*	WD	77847	62843	71732	77848
5919	*	**SS**	P	*SW*	WD	77849	62844	71718	77850
5920	*	**SS**	P	*SW*	WD	77851	62845	71733	77852

CLASS 456   BREL YORK

Inner suburban units previously operated by Southern, but now operated
by South Western Railway.

Formation: DMS–DTS.
Construction: Steel underframe, aluminium alloy body & roof.
Traction Motors: Two GEC507-21J of 185 kW, some recovered from Class 405s.
Wheel Arrangement: 2-Bo + 2-2.   **Dimensions:** 20.61 x 2.82 m.
Braking: Disc.   **Couplers:** Tightlock.
Bogies: P7 (motor) and T3 (trailer).   **Control System:** GTO Chopper.
Gangways: Within unit.   **Maximum Speed:** 75 mph.
Doors: Sliding.
Seating Layout: 2+2 facing/unidirectional.
Heating & Ventilation: Convection heating.
Multiple Working: Within class and with Class 455.

DMS. Lot No. 31073 1990–91. –/59. 43.3 t.
DTS. Lot No. 31074 1990–91. –/54(+5). 32.3 t.

456 001	**SS**	P	*SW*	WD	64735	78250
456 002	**SS**	P	*SW*	WD	64736	78251
456 003	**SS**	P	*SW*	WD	64737	78252
456 004	**SS**	P	*SW*	WD	64738	78253
456 005	**SS**	P	*SW*	WD	64739	78254
456 006	**SS**	P	*SW*	WD	64740	78255
456 007	**SS**	P	*SW*	WD	64741	78256
456 008	**SS**	P	*SW*	WD	64742	78257
456 009	**SS**	P	*SW*	WD	64743	78258
456 010	**SS**	P	*SW*	WD	64744	78259
456 011	**SS**	P	*SW*	WD	64745	78260
456 012	**SS**	P	*SW*	WD	64746	78261
456 013	**SS**	P	*SW*	WD	64747	78262
456 014	**SS**	P	*SW*	WD	64748	78263
456 015	**SS**	P	*SW*	WD	64749	78264
456 016	**SS**	P	*SW*	WD	64750	78265
456 017	**SS**	P	*SW*	WD	64751	78266
456 018	**SS**	P	*SW*	WD	64752	78267
456 019	**SS**	P	*SW*	WD	64753	78268
456 020	**SS**	P	*SW*	WD	64754	78269
456 021	**SS**	P	*SW*	WD	64755	78270
456 022	**SS**	P	*SW*	WD	64756	78271
456 023	**SS**	P	*SW*	WD	64757	78272
456 024	**SS**	P	*SW*	WD	64758	78273

CLASS 458   JUNIPER   ALSTOM BIRMINGHAM

Outer suburban units. Between 2013 and 2016 the fleet of 30 4-car Class 458 units and the former Gatwick Express fleet of eight 8-car Class 460 units was combined to form a fleet of 36 5-car Standard Class only Class 458/5s. The work was carried out at Wabtec Doncaster and Brush Loughborough. Former Class 460 driving cars 67901/903/907/908 were not included in this programme and have been scrapped.

After lengthening each unit was renumbered into the 458 5xx series. All individual vehicles retained their original numbers.

Formation: DMC–TS*–TS–MS–DMC (* ex-Class 460 in 458 501–530).
Construction: Steel.   **Dimensions:** 21.16 or 21.06 x 2.80 m.
Traction Motors: Two Alstom ONIX 800 asynchronous of 270 kW.
Wheel Arrangement: 2-Bo + 2-2 + 2-2 + Bo-2 + Bo-2.
Braking: Disc & regenerative.   **Control System:** IGBT Inverter.
Bogies: ACR.   **Doors:** Sliding plug.
Gangways: Throughout.
Couplers: Voith 136.
Maximum Speed: 75 mph.
Heating & Ventilation: Air conditioning. **Multiple Working:** Within class.
Seating Layout: 2+2 facing/unidirectional.

DMC(A). Alstom 1998–2000. –/60. 45.7 t.
TS. Alstom 1998–99. 458 501–530 –/56; 458 531–536 –/52 1T. 34.4 t.
TS. Alstom 1998–2000. –/42 1TD 2W. 34.1 t.

MS. Alstom 1998–2000. 458 501–530 –56 1T; 458 531–536 –/56. 40.1 t.
DMC(B). Alstom 1998–2000. –/60. 44.9 t.

458 501	**SD**	P	*SW*	WD	67601	74431	74001	74101	67701
458 502	**SD**	P	*SW*	WD	67602	74421	74002	74102	67702
458 503	**SD**	P	*SW*	WD	67603	74441	74003	74103	67703
458 504	**SD**	P	*SW*	WD	67604	74451	74004	74104	67704
458 505	**SD**	P	*SW*	WD	67605	74425	74005	74105	67705
458 506	**SD**	P	*SW*	WD	67606	74436	74006	74106	67706
458 507	**SD**	P	*SW*	WD	67607	74428	74007	74107	67707
458 508	**SD**	P	*SW*	WD	67608	74433	74008	74108	67708
458 509	**SD**	P	*SW*	WD	67609	74452	74009	74109	67709
458 510	**SD**	P	*SW*	WD	67610	74405	74010	74110	67710
458 511	**SD**	P	*SW*	WD	67611	74435	74011	74111	67711
458 512	**SD**	P	*SW*	WD	67612	74427	74012	74112	67712
458 513	**SD**	P	*SW*	WD	67613	74437	74013	74113	67713
458 514	**SD**	P	*SW*	WD	67614	74407	74014	74114	67714
458 515	**SD**	P	*SW*	WD	67615	74404	74015	74115	67715
458 516	**SD**	P	*SW*	WD	67616	74406	74016	74116	67716
458 517	**SD**	P	*SW*	WD	67617	74426	74017	74117	67717
458 518	**SD**	P	*SW*	WD	67618	74432	74018	74118	67718
458 519	**SD**	P	*SW*	WD	67619	74403	74019	74119	67719
458 520	**SD**	P	*SW*	WD	67620	74401	74020	74120	67720
458 521	**SD**	P	*SW*	WD	67621	74438	74021	74121	67721
458 522	**SD**	P	*SW*	WD	67622	74424	74022	74122	67722
458 523	**SD**	P	*SW*	WD	67623	74434	74023	74123	67723
458 524	**SD**	P	*SW*	WD	67624	74402	74024	74124	67724
458 525	**SD**	P	*SW*	WD	67625	74422	74025	74125	67725
458 526	**SD**	P	*SW*	WD	67626	74442	74026	74126	67726
458 527	**SD**	P	*SW*	WD	67627	74412	74027	74127	67727
458 528	**SD**	P	*SW*	WD	67628	74408	74028	74128	67728
458 529	**SD**	P	*SW*	WD	67629	74423	74029	74129	67729
458 530	**SD**	P	*SW*	WD	67630	74411	74030	74130	67730

The following units were converted entirely from Class 460s.

458 531	**SD**	P	*SW*	WD	67913	74418	74446	74458	67912
458 532	**SD**	P	*SW*	WD	67904	74417	74447	74457	67905
458 533	**SD**	P	*SW*	WD	67917	74413	74443	74453	67916
458 534	**SD**	P	*SW*	WD	67914	74414	74444	74454	67918
458 535	**SD**	P	*SW*	WD	67915	74415	74445	74455	67911
458 536	**SD**	P	*SW*	WD	67906	74416	74448	74456	67902

CLASS 465   NETWORKER

Inner/outer suburban units.

Formation: DMS–TS–TS–DMS.
Construction: Welded aluminium alloy.
Traction Motors: Four Hitachi asynchronous of 280 kW (Classes 465/0 and 465/1) or Four GEC-Alsthom G352BY of 280 kW (Classes 465/2 and 465/9).
Wheel Arrangement: Bo-Bo + 2-2 + 2-2 + Bo-Bo.
Braking: Disc & rheostatic and regenerative (Classes 465/0 and 465/1 only).

Bogies: BREL P3/T3 (465/0 and 465/1), SRP BP62/BT52 (465/2 and 465/9).
Dimensions: 20.89/20.06 x 2.81 m.
Control System: IGBT Inverter (465/0 and 465/1) or 1992-type GTO Inverter.
Gangways: Within unit.   **Couplers:** Tightlock.
Doors: Sliding plug.   **Maximum Speed:** 75 mph.
Seating Layout: 3+2 facing/unidirectional.
Multiple Working: Within class and with Class 466.

64759–808. DMS(A). Lot No. 31100 BREL York 1991–93. –/86. 39.2t.
64809–858. DMS(B). Lot No. 31100 BREL York 1991–93. –/86. 39.2t.
65734–749. DMS(A). Lot No. 31103 Metro-Cammell 1991–93. –/86. 39.2t.
65784–799. DMS(B). Lot No. 31103 Metro-Cammell 1991–93. –/86. 39.2t.
65800–846. DMS(A). Lot No. 31130 ABB York 1993–94. –/86. 39.2t.
65847–893. DMS(B). Lot No. 31130 ABB York 1993–94. –/86. 39.2t.
72028–126 (even nos.) TS. Lot No. 31102 BREL York 1991–93. –/90. 27.2t.
72029–127 (odd nos.) TS. Lot No. 31101 BREL York 1991–93. –/86 1T (* –/65(+7) 1TD 2W, † –/78(+4) 1T 2W). 28.0 t (* 29.6 t).
72787–817 (odd nos.) TS. Lot No. 31104 Metro-Cammell 1991–92. –/86 1T (* –/65(+7) 1TD 2W). 28.0 t (* 30.2 t).
72788–818 (even nos.) TS. Lot No. 31105 Metro-Cammell 1991–92. –/90. 29.4t.
72900–992 (even nos.) TS. Lot No. 31102 ABB York 1993–94. –/90. 27.2t.
72901–993 (odd nos.) TS. Lot No. 31101 ABB York 1993–94. –/86 1T (* –/65(+7) 1TD 2W). 28.0t (* 29.6 t).

* Fitted with universal access toilet to meet the 2020 accessibility regulations.
† Part modified to meet the 2020 accessibility regulations. Wheelchair spaces installed but new toilet not yet fitted.

Class 465/0. Built by BREL/ABB.

465001	*	**SE**	E	*SE*	SG	64759	72028	72029	64809
465002	*	**SE**	E	*SE*	SG	64760	72030	72031	64810
465003	*	**SE**	E	*SE*	SG	64761	72032	72033	64811
465004	†	**SE**	E	*SE*	SG	64762	72034	72035	64812
465005	†	**SE**	E	*SE*	SG	64763	72036	72037	64813
465006	*	**SE**	E	*SE*	SG	64764	72038	72039	64814
465007	*	**SE**	E	*SE*	SG	64765	72040	72041	64815
465008	†	**SE**	E	*SE*	SG	64766	72042	72043	64816
465009	†	**SE**	E	*SE*	SG	64767	72044	72045	64817
465010	†	**SE**	E	*SE*	SG	64768	72046	72047	64818
465011	*	**SE**	E	*SE*	SG	64769	72048	72049	64819
465012	†	**SE**	E	*SE*	SG	64770	72050	72051	64820
465013	*	**SE**	E	*SE*	SG	64771	72052	72053	64821
465014	*	**SE**	E	*SE*	SG	64772	72054	72055	64822
465015	†	**SE**	E	*SE*	SG	64773	72056	72057	64823
465016	*	**SE**	E	*SE*	SG	64774	72058	72059	64824
465017	†	**SE**	E	*SE*	SG	64775	72060	72061	64825
465018	*	**SE**	E	*SE*	SG	64776	72062	72063	64826
465019	†	**SE**	E	*SE*	SG	64777	72064	72065	64827
465020	†	**SE**	E	*SE*	SG	64778	72066	72067	64828
465021	*	**SE**	E	*SE*	SG	64779	72068	72069	64829
465022	*	**SE**	E	*SE*	SG	64780	72070	72071	64830

465023	†	**SE**	E	*SE*	SG	64781	72072	72073	64831
465024	*	**SE**	E	*SE*	SG	64782	72074	72075	64832
465025	†	**SE**	E	*SE*	SG	64783	72076	72077	64833
465026	*	**SE**	E	*SE*	SG	64784	72078	72079	64834
465027	†	**SE**	E	*SE*	SG	64785	72080	72081	64835
465028	†	**SE**	E	*SE*	SG	64786	72082	72083	64836
465029	†	**SE**	E	*SE*	SG	64787	72084	72085	64837
465030	*	**SE**	E	*SE*	SG	64788	72086	72087	64838
465031	†	**SE**	E	*SE*	SG	64789	72088	72089	64839
465032	†	**SE**	E	*SE*	SG	64790	72090	72091	64840
465033	†	**SE**	E	*SE*	SG	64791	72092	72093	64841
465034	†	**SE**	E	*SE*	SG	64792	72094	72095	64842
465035	*	**SE**	E	*SE*	SG	64793	72096	72097	64843
465036	*	**SE**	E	*SE*	SG	64794	72098	72099	64844
465037	†	**SE**	E	*SE*	SG	64795	72100	72101	64845
465038	†	**SE**	E	*SE*	SG	64796	72102	72103	64846
465039	†	**SE**	E	*SE*	SG	64797	72104	72105	64847
465040	†	**SE**	E	*SE*	SG	64798	72106	72107	64848
465041	†	**SE**	E	*SE*	SG	64799	72108	72109	64849
465042	†	**SE**	E	*SE*	SG	64800	72110	72111	64850
465043	†	**SE**	E	*SE*	SG	64801	72112	72113	64851
465044	†	**SE**	E	*SE*	SG	64802	72114	72115	64852
465045	*	**SE**	E	*SE*	SG	64803	72116	72117	64853
465046	*	**SE**	E	*SE*	SG	64804	72118	72119	64854
465047	†	**SE**	E	*SE*	SG	64805	72120	72121	64855
465048	†	**SE**	E	*SE*	SG	64806	72122	72123	64856
465049	*	**SE**	E	*SE*	SG	64807	72124	72125	64857
465050	†	**SE**	E	*SE*	SG	64808	72126	72127	64858

Class 465/1. Built by BREL/ABB. Similar to Class 465/0 but with detail differences.

465151	*	**SE**	E	*SE*	SG	65800	72900	72901	65847
465152	*	**SE**	E	*SE*	SG	65801	72902	72903	65848
465153	*	**SE**	E	*SE*	SG	65802	72904	72905	65849
465154	*	**SE**	E	*SE*	SG	65803	72906	72907	65850
465155	*	**SE**	E	*SE*	SG	65804	72908	72909	65851
465156	*	**SE**	E	*SE*	SG	65805	72910	72911	65852
465157	*	**SE**	E	*SE*	SG	65806	72912	72913	65853
465158	*	**SE**	E	*SE*	SG	65807	72914	72915	65854
465159	*	**SE**	E	*SE*	SG	65808	72916	72917	65855
465160	*	**SE**	E	*SE*	SG	65809	72918	72919	65856
465161	*	**SE**	E	*SE*	SG	65810	72920	72921	65857
465162	*	**SE**	E	*SE*	SG	65811	72922	72923	65858
465163	*	**SE**	E	*SE*	SG	65812	72924	72925	65859
465164	*	**SE**	E	*SE*	SG	65813	72926	72927	65860
465165	*	**SE**	E	*SE*	SG	65814	72928	72929	65861
465166	*	**SE**	E	*SE*	SG	65815	72930	72931	65862
465167	*	**SE**	E	*SE*	SG	65816	72932	72933	65863
465168	*	**SE**	E	*SE*	SG	65817	72934	72935	65864
465169	*	**SE**	E	*SE*	SG	65818	72936	72937	65865
465170	*	**SE**	E	*SE*	SG	65819	72938	72939	65866

465 171	*	**SE**	E	*SE*	SG	65820	72940	72941	65867
465 172	*	**SE**	E	*SE*	SG	65821	72942	72943	65868
465 173	*	**SE**	E	*SE*	SG	65822	72944	72945	65869
465 174	*	**SE**	E	*SE*	SG	65823	72946	72947	65870
465 175	*	**SE**	E	*SE*	SG	65824	72948	72949	65871
465 176	*	**SE**	E	*SE*	SG	65825	72950	72951	65872
465 177	*	**SE**	E	*SE*	SG	65826	72952	72953	65873
465 178	*	**SE**	E	*SE*	SG	65827	72954	72955	65874
465 179	*	**SE**	E	*SE*	SG	65828	72956	72957	65875
465 180	*	**SE**	E	*SE*	SG	65829	72958	72959	65876
465 181	*	**SE**	E	*SE*	SG	65830	72960	72961	65877
465 182	*	**SE**	E	*SE*	SG	65831	72962	72963	65878
465 183	*	**SE**	E	*SE*	SG	65832	72964	72965	65879
465 184	*	**SE**	E	*SE*	SG	65833	72966	72967	65880
465 185	*	**SE**	E	*SE*	SG	65834	72968	72969	65881
465 186	*	**SE**	E	*SE*	SG	65835	72970	72971	65882
465 187	*	**SE**	E	*SE*	SG	65836	72972	72973	65883
465 188	*	**SE**	E	*SE*	SG	65837	72974	72975	65884
465 189	*	**SE**	E	*SE*	SG	65838	72976	72977	65885
465 190	*	**SE**	E	*SE*	SG	65839	72978	72979	65886
465 191	*	**SE**	E	*SE*	SG	65840	72980	72981	65887
465 192	*	**SE**	E	*SE*	SG	65841	72982	72983	65888
465 193	*	**SE**	E	*SE*	SG	65842	72984	72985	65889
465 194	*	**SE**	E	*SE*	SG	65843	72986	72987	65890
465 195	*	**SE**	E	*SE*	SG	65844	72988	72989	65891
465 196	*	**SE**	E	*SE*	SG	65845	72990	72991	65892
465 197	*	**SE**	E	*SE*	SG	65846	72992	72993	65893

Class 465/2. Built by Metro-Cammell. **Dimensions:** 20.80/20.15 x 2.81 m.

465 235	*	**SE**	A	*SE*	SG	65734	72787	72788	65784
465 236	*	**SE**	A	*SE*	SG	65735	72789	72790	65785
465 237	*	**SE**	A	*SE*	SG	65736	72791	72792	65786
465 238	*	**SE**	A	*SE*	SG	65737	72793	72794	65787
465 239	*	**SE**	A	*SE*	SG	65738	72795	72796	65788
465 240	*	**SE**	A	*SE*	SG	65739	72797	72798	65789
465 241	*	**SE**	A	*SE*	SG	65740	72799	72800	65790
465 242	*	**SE**	A	*SE*	SG	65741	72801	72802	65791
465 243	*	**SE**	A	*SE*	SG	65742	72803	72804	65792
465 244	*	**SE**	A	*SE*	SG	65743	72805	72806	65793
465 245	*	**SE**	A	*SE*	SG	65744	72807	72808	65794
465 246	*	**SE**	A	*SE*	SG	65745	72809	72810	65795
465 247	*	**SE**	A	*SE*	SG	65746	72811	72812	65796
465 248	*	**SE**	A	*SE*	SG	65747	72813	72814	65797
465 249	*	**SE**	A	*SE*	SG	65748	72815	72816	65798
465 250	*	**SE**	A	*SE*	SG	65749	72817	72818	65799

Class 465/9. Built by Metro-Cammell. Refurbished 2005 for longer distance services, with the addition of First Class. Fitted with universal access toilet to meet the 2020 accessibility regulations. Details as Class 465/0 unless stated.

Formation: DMC–TS–TS–DMC.
Seating Layout: 1: 2+2 facing/unidirectional, 2: 3+2 facing/unidirectional.

65700–733. DMC(A). Lot No. 31103 Metro-Cammell 1991–93. 12/68. 39.2t.
72719–785 (odd nos.) TS(A). Lot No. 31104 Metro-Cammell 1991–92. –/65(+7) 1TD 2W. 30.3t.
72720–786 (even nos.) TS(B). Lot No. 31105 Metro-Cammell 1991–92. –/90. 29.5t.
65750–783. DMC(B). Lot No. 31103 Metro-Cammell 1991–93. 12/68. 39.2t.

465901	(465201)	**SE**	A	*SE*	SG	65700	72719	72720	65750
465902	(465202)	**SE**	A	*SE*	SG	65701	72721	72722	65751
465903	(465203)	**SE**	A	*SE*	SG	65702	72723	72724	65752
465904	(465204)	**SE**	A	*SE*	SG	65703	72725	72726	65753
465905	(465205)	**SE**	A	*SE*	SG	65704	72727	72728	65754
465906	(465206)	**SE**	A	*SE*	SG	65705	72729	72730	65755
465907	(465207)	**SE**	A	*SE*	SG	65706	72731	72732	65756
465908	(465208)	**SE**	A	*SE*	SG	65707	72733	72734	65757
465909	(465209)	**SE**	A	*SE*	SG	65708	72735	72736	65758
465910	(465210)	**SE**	A	*SE*	SG	65709	72737	72738	65759
465911	(465211)	**SE**	A	*SE*	SG	65710	72739	72740	65760
465912	(465212)	**SE**	A	*SE*	SG	65711	72741	72742	65761
465913	(465213)	**SE**	A	*SE*	SG	65712	72743	72744	65762
465914	(465214)	**SE**	A	*SE*	SG	65713	72745	72746	65763
465915	(465215)	**SE**	A	*SE*	SG	65714	72747	72748	65764
465916	(465216)	**SE**	A	*SE*	SG	65715	72749	72750	65765
465917	(465217)	**SE**	A	*SE*	SG	65716	72751	72752	65766
465918	(465218)	**SE**	A	*SE*	SG	65717	72753	72754	65767
465919	(465219)	**SE**	A	*SE*	SG	65718	72755	72756	65768
465920	(465220)	**SE**	A	*SE*	SG	65719	72757	72758	65769
465921	(465221)	**SE**	A	*SE*	SG	65720	72759	72760	65770
465922	(465222)	**SE**	A	*SE*	SG	65721	72761	72762	65771
465923	(465223)	**SE**	A	*SE*	SG	65722	72763	72764	65772
465924	(465224)	**SE**	A	*SE*	SG	65723	72765	72766	65773
465925	(465225)	**SE**	A	*SE*	SG	65724	72767	72768	65774
465926	(465226)	**SE**	A	*SE*	SG	65725	72769	72770	65775
465927	(465227)	**SE**	A	*SE*	SG	65726	72771	72772	65776
465928	(465228)	**SE**	A	*SE*	SG	65727	72773	72774	65777
465929	(465229)	**SE**	A	*SE*	SG	65728	72775	72776	65778
465930	(465230)	**SE**	A	*SE*	SG	65729	72777	72778	65779
465931	(465231)	**SE**	A	*SE*	SG	65730	72779	72780	65780
465932	(465232)	**SE**	A	*SE*	SG	65731	72781	72782	65781
465933	(465233)	**SE**	A	*SE*	SG	65732	72783	72784	65782
465934	(465234)	**SE**	A	*SE*	SG	65733	72785	72786	65783

CLASS 466   NETWORKER   GEC-ALSTHOM

Inner/outer suburban units.

Formation: DMS–DTS.
Construction: Welded aluminium alloy.
Traction Motors: Two GEC-Alsthom G352AY asynchronous of 280kW.
Wheel Arrangement: Bo-Bo + 2-2.   **Couplers:** Tightlock.
Braking: Disc, rheostatic & regen.   **Control System:** 1992-type GTO Inverter.

Dimensions: 20.80 x 2.80 m.   **Maximum Speed:** 75 mph.
Bogies: BREL P3/T3.   **Doors:** Sliding plug.
Gangways: Within unit.
Seating Layout: 3+2 facing/unidirectional.
Multiple Working: Within class and with Class 465.

DMS. Lot No. 31128 Birmingham 1993–94. –/86. 40.6t.
DTS. Lot No. 31129 Birmingham 1993–94. –/82 1T. 31.4t.

466001	**SE**	A	*SE*	SG	64860	78312
466002	**SE**	A	*SE*	SG	64861	78313
466003	**SE**	A	*SE*	SG	64862	78314
466004	**SE**	A	*SE*	SG	64863	78315
466005	**SE**	A	*SE*	SG	64864	78316
466006	**SE**	A	*SE*	SG	64865	78317
466007	**SE**	A	*SE*	SG	64866	78318
466008	**SE**	A	*SE*	SG	64867	78319
466009	**SE**	A	*SE*	SG	64868	78320
466010	**SE**	A	*SE*	SG	64869	78321
466011	**SE**	A	*SE*	SG	64870	78322
466012	**SE**	A	*SE*	SG	64871	78323
466013	**SE**	A	*SE*	SG	64872	78324
466014	**SE**	A	*SE*	SG	64873	78325
466015	**SE**	A	*SE*	SG	64874	78326
466016	**SE**	A	*SE*	SG	64875	78327
466017	**SE**	A	*SE*	SG	64876	78328
466018	**SE**	A	*SE*	SG	64877	78329
466019	**SE**	A	*SE*	SG	64878	78330
466020	**SE**	A	*SE*	SG	64879	78331
466021	**SE**	A	*SE*	SG	64880	78332
466022	**SE**	A	*SE*	SG	64881	78333
466023	**SE**	A	*SE*	SG	64882	78334
466024	**SE**	A	*SE*	SG	64883	78335
466025	**SE**	A	*SE*	SG	64884	78336
466026	**SE**	A	*SE*	SG	64885	78337
466027	**SE**	A	*SE*	SG	64886	78338
466028	**SE**	A	*SE*	SG	64887	78339
466029	**SE**	A	*SE*	SG	64888	78340
466030	**SE**	A	*SE*	SG	64889	78341
466031	**SE**	A	*SE*	SG	64890	78342
466032	**SE**	A	*SE*	SG	64891	78343
466033	**SE**	A	*SE*	SG	64892	78344
466034	**SE**	A	*SE*	SG	64893	78345
466035	**SE**	A	*SE*	SG	64894	78346
466036	**SE**	A	*SE*	SG	64895	78347
466037	**SE**	A	*SE*	SG	64896	78348
466038	**SE**	A	*SE*	SG	64897	78349
466039	**SE**	A	*SE*	SG	64898	78350
466040	**SE**	A	*SE*	SG	64899	78351
466041	**SE**	A	*SE*	SG	64900	78352
466042	**SE**	A	*SE*	SG	64901	78353
466043	**SE**	A	*SE*	SG	64902	78354

CLASS 483   METRO-CAMMELL

Built 1938 onwards for LTE. Converted 1989–90 for the Isle of Wight Line.

Formation: DMS–DMS.
System: 660 V DC third rail.
Construction: Steel.
Wheel arrangement: A1-1A + A1-1A.
Traction Motors: Two Crompton Parkinson/GEC/BTH LT100 of 125 kW.
Braking: Tread.
Dimensions: 16.15 x 2.69 m.
Bogies: LT design.
Couplers: Wedgelock.
Gangways: None. End doors.
Control System: Pneumatic Camshaft Motor (PCM).
Doors: Sliding.
Maximum Speed: 45 mph.
Seating Layout: Longitudinal or 2+2 facing/unidirectional.
Multiple Working: Within class.
The last three numbers of the unit number only are carried.

Former London Underground numbers are shown in parentheses.

DMS(A). Lot No. 31071. –/40. 27.4 t.
DMS(B). Lot No. 31072. –/42. 27.4 t.

483 002	**LT**	SW		RY (S)	122	(10221)	225	(11142)	RAPTOR
483 004	**LT**	SW	*SW*	RY	124	(10205)	224	(11205)
483 006	**LT**	SW	*SW*	RY	126	(10297)	226	(11297)
483 007	**LT**	SW	*SW*	RY	127	(10291)	227	(11291)
483 008	**LT**	SW	*SW*	RY	128	(10255)	228	(11255)
483 009	**LT**	SW		RY (S)	129	(10229)	229	(11229)

CLASS 484 D-TRAIN METRO-CAMMELL/VIVARAIL

South Western Railway has five 2-car D-Trains on order for the Isle of Wight Line, due for delivery 2020–21. Similar to the converted Class 230 DMUs or diesel-battery units, these will be straight third-rail EMUs, rebuilt from former London Underground D78 stock. Full details awaited.

Formation: DMS–DMS.
System: 660 V DC third rail.
Construction: Aluminium.
Wheel Arrangement: Bo-Bo + Bo-Bo.
Traction motors: LT118.
Couplers: LUL automatic wedgelock.
Braking: Rheostatic & Dynamic.
Dimensions: 18.37 x 2.85 m.
Bogies: Bombardier FLEXX1000 flexible-frame.
Gangways: Within unit only.
Control System: IGBT Inverter.
Doors: Sliding.
Maximum Speed: 60 mph.
Seating Layout: Longitudinal or 2+2 facing.
Multiple Working: Within class.

DMS(A). Metro-Cammell Birmingham 1979–83.
DMS(B). Metro-Cammell Birmingham 1979–83.

484 001
484 002
484 003
484 004
484 005

CLASS 507 BREL YORK

Formation: BDMS–TS–DMS.
Construction: Steel underframe, aluminium alloy body and roof.
Traction Motors: Four GEC G310AZ of 82.125 kW.
Wheel Arrangement: Bo-Bo + 2-2 + Bo-Bo.
Braking: Disc & rheostatic.   **Dimensions:** 20.18 x 2.82 m.
Bogies: BX1.   **Couplers:** Tightlock.
Gangways: Within unit + end doors. **Control System:** Camshaft.
Doors: Sliding.   **Maximum Speed:** 75 mph.
Seating Layout: All refurbished with 2+2 high-back facing seating.
Multiple Working: Within class and with Class 508.

Fitted with tripcocks for operating on the Merseyrail Wirral Lines.

Advertising livery: 507 002 Liverpool Hope University (white).

BDMS. Lot No. 30906 1978–80. –/56(+3) 1W. 37.0 t.
TS. Lot No. 30907 1978–80. –/74. 25.5 t.
DMS. Lot No. 30908 1978–80. –/56(+3) 1W. 35.5 t.

507 001	**MY**	A	*ME*	BD	64367	71342	64405
507 002	**AL**	A	*ME*	BD	64368	71343	64406
507 003	**MY**	A	*ME*	BD	64369	71344	64407
507 004	**MY**	A	*ME*	BD	64388	71345	64408
507 005	**MY**	A	*ME*	BD	64371	71346	64409
507 006	**MY**	A	*ME*	BD	64372	71347	64410
507 007	**MY**	A	*ME*	BD	64373	71348	64411
507 008	**MY**	A	*ME*	BD	64374	71349	64412
507 009	**MY**	A	*ME*	BD	64375	71350	64413
507 010	**MY**	A	*ME*	BD	64376	71351	64414
507 011	**MY**	A	*ME*	BD	64377	71352	64415
507 012	**MY**	A	*ME*	BD	64378	71353	64416
507 013	**MY**	A	*ME*	BD	64379	71354	64417
507 014	**MY**	A	*ME*	BD	64380	71355	64418
507 015	**MY**	A	*ME*	BD	64381	71356	64419
507 016	**MY**	A	*ME*	BD	64382	71357	64420
507 017	**MY**	A	*ME*	BD	64383	71358	64421
507 018	**MY**	A	*ME*	BD	64384	71359	64422
507 019	**MY**	A	*ME*	BD	64385	71360	64423
507 020	**MY**	A	*ME*	BD	64386	71361	64424
507 021	**MY**	A	*ME*	BD	64387	71362	64425
507 023	**MY**	A	*ME*	BD	64389	71364	64427
507 024	**MY**	A	*ME*	BD	64390	71365	64428
507 025	**MY**	A	*ME*	BD	64391	71366	64429
507 026	**MY**	A	*ME*	BD	64392	71367	64430
507 027	**MY**	A	*ME*	BD	64393	71368	64431
507 028	**MY**	A	*ME*	BD	64394	71369	64432
507 029	**MY**	A	*ME*	BD	64395	71370	64433
507 030	**MY**	A	*ME*	BD	64396	71371	64434
507 031	**MY**	A	*ME*	BD	64397	71372	64435
507 032	**MY**	A	*ME*	BD	64398	71373	64436
507 033	**MY**	A	*ME*	BD	64399	71374	64437

Names:

507 004   Bob Paisley
507 008   Harold Wilson
507 009   Dixie Dean
507 016   Merseyrail – celebrating the first ten years (2003–2013)
507 020   John Peel
507 021   Red Rum
507 023   Operations Inspector Stuart Mason
507 026   Councillor George Howard
507 033   Councillor Jack Spriggs

CLASS 508   BREL YORK

Formation: DMS–TS–BDMS.
Construction: Steel underframe, aluminium alloy body and roof.
Traction Motors: Four GEC G310AZ of 82.125 kW.
Wheel Arrangement: Bo-Bo + 2-2 + Bo-Bo.
Braking: Disc & rheostatic.   **Dimensions:** 20.18 x 2.82 m.
Bogies: BX1.   **Couplers:** Tightlock.
Gangways: Within unit + end doors. **Control System:** Camshaft.
Doors: Sliding.   **Maximum Speed:** 75 mph.
Seating Layout: All refurbished with 2+2 high-back facing seating.
Multiple Working: Within class and with Class 507.

Fitted with tripcocks for operating on the Merseyrail Wirral Lines.

Advertising livery: 508 111 Beatles Story (blue).

DMS. Lot No. 30979 1979–80. –/56(+3) 1W. 36.0 t.
TS. Lot No. 30980 1979–80. –/74. 26.5 t.
BDMS. Lot No. 30981 1979–80. –/56(+3) 1W. 36.5 t.

508 103	**MY**	A	*ME*	BD	64651	71485	64694
508 104	**MY**	A	*ME*	BD	64652	71486	64695
508 108	**MY**	A	*ME*	BD	64656	71490	64699
508 110	**MY**	A	*ME*	BD	64658	71492	64701
508 111	**AL**	A	*ME*	BD	64659	71493	64702
508 112	**MY**	A	*ME*	BD	64660	71494	64703
508 114	**MY**	A	*ME*	BD	64662	71496	64705
508 115	**MY**	A	*ME*	BD	64663	71497	64706
508 117	**MY**	A	*ME*	BD	64665	71499	64708
508 120	**MY**	A	*ME*	BD	64668	71502	64711
508 122	**MY**	A	*ME*	BD	64670	71504	64713
508 123	**MY**	A	*ME*	BD	64671	71505	64714
508 124	**MY**	A	*ME*	BD	64672	71506	64715
508 125	**MY**	A	*ME*	BD	64673	71507	64716
508 126	**MY**	A	*ME*	BD	64674	71508	64717
508 127	**MY**	A	*ME*	BD	64675	71509	64718
508 128	**MY**	A	*ME*	BD	64676	71510	64719
508 130	**MY**	A	*ME*	BD	64678	71512	64721
508 131	**MY**	A	*ME*	BD	64679	71513	64722
508 134	**MY**	A	*ME*	BD	64682	71516	64725

508 136	**MY**	A	*ME*	BD	64684	71518 64727
508 137	**MY**	A	*ME*	BD	64685	71519 64728
508 138	**MY**	A	*ME*	BD	64686	71520 64729
508 139	**MY**	A	*ME*	BD	64687	71521 64730
508 140	**MY**	A	*ME*	BD	64688	71522 64731
508 141	**MY**	A	*ME*	BD	64689	71523 64732
508 143	**MY**	A	*ME*	BD	64691	71525 64734

Names:

508 111	The Beatles	508 136	Wilfred Owen MC
508 123	William Roscoe		

3. DUAL VOLTAGE OR 25 kV AC OVERHEAD UNITS

The Class 7xx series is being used for some new-build EMUs built from 2014 onwards as freight wagons take up many of the remaining potential Class 3xx series'.

CLASS 700   DESIRO CITY   SIEMENS

The Class 700s are the large new fleet of EMUs for Govia Thameslink. The first unit was delivered in summer 2015, the first entered traffic in spring 2016 and all units had been accepted into traffic by summer 2018. The units are financed by Cross London Trains (a consortium of Siemens Project Ventures, Innisfree Ltd and 3i Infrastructure Ltd).

Formation (8-car): DMC–PTS–MS–TS–TS–MS–PTS–DMC or
(12-car): DMC–PTS–MS–MS–TS–TS–TS–TS–MS–MS–PTS–DMC.
Systems: 25 kV AC overhead/750 V DC third rail.
Construction: Aluminium.
Traction Motors: Four Siemens asynchronous of 200 kW.
Wheel Arrangement (8-car): Bo-Bo + 2-2 + Bo-Bo + 2-2 + 2-2 + Bo-Bo + 2-2 + Bo-Bo. **(12-car):** Bo-Bo + 2-2 + Bo-Bo + Bo-Bo + 2-2 + 2-2 + 2-2 + 2-2 + Bo-Bo + Bo-Bo + 2-2 + Bo-Bo.
Braking: Disc, tread & regenerative. **Dimensions:** 20.52/20.16 m x 2.80 m.
Bogies: Siemens SF7000 inside-frame. **Couplers:** Dellner 12.
Gangways: Within unit.   **Control System:** IGBT Inverter.
Doors: Sliding plug.   **Maximum Speed:** 100 mph.
Heating & ventilation: Air conditioning.
Seating Layout: 2+2 facing/unidirectional.
Multiple Working: Within class and with Classes 707 and 717.

Class 700/0. 8-car units.

DMC(A). Siemens Krefeld 2014–18. 26/16(+3). 38.5 t.
PTS. Siemens Krefeld 2014–18. –/54 1T. 33.1 t.
MS. Siemens Krefeld 2014–18. –/64. 36.2 t.
TS. Siemens Krefeld 2014–18. –/56(+3). 28.7 t.
TS(W). Siemens Krefeld 2014–18. –/40(+8) 1TD 2W. 29.1 t.

MS. Siemens Krefeld 2014–18. –/64. 36.2 t.
PTS. Siemens Krefeld 2014–18. –/54 1T. 33.2 t.
DMC(B). Siemens Krefeld 2014–18. 26/16(+3). 38.5 t.

700 001	**TL** CT *TL* TB	401001	402001	403001	406001
		407001	410001	411001	412001
700 002	**TL** CT *TL* TB	401002	402002	403002	406002
		407002	410002	411002	412002
700 003	**TL** CT *TL* TB	401003	402003	403003	406003
		407003	410003	411003	412003
700 004	**TL** CT *TL* TB	401004	402004	403004	406004
		407004	410004	411004	412004
700 005	**TL** CT *TL* TB	401005	402005	403005	406005
		407005	410005	411005	412005
700 006	**TL** CT *TL* TB	401006	402006	403006	406006
		407006	410006	411006	412006
700 007	**TL** CT *TL* TB	401007	402007	403007	406007
		407007	410007	411007	412007
700 008	**TL** CT *TL* TB	401008	402008	403008	406008
		407008	410008	411008	412008
700 009	**TL** CT *TL* TB	401009	402009	403009	406009
		407009	410009	411009	412009
700 010	**TL** CT *TL* TB	401010	402010	403010	406010
		407010	410010	411010	412010
700 011	**TL** CT *TL* TB	401011	402011	403011	406011
		407011	410011	411011	412011
700 012	**TL** CT *TL* TB	401012	402012	403012	406012
		407012	410012	411012	412012
700 013	**TL** CT *TL* TB	401013	402013	403013	406013
		407013	410013	411013	412013
700 014	**TL** CT *TL* TB	401014	402014	403014	406014
		407014	410014	411014	412014
700 015	**TL** CT *TL* TB	401015	402015	403015	406015
		407015	410015	411015	412015
700 016	**TL** CT *TL* TB	401016	402016	403016	406016
		407016	410016	411016	412016
700 017	**TL** CT *TL* TB	401017	402017	403017	406017
		407017	410017	411017	412017
700 018	**TL** CT *TL* TB	401018	402018	403018	406018
		407018	410018	411018	412018
700 019	**TL** CT *TL* TB	401019	402019	403019	406019
		407019	410019	411019	412019
700 020	**TL** CT *TL* TB	401020	402020	403020	406020
		407020	410020	411020	412020
700 021	**TL** CT *TL* TB	401021	402021	403021	406021
		407021	410021	411021	412021
700 022	**TL** CT *TL* TB	401022	402022	403022	406022
		407022	410022	411022	412022
700 023	**TL** CT *TL* TB	401023	402023	403023	406023
		407023	410023	411023	412023

700 024	**TL** CT *TL* TB	401024	402024	403024	406024		
		407024	410024	411024	412024		
700 025	**TL** CT *TL* TB	401025	402025	403025	406025		
		407025	410025	411025	412025		
700 026	**TL** CT *TL* TB	401026	402026	403026	406026		
		407026	410026	411026	412026		
700 027	**TL** CT *TL* TB	401027	402027	403027	406027		
		407027	410027	411027	412027		
700 028	**TL** CT *TL* TB	401028	402028	403028	406028		
		407028	410028	411028	412028		
700 029	**TL** CT *TL* TB	401029	402029	403029	406029		
		407029	410029	411029	412029		
700 030	**TL** CT *TL* TB	401030	402030	403030	406030		
		407030	410030	411030	412030		
700 031	**TL** CT *TL* TB	401031	402031	403031	406031		
		407031	410031	411031	412031		
700 032	**TL** CT *TL* TB	401032	402032	403032	406032		
		407032	410032	411032	412032		
700 033	**TL** CT *TL* TB	401033	402033	403033	406033		
		407033	410033	411033	412033		
700 034	**TL** CT *TL* TB	401034	402034	403034	406034		
		407034	410034	411034	412034		
700 035	**TL** CT *TL* TB	401035	402035	403035	406035		
		407035	410035	411035	412035		
700 036	**TL** CT *TL* TB	401036	402036	403036	406036		
		407036	410036	411036	412036		
700 037	**TL** CT *TL* TB	401037	402037	403037	406037		
		407037	410037	411037	412037		
700 038	**TL** CT *TL* TB	401038	402038	403038	406038		
		407038	410038	411038	412038		
700 039	**TL** CT *TL* TB	401039	402039	403039	406039		
		407039	410039	411039	412039		
700 040	**TL** CT *TL* TB	401040	402040	403040	406040		
		407040	410040	411040	412040		
700 041	**TL** CT *TL* TB	401041	402041	403041	406041		
		407041	410041	411041	412041		
700 042	**TL** CT *TL* TB	401042	402042	403042	406042		
		407042	410042	411042	412042		
700 043	**TL** CT *TL* TB	401043	402043	403043	406043		
		407043	410043	411043	412043		
700 044	**TL** CT *TL* TB	401044	402044	403044	406044		
		407044	410044	411044	412044		
700 045	**TL** CT *TL* TB	401045	402045	403045	406045		
		407045	410045	411045	412045		
700 046	**TL** CT *TL* TB	401046	402046	403046	406046		
		407046	410046	411046	412046		
700 047	**TL** CT *TL* TB	401047	402047	403047	406047		
		407047	410047	411047	412047		
700 048	**TL** CT *TL* TB	401048	402048	403048	406048		
		407048	410048	411048	412048		

700 049	**TL**	CT	*TL*	TB	401049	402049	403049	406049		
					407049	410049	411049	412049		
700 050	**TL**	CT	*TL*	TB	401050	402050	403050	406050		
					407050	410050	411050	412050		
700 051	**TL**	CT	*TL*	TB	401051	402051	403051	406051		
					407051	410051	411051	412051		
700 052	**TL**	CT	*TL*	TB	401052	402052	403052	406052		
					407052	410052	411052	412052		
700 053	**TL**	CT	*TL*	TB	401053	402053	403053	406053		
					407053	410053	411053	412053		
700 054	**TL**	CT	*TL*	TB	401054	402054	403054	406054		
					407054	410054	411054	412054		
700 055	**TL**	CT	*TL*	TB	401055	402055	403055	406055		
					407055	410055	411055	412055		
700 056	**TL**	CT	*TL*	TB	401056	402056	403056	406056		
					407056	410056	411056	412056		
700 057	**TL**	CT	*TL*	TB	401057	402057	403057	406057		
					407057	410057	411057	412057		
700 058	**TL**	CT	*TL*	TB	401058	402058	403058	406058		
					407058	410058	411058	412058		
700 059	**TL**	CT	*TL*	TB	401059	402059	403059	406059		
					407059	410059	411059	412059		
700 060	**TL**	CT	*TL*	TB	401060	402060	403060	406060		
					407060	410060	411060	412060		

Class 700/1. 12-car units.

DMC(A). Siemens Krefeld 2013–18. 26/20. 38.2 t.
PTS. Siemens Krefeld 2013–18. –/54 1T. 34.4 t.
MS. Siemens Krefeld 2013–18. –/60(+3). 36.0 t.
MS. Siemens Krefeld 2013–18. –/56 1T. 35.8 t.
TS. Siemens Krefeld 2013–18. –/64. 26.8 t.
TS. Siemens Krefeld 2013–18. –/56(+3). 28.3 t.
TS(W). Siemens Krefeld 2013–18. –/38(+9) 1TD 2W. 28.7 t.
TS. Siemens Krefeld 2013–18. –/64. 27.9 t.
MS. Siemens Krefeld 2013–18. –/56 1T. 35.6 t.
MS. Siemens Krefeld 2013–18. –/60(+3). 35.3 t.
PTS. Siemens Krefeld 2013–18. –/54 1T. 34.4 t.
DMC(B). Siemens Krefeld 2013–18. 26/20. 38.2 t.

700 101	**TL**	CT	*TL*	TB	401101 402101 403101 404101 405101 406101
					407101 408101 409101 410101 411101 412101
700 102	**TL**	CT	*TL*	TB	401102 402102 403102 404102 405102 406102
					407102 408102 409102 410102 411102 412102
700 103	**TL**	CT	*TL*	TB	401103 402103 403103 404103 405103 406103
					407103 408103 409103 410103 411103 412103
700 104	**TL**	CT	*TL*	TB	401104 402104 403104 404104 405104 406104
					407104 408104 409104 410104 411104 412104
700 105	**TL**	CT	*TL*	TB	401105 402105 403105 404105 405105 406105
					407105 408105 409105 410105 411105 412105
700 106	**TL**	CT	*TL*	TB	401106 402106 403106 404106 405106 406106
					407106 408106 409106 410106 411106 412106

700 107	**TL** CT *TL*	TB	401107	402107	403107	404107	405107	406107	
			407107	408107	409107	410107	411107	412107	
700 108	**TL** CT *TL*	TB	401108	402108	403108	404108	405108	406108	
			407108	408108	409108	410108	411108	412108	
700 109	**TL** CT *TL*	TB	401109	402109	403109	404109	405109	406109	
			407109	408109	409109	410109	411109	412109	
700 110	**TL** CT *TL*	TB	401110	402110	403110	404110	405110	406110	
			407110	408110	409110	410110	411110	412110	
700 111	**TL** CT *TL*	TB	401111	402111	403111	404111	405111	406111	
			407111	408111	409111	410111	411111	412111	
700 112	**TL** CT *TL*	TB	401112	402112	403112	404112	405112	406112	
			407112	408112	409112	410112	411112	412112	
700 113	**TL** CT *TL*	TB	401113	402113	403113	404113	405113	406113	
			407113	408113	409113	410113	411113	412113	
700 114	**TL** CT *TL*	TB	401114	402114	403114	404114	405114	406114	
			407114	408114	409114	410114	411114	412114	
700 115	**TL** CT *TL*	TB	401115	402115	403115	404115	405115	406115	
			407115	408115	409115	410115	411115	412115	
700 116	**TL** CT *TL*	TB	401116	402116	403116	404116	405116	406116	
			407116	408116	409116	410116	411116	412116	
700 117	**TL** CT *TL*	TB	401117	402117	403117	404117	405117	406117	
			407117	408117	409117	410117	411117	412117	
700 118	**TL** CT *TL*	TB	401118	402118	403118	404118	405118	406118	
			407118	408118	409118	410118	411118	412118	
700 119	**TL** CT *TL*	TB	401119	402119	403119	404119	405119	406119	
			407119	408119	409119	410119	411119	412119	
700 120	**TL** CT *TL*	TB	401120	402120	403120	404120	405120	406120	
			407120	408120	409120	410120	411120	412120	
700 121	**TL** CT *TL*	TB	401121	402121	403121	404121	405121	406121	
			407121	408121	409121	410121	411121	412121	
700 122	**TL** CT *TL*	TB	401122	402122	403122	404122	405122	406122	
			407122	408122	409122	410122	411122	412122	
700 123	**TL** CT *TL*	TB	401123	402123	403123	404123	405123	406123	
			407123	408123	409123	410123	411123	412123	
700 124	**TL** CT *TL*	TB	401124	402124	403124	404124	405124	406124	
			407124	408124	409124	410124	411124	412124	
700 125	**TL** CT *TL*	TB	401125	402125	403125	404125	405125	406125	
			407125	408125	409125	410125	411125	412125	
700 126	**TL** CT *TL*	TB	401126	402126	403126	404126	405126	406126	
			407126	408126	409126	410126	411126	412126	
700 127	**TL** CT *TL*	TB	401127	402127	403127	404127	405127	406127	
			407127	408127	409127	410127	411127	412127	
700 128	**TL** CT *TL*	TB	401128	402128	403128	404128	405128	406128	
			407128	408128	409128	410128	411128	412128	
700 129	**TL** CT *TL*	TB	401129	402129	403129	404129	405129	406129	
			407129	408129	409129	410129	411129	412129	
700 130	**TL** CT *TL*	TB	401130	402130	403130	404130	405130	406130	
			407130	408130	409130	410130	411130	412130	
700 131	**TL** CT *TL*	TB	401131	402131	403131	404131	405131	406131	
			407131	408131	409131	410131	411131	412131	

700 132	**TL** CT *TL*	TB	401132	402132	403132	404132	405132	406132		
			407132	408132	409132	410132	411132	412132		
700 133	**TL** CT *TL*	TB	401133	402133	403133	404133	405133	406133		
			407133	408133	409133	410133	411133	412133		
700 134	**TL** CT *TL*	TB	401134	402134	403134	404134	405134	406134		
			407134	408134	409134	410134	411134	412134		
700 135	**TL** CT *TL*	TB	401135	402135	403135	404135	405135	406135		
			407135	408135	409135	410135	411135	412135		
700 136	**TL** CT *TL*	TB	401136	402136	403136	404136	405136	406136		
			407136	408136	409136	410136	411136	412136		
700 137	**TL** CT *TL*	TB	401137	402137	403137	404137	405137	406137		
			407137	408137	409137	410137	411137	412137		
700 138	**TL** CT *TL*	TB	401138	402138	403138	404138	405138	406138		
			407138	408138	409138	410138	411138	412138		
700 139	**TL** CT *TL*	TB	401139	402139	403139	404139	405139	406139		
			407139	408139	409139	410139	411139	412139		
700 140	**TL** CT *TL*	TB	401140	402140	403140	404140	405140	406140		
			407140	408140	409140	410140	411140	412140		
700 141	**TL** CT *TL*	TB	401141	402141	403141	404141	405141	406141		
			407141	408141	409141	410141	411141	412141		
700 142	**TL** CT *TL*	TB	401142	402142	403142	404142	405142	406142		
			407142	408142	409142	410142	411142	412142		
700 143	**TL** CT *TL*	TB	401143	402143	403143	404143	405143	406143		
			407143	408143	409143	410143	411143	412143		
700 144	**TL** CT *TL*	TB	401144	402144	403144	404144	405144	406144		
			407144	408144	409144	410144	411144	412144		
700 145	**TL** CT *TL*	TB	401145	402145	403145	404145	405145	406145		
			407145	408145	409145	410145	411145	412145		
700 146	**TL** CT *TL*	TB	401146	402146	403146	404146	405146	406146		
			407146	408146	409146	410146	411146	412146		
700 147	**TL** CT *TL*	TB	401147	402147	403147	404147	405147	406147		
			407147	408147	409147	410147	411147	412147		
700 148	**TL** CT *TL*	TB	401148	402148	403148	404148	405148	406148		
			407148	408148	409148	410148	411148	412148		
700 149	**TL** CT *TL*	TB	401149	402149	403149	404149	405149	406149		
			407149	408149	409149	410149	411149	412149		
700 150	**TL** CT *TL*	TB	401150	402150	403150	404150	405150	406150		
			407150	408150	409150	410150	411150	412150		
700 151	**TL** CT *TL*	TB	401151	402151	403151	404151	405151	406151		
			407151	408151	409151	410151	411151	412151		
700 152	**TL** CT *TL*	TB	401152	402152	403152	404152	405152	406152		
			407152	408152	409152	410152	411152	412152		
700 153	**TL** CT *TL*	TB	401153	402153	403153	404153	405153	406153		
			407153	408153	409153	410153	411153	412153		
700 154	**TL** CT *TL*	TB	401154	402154	403154	404154	405154	406154		
			407154	408154	409154	410154	411154	412154		
700 155	**TL** CT *TL*	TB	401155	402155	403155	404155	405155	406155		
			407155	408155	409155	410155	411155	412155		

CLASS 701   AVENTRA   BOMBARDIER DERBY

South Western Railway has 60 10-car and 30 5-car Aventra EMUs on order from Bombardier, financed by Rock Rail. They are due to enter service in 2020–21. The units will be used mainly on inner and outer suburban duties, replacing Classes 455, 456, 458 and 707. Full details awaited.

Formation:
Systems: 750 V DC third rail.
Construction: Aluminium.
Traction Motors: Two Bombardier asynchronous of 250 kW.
Wheel Arrangement:
Braking: Disc & regenerative   **Dimensions:** 20.88/19.90 m x 2.78 m.
Bogies: FLEXX B5000 inside-frame.   **Couplers:** Dellner.
Gangways: Within unit.   **Control System:** IGBT Inverter.
Doors: Sliding plug.   **Maximum Speed:** 100 mph.
Heating & ventilation: Air conditioning.
Seating Layout: 2+2 facing/unidirectional.
Multiple Working: Within class.

Class 710/1. 10-car units.

701 001	RR	480001	481001	482001	483001	484001
		485001	486001	487001	488001	489001
701 002	RR	480002	481002	482002	483002	484002
		485002	486002	487002	488002	489002
701 003	RR	480003	481003	482003	483003	484003
		485003	486003	487003	488003	489003
701 004	RR	480004	481004	482004	483004	484004
		485004	486004	487004	488004	489004
701 005	RR	480005	481005	482005	483005	484005
		485005	486005	487005	488005	489005
701 006	RR	480006	481006	482006	483006	484006
		485006	486006	487006	488006	489006
701 007	RR	480007	481007	482007	483007	484007
		485007	486007	487007	488007	489007
701 008	RR	480008	481008	482008	483008	484008
		485008	486008	487008	488008	489008
701 009	RR	480009	481009	482009	483009	484009
		485009	486009	487009	488009	489009
701 010	RR	480010	481010	482010	483010	484010
		485010	486010	487010	488010	489010
701 011	RR	480011	481011	482011	483011	484011
		485011	486011	487011	488011	489011
701 012	RR	480012	481012	482012	483012	484012
		485012	486012	487012	488012	489012
701 013	RR	480013	481013	482013	483013	484013
		485013	486013	487013	488013	489013
701 014	RR	480014	481014	482014	483014	484014
		485014	486014	487014	488014	489014
701 015	RR	480015	481015	482015	483015	484015
		485015	486015	487015	488015	489015

701 016	RR	480016	481016	482016	483016	484016
		485016	486016	487016	488016	489016
701 017	RR	480017	481017	482017	483017	484017
		485017	486017	487017	488017	489017
701 018	RR	480018	481018	482018	483018	484018
		485018	486018	487018	488018	489018
701 019	RR	480019	481019	482019	483019	484019
		485019	486019	487019	488019	489019
701 020	RR	480020	481020	482020	483020	484020
		485020	486020	487020	488020	489020
701 021	RR	480021	481021	482021	483021	484021
		485021	486021	487021	488021	489021
701 022	RR	480022	481022	482022	483022	484022
		485022	486022	487022	488022	489022
701 023	RR	480023	481023	482023	483023	484023
		485023	486023	487023	488023	489023
701 024	RR	480024	481024	482024	483024	484024
		485024	486024	487024	488024	489024
701 025	RR	480025	481025	482025	483025	484025
		485025	486025	487025	488025	489025
701 026	RR	480026	481026	482026	483026	484026
		485026	486026	487026	488026	489026
701 027	RR	480027	481027	482027	483027	484027
		485027	486027	487027	488027	489027
701 028	RR	480028	481028	482028	483028	484028
		485028	486028	487028	488028	489028
701 029	RR	480029	481029	482029	483029	484029
		485029	486029	487029	488029	489029
701 030	RR	480030	481030	482030	483030	484030
		485030	486030	487030	488030	489030
701 031	RR	480031	481031	482031	483031	484031
		485031	486031	487031	488031	489031
701 032	RR	480032	481032	482032	483032	484032
		485032	486032	487032	488032	489032
701 033	RR	480033	481033	482033	483033	484033
		485033	486033	487033	488033	489033
701 034	RR	480034	481034	482034	483034	484034
		485034	486034	487034	488034	489034
701 035	RR	480035	481035	482035	483035	484035
		485035	486035	487035	488035	489035
701 036	RR	480036	481036	482036	483036	484036
		485036	486036	487036	488036	489036
701 037	RR	480037	481037	482037	483037	484037
		485037	486037	487037	488037	489037
701 038	RR	480038	481038	482038	483038	484038
		485038	486038	487038	488038	489038
701 039	RR	480039	481039	482039	483039	484039
		485039	486039	487039	488039	489039
701 040	RR	480040	481040	482040	483040	484040
		485040	486040	487040	488040	489040

701 041	RR	480041	481041	482041	483041	484041
		485041	486041	487041	488041	489041
701 042	RR	480042	481042	482042	483042	484042
		485042	486042	487042	488042	489042
701 043	RR	480043	481043	482043	483043	484043
		485043	486043	487043	488043	489043
701 044	RR	480044	481044	482044	483044	484044
		485044	486044	487044	488044	489044
701 045	RR	480045	481045	482045	483045	484045
		485045	486045	487045	488045	489045
701 046	RR	480046	481046	482046	483046	484046
		485046	486046	487046	488046	489046
701 047	RR	480047	481047	482047	483047	484047
		485047	486047	487047	488047	489047
701 048	RR	480048	481048	482048	483048	484048
		485048	486048	487048	488048	489048
701 049	RR	480049	481049	482049	483049	484049
		485049	486049	487049	488049	489049
701 050	RR	480050	481050	482050	483050	484050
		485050	486050	487050	488050	489050
701 051	RR	480051	481051	482051	483051	484051
		485051	486051	487051	488051	489051
701 052	RR	480052	481052	482052	483052	484052
		485052	486052	487052	488052	489052
701 053	RR	480053	481053	482053	483053	484053
		485053	486053	487053	488053	489053
701 054	RR	480054	481054	482054	483054	484054
		485054	486054	487054	488054	489054
701 055	RR	480055	481055	482055	483055	484055
		485055	486055	487055	488055	489055
701 056	RR	480056	481056	482056	483056	484056
		485056	486056	487056	488056	489056
701 057	RR	480057	481057	482057	483057	484057
		485057	486057	487057	488057	489057
701 058	RR	480058	481058	482058	483058	484058
		485058	486058	487058	488058	489058
701 059	RR	480059	481059	482059	483059	484059
		485059	486059	487059	488059	489059
701 060	RR	480060	481060	482060	483060	484060
		485060	486060	487060	488060	489060

Class 710/5. 5-car units.

701 501	RR	480101	481101	482101	483101	484101
701 502	RR	480102	481102	482102	483102	484102
701 503	RR	480103	481103	482103	483103	484103
701 504	RR	480104	481104	482104	483104	484104
701 505	RR	480105	481105	482105	483105	484105
701 506	RR	480106	481106	482106	483106	484106
701 507	RR	480107	481107	482107	483107	484107
701 508	RR	480108	481108	482108	483108	484108
701 509	RR	480109	481109	482109	483109	484109

701510	RR		480110	481110	482110	483110	484110
701511	RR		480111	481111	482111	483111	484111
701512	RR		480112	481112	482112	483112	484112
701513	RR		480113	481113	482113	483113	484113
701514	RR		480114	481114	482114	483114	484114
701515	RR		480115	481115	482115	483115	484115
701516	RR		480116	481116	482116	483116	484116
701517	RR		480117	481117	482117	483117	484117
701518	RR		480118	481118	482118	483118	484118
701519	RR		480119	481119	482119	483119	484119
701520	RR		480120	481120	482120	483120	484120
701521	RR		480121	481121	482121	483121	484121
701522	RR		480122	481122	482122	483122	484122
701523	RR		480123	481123	482123	483123	484123
701524	RR		480124	481124	482124	483124	484124
701525	RR		480125	481125	482125	483125	484125
701526	RR		480126	481126	482126	483126	484126
701527	RR		480127	481127	482127	483127	484127
701528	RR		480128	481128	482128	483128	484128
701529	RR		480129	481129	482129	483129	484129
701530	RR		480130	481130	482130	483130	484130

CLASS 707   DESIRO CITY   SIEMENS

South Western Railway suburban units. Built with the capability to be easily converted to dual voltage units.

Formation: DMS–TS–TS–(P)TS–DMS.
Systems: 750 V DC third rail but with 25 kV AC overhead capability.
Construction: Aluminium.
Traction Motors: Four Siemens asynchronous of 200 kW.
Wheel Arrangement: Bo-Bo + 2-2 + 2-2 + 2-2 + Bo-Bo.
Braking: Disc, tread & regenerative.   **Dimensions:** 20.00/20.16 m x 2.80 m.
Bogies: Siemens SF7000 inside-frame.   **Couplers:** Dellner 12.
Gangways: Within unit.   **Control System:** IGBT Inverter.
Doors: Sliding plug.   **Maximum Speed:** 100 mph.
Heating & ventilation: Air conditioning.
Seating Layout: 2+2/2+1 facing/unidirectional.
Multiple Working: Within class and with Classes 700 and 717.

DMS(A). Siemens Krefeld 2015–17. –/46. 37.9 t.
TS. Siemens Krefeld 2015–17. –/64. 28.3 t.
TS. Siemens Krefeld 2015–17. –/53(+4) 2W. 28.5 t.
(P)TS. Siemens Krefeld 2015–17. –/62. 27.7 t.
DMS(B). Siemens Krefeld 2015–17. –/46. 37.9 t.

707001	SS	A	SW	WD	421001	422001	423001	424001	425001
707002	SS	A	SW	WD	421002	422002	423002	424002	425002
707003	SS	A	SW	WD	421003	422003	423003	424003	425003
707004	SS	A	SW	WD	421004	422004	423004	424004	425004
707005	SS	A	SW	WD	421005	422005	423005	424005	425005
707006	SS	A	SW	WD	421006	422006	423006	424006	425006

707 007	**SS**	A	*SW*	WD	421007	422007	423007	424007	425007
707 008	**SS**	A	*SW*	WD	421008	422008	423008	424008	425008
707 009	**SS**	A	*SW*	WD	421009	422009	423009	424009	425009
707 010	**SS**	A	*SW*	WD	421010	422010	423010	424010	425010
707 011	**SS**	A	*SW*	WD	421011	422011	423011	424011	425011
707 012	**SS**	A	*SW*	WD	421012	422012	423012	424012	425012
707 013	**SS**	A	*SW*	WD	421013	422013	423013	424013	425013
707 014	**SS**	A	*SW*	WD	421014	422014	423014	424014	425014
707 015	**SS**	A	*SW*	WD	421015	422015	423015	424015	425015
707 016	**SS**	A	*SW*	WD	421016	422016	423016	424016	425016
707 017	**SS**	A	*SW*	WD	421017	422017	423017	424017	425017
707 018	**SS**	A	*SW*	WD	421018	422018	423018	424018	425018
707 019	**SS**	A	*SW*	WD	421019	422019	423019	424019	425019
707 020	**SS**	A	*SW*	WD	421020	422020	423020	424020	425020
707 021	**SS**	A	*SW*	WD	421021	422021	423021	424021	425021
707 022	**SS**	A	*SW*	WD	421022	422022	423022	424022	425022
707 023	**SS**	A	*SW*	WD	421023	422023	423023	424023	425023
707 024	**SS**	A	*SW*	WD	421024	422024	423024	424024	425024
707 025	**SS**	A	*SW*	WD	421025	422025	423025	424025	425025
707 026	**SS**	A	*SW*	WD	421026	422026	423026	424026	425026
707 027	**SS**	A	*SW*	WD	421027	422027	423027	424027	425027
707 028	**SS**	A	*SW*	WD	421028	422028	423028	424028	425028
707 029	**SS**	A	*SW*	WD	421029	422029	423029	424029	425029
707 030	**SS**	A	*SW*	WD	421030	422030	423030	424030	425030

CLASS 710   AVENTRA   BOMBARDIER DERBY

These suburban 4-car Aventras are now being delivered to London Overground for use on Gospel Oak–Barking, London Euston–Watford Junction London and Liverpool Street local services. There are a mix of AC only and dual-voltage units. The first trains (710/2s) entered service in spring 2019, with the remainder due to follow in 2019–20.

Originally 45 4-car units were ordered. In 2018 an extra three 4-cars and six 5-cars were ordered.

Formation: DMS–MS–PMS–DMS or DMS–MS–PMS–MS–DMS.
Systems: Class 710/1 25 kV AC overhead only. Class 710/2 25 kV AC overhead and 750 V DC third rail.
Construction: Aluminium.
Traction Motors: Two Bombardier asynchronous of 265 kW.
Wheel Arrangement: Bo-2 + 2-Bo + Bo-2 (+ 2-Bo) + 2-Bo.
Braking: Disc & regenerative   **Dimensions:** 21.45/19.99 m x 2.78 m.
Bogies: FLEXX B5000 inside-frame.   **Couplers:** Dellner 12.
Gangways: Within unit.   **Control System:** IGBT Inverter.
Doors: Sliding plug.   **Maximum Speed:** 75 mph.
Heating & ventilation: Air conditioning.
Seating Layout: Longitudinal ("tube style") low density.
Multiple Working: Within class.

Class 710/1. 25 kV AC only 4-car units.

DMS(A). Bombardier Derby 2017–19. –/40(+6).   t.
MS. Bombardier Derby 2017–19. –/46.   t.
PMS. Bombardier Derby 2017–19. –/45(+6) 2W.   t.
DMS(B). Bombardier Derby 2017–19. –/40(+6).   t.

710101	**LD**	RF		431101	431201	431301	431501
710102	**LD**	RF		431102	431202	431302	431502
710103	**LD**	RF		431103	431203	431303	431503
710104	**LD**	RF		431104	431204	431304	431504
710105	**LD**	RF		431105	431205	431305	431505
710106	**LD**	RF		431106	431206	431306	431506
710107	**LD**	RF		431107	431207	431307	431507
710108	**LD**	RF		431108	431208	431308	431508
710109	**LD**	RF		431109	431209	431309	431509
710110	**LD**	RF		431110	431210	431310	431510
710111	**LD**	RF		431111	431211	431311	431511
710112	**LD**	RF		431112	431212	431312	431512
710113	**LD**	RF		431113	431213	431313	431513
710114	**LD**	RF		431114	431214	431314	431514
710115	**LD**	RF		431115	431215	431315	431515
710116	**LD**	RF		431116	431216	431316	431516
710117	**LD**	RF		431117	431217	431317	431517
710118	**LD**	RF		431118	431218	431318	431518
710119	**LD**	RF		431119	431219	431319	431519
710120	**LD**	RF		431120	431220	431320	431520
710121	**LD**	RF		431121	431221	431321	431521
710122	**LD**	RF		431122	431222	431322	431522
710123	**LD**	RF		431123	431223	431323	431523
710124	**LD**	RF		431124	431224	431324	431524
710125	**LD**	RF		431125	431225	431325	431525
710126	**LD**	RF		431126	431226	431326	431526
710127	**LD**	RF		431127	431227	431327	431527
710128	**LD**	RF		431128	431228	431328	431528
710129	**LD**	RF		431129	431229	431329	431529
710130	**LD**	RF		431130	431230	431330	431530

Class 710/2. 25 kV AC/750 V DC 4-car units.

DMS(A). Bombardier Derby 2017–19. –/40(+6). 43.5 t.
MS. Bombardier Derby 2017–19. –/46. 32.3 t.
PMS. Bombardier Derby 2017–19. –/45(+6) 2W. 38.5 t.
DMS(B). Bombardier Derby 2017–19. –/40(+6).43.5 t.

710256	**LD**	RF			432156	432256	432356	432556
710257	**LD**	RF	*LO*	WN	432157	432257	432357	432557
710258	**LD**	RF	*LO*	WN	432158	432258	432358	432558
710259	**LD**	RF			432159	432259	432359	432559
710260	**LD**	RF	*LO*	WN	432160	432260	432360	432560
710261	**LD**	RF	*LO*	WN	432161	432261	432361	432561
710262	**LD**	RF	*LO*	WN	432162	432262	432362	432562
710263	**LD**	RF	*LO*	WN	432163	432263	432363	432563

710264	**LD**	RF	*LO*	WN	432164	432264	432364	432564
710265	**LD**	RF	*LO*	WN	432165	432265	432365	432565
710266	**LD**	RF	*LO*	WN	432166	432266	432366	432566
710267	**LD**	RF	*LO*	WN	432167	432267	432367	432567
710268	**LD**	RF	*LO*	WN	432168	432268	432368	432568
710269	**LD**	RF	*LO*	WN	432169	432269	432369	432569
710270	**LD**	RF			432170	432270	432370	432570
710271	**LD**	RF			432171	432271	432371	432571
710272	**LD**	RF			432172	432272	432372	432572
710273	**LD**	RF			432173	432273	432373	432573

Class 710/2. 25 kV AC/750 V DC 5-car units.

DMS(A). Bombardier Derby 2019–20. –/40(+6).   t.
MS. Bombardier Derby 2019–20. –/46.   t.
PMS. Bombardier Derby 2019–20. –/45(+6) 2W.   t.
MS. Bombardier Derby 2019–20. –/–.   t.
DMS(B). Bombardier Derby 2019–20. –/40(+6).   t.

710274	**LD**	RF	432174	432274	432374	432474	432574
710275	**LD**	RF	432175	432275	432375	432475	432575
710276	**LD**	RF	432176	432276	432376	432476	432576
710277	**LD**	RF	432177	432277	432377	432477	432577
710278	**LD**	RF	432178	432278	432378	432478	432578
710279	**LD**	RF	432179	432279	432379	432479	432579

CLASS 717   DESIRO CITY   SIEMENS

New dual-voltage 6-car units used on Great Northern services from London Moorgate. The design is based on Classes 700/707, but has emergency end doors for tunnel operation. Fitted with tripcocks for operation between Moorgate and Drayton Park.

Formation: DMS–TS–TS–MS–PTS–DMS.
Systems: 25 kV AC overhead and 750 V DC third rail.
Construction: Aluminium.
Traction Motors: Four Siemens asynchronous of 200 kW.
Wheel Arrangement: Bo-Bo + 2-2 + 2-2 + Bo-Bo + 2-2 + Bo-Bo.
Braking: Disc, tread & regenerative.   **Dimensions:** 20.00 x 2.80 m.
Bogies: Siemens SF7000 inside-frame. **Couplers:** Dellner 12.
Gangways: Within unit + end doors. **Control System:** IGBT Inverter.
Doors: Sliding plug.   **Maximum Speed:** 85 mph.
Heating & ventilation: Air conditioning.
Seating Layout: 2+2 facing/unidirectional.
Multiple Working: Within class and with Classes 700 and 707.

DMS(A). Siemens Krefeld 2017–18. –/52(+4). 38.8 t.
TS. Siemens Krefeld 2017–18. –/68. 28.8 t.
TS. Siemens Krefeld 2017–18. –/61(+4) 2W. 28.7 t.
MS. Siemens Krefeld 2017–18. –/68. 35.5 t.
PTO. Siemens Krefeld 2017–18. –/61(+3). 33.9 t.
DMS(B). Siemens Krefeld 2017–18. –/52(+4). 38.8 t.

717001	**TL**	RR	*GN*	HE	451001 452001 453001 454001 455001 456001
717002	**TL**	RR	*GN*	HE	451002 452002 453002 454002 455002 456002
717003	**TL**	RR	*GN*	HE	451003 452003 453003 454003 455003 456003
717004	**TL**	RR	*GN*	HE	451004 452004 453004 454004 455004 456004
717005	**TL**	RR	*GN*	HE	451005 452005 453005 454005 455005 456005
717006	**TL**	RR	*GN*	HE	451006 452006 453006 454006 455006 456006
717007	**TL**	RR	*GN*	HE	451007 452007 453007 454007 455007 456007
717008	**TL**	RR	*GN*	HE	451008 452008 453008 454008 455008 456008
717009	**TL**	RR	*GN*	HE	451009 452009 453009 454009 455009 456009
717010	**TL**	RR	*GN*	HE	451010 452010 453010 454010 455010 456010
717011	**TL**	RR	*GN*	HE	451011 452011 453011 454011 455011 456011
717012	**TL**	RR	*GN*	HE	451012 452012 453012 454012 455012 456012
717013	**TL**	RR	*GN*	HE	451013 452013 453013 454013 455013 456013
717014	**TL**	RR	*GN*	HE	451014 452014 453014 454014 455014 456014
717015	**TL**	RR	*GN*	HE	451015 452015 453015 454015 455015 456015
717016	**TL**	RR	*GN*	HE	451016 452016 453016 454016 455016 456016
717017	**TL**	RR	*GN*	HE	451017 452017 453017 454017 455017 456017
717018	**TL**	RR	*GN*	HE	451018 452018 453018 454018 455018 456018
717019	**TL**	RR	*GN*	HE	451019 452019 453019 454019 455019 456019
717020	**TL**	RR	*GN*	HE	451020 452020 453020 454020 455020 456020
717021	**TL**	RR	*GN*	HE	451021 452021 453021 454021 455021 456021
717022	**TL**	RR	*GN*	HE	451022 452022 453022 454022 455022 456022
717023	**TL**	RR	*GN*	HE	451023 452023 453023 454023 455023 456023
717024	**TL**	RR	*GN*	HE	451024 452024 453024 454024 455024 456024
717025	**TL**	RR	*GN*	HE	451025 452025 453025 454025 455025 456025

CLASS 720   AVENTRA   BOMBARDIER DERBY

This large fleet of Aventra EMUs was ordered by Greater Anglia in 2016 to replace its entire Class 317, 321, 360 and 379 fleets on outer suburban and medium-distance services. The units will be around a year late entering service owing to Bombardier Aventra software issues. They are expected to enter service from spring 2020. Full details awaited.

Formation (10-car): DMS–PMS–MS–MS–TS–MS–PMS–MS–MS–DTS or
(5-car): DMS–PMS–MS–MS–DTS.
Systems: 25 kV AC overhead.
Construction: Aluminium.
Traction Motors: Two Bombardier asynchronous of 265 kW.
Wheel Arrangement:
Braking: Disc & regenerative   **Dimensions:** 24.47/24.21 x 2.78 m.
Bogies: FLEXX B5000 inside-frame.   **Couplers:** Dellner 12.
Gangways: Within unit.   **Control System:** IGBT Inverter.
Doors: Sliding plug.   **Maximum Speed:** 100 mph.
Heating & ventilation: Air conditioning.
Seating Layout: 3+2 facing/unidirectional.
Multiple Working: Within class.

Class 720/1. 10-car units.

DMS. Bombardier Derby 2019–20.   t.
PMS(A). Bombardier Derby 2019–20.   t.
MS(A). Bombardier Derby 2019–20.   t.
MS(B). Bombardier Derby 2019–20.   t.
TS. Bombardier Derby 2019–20.   t.
MS(C). Bombardier Derby 2019–20.   t.
PMS(B). Bombardier Derby 2019–20.   t.
MS(D). Bombardier Derby 2019–20.   t.
MS(E). Bombardier Derby 2019–20.   t.
DTS. Bombardier Derby 2019–20.   t.

720 101	**GR**	A	450101	451101	452101	453101	454101
			455101	456101	457101	458101	459101
720 102	**GR**	A	450102	451102	452102	453102	454102
			455102	456102	457102	458102	459102
720 103	**GR**	A	450103	451103	452103	453103	454103
			455103	456103	457103	458103	459103
720 104	**GR**	A	450104	451104	452104	453104	454104
			455104	456104	457104	458104	459104
720 105	**GR**	A	450105	451105	452105	453105	454105
			455105	456105	457105	458105	459105
720 106	**GR**	A	450106	451106	452106	453106	454106
			455106	456106	457106	458106	459106
720 107	**GR**	A	450107	451107	452107	453107	454107
			455107	456107	457107	458107	459107
720 108	**GR**	A	450108	451108	452108	453108	454108
			455108	456108	457108	458108	459108
720 109	**GR**	A	450109	451109	452109	453109	454109
			455109	456109	457109	458109	459109
720 110	**GR**	A	450110	451110	452110	453110	454110
			455110	456110	457110	458110	459110
720 111	**GR**	A	450111	451111	452111	453111	454111
			455111	456111	457111	458111	459111
720 112	**GR**	A	450112	451112	452112	453112	454112
			455112	456112	457112	458112	459112
720 113	**GR**	A	450113	451113	452113	453113	454113
			455113	456113	457113	458113	459113
720 114	**GR**	A	450114	451114	452114	453114	454114
			455114	456114	457114	458114	459114
720 115	**GR**	A	450115	451115	452115	453115	454115
			455115	456115	457115	458115	459115
720 116	**GR**	A	450116	451116	452116	453116	454116
			455116	456116	457116	458116	459116
720 117	**GR**	A	450117	451117	452117	453117	454117
			455117	456117	457117	458117	459117
720 118	**GR**	A	450118	451118	452118	453118	454118
			455118	456118	457118	458118	459118
720 119	**GR**	A	450119	451119	452119	453119	454119
			455119	456119	457119	458119	459119

720 120	**GR**	A	450120	451120	452120	453120	454120
			455120	456120	457120	458120	459120
720 121	**GR**	A	450121	451121	452121	453121	454121
			455121	456121	457121	458121	459121
720 122	**GR**	A	450122	451122	452122	453122	454122
			455122	456122	457122	458122	459122

Class 720/5. 5-car units.

DMS. Bombardier Derby 2018–20.   t.
PMS. Bombardier Derby 2018–20.   t.
MS(A). Bombardier Derby 2018–20.   t.
MS(B). Bombardier Derby 2018–20.   t.
DTS. Bombardier Derby 2018–20.   t.

720 501	**GR**	A	450501	451501	452501	453501	459501
720 502	**GR**	A	450502	451502	452502	453502	459502
720 503	**GR**	A	450503	451503	452503	453503	459503
720 504	**GR**	A	450504	451504	452504	453504	459504
720 505	**GR**	A	450505	451505	452505	453505	459505
720 506	**GR**	A	450506	451506	452506	453506	459506
720 507	**GR**	A	450507	451507	452507	453507	459507
720 508	**GR**	A	450508	451508	452508	453508	459508
720 509	**GR**	A	450509	451509	452509	453509	459509
720 510	**GR**	A	450510	451510	452510	453510	459510
720 511	**GR**	A	450511	451511	452511	453511	459511
720 512	**GR**	A	450512	451512	452512	453512	459512
720 513	**GR**	A	450513	451513	452513	453513	459513
720 514	**GR**	A	450514	451514	452514	453514	459514
720 515	**GR**	A	450515	451515	452515	453515	459515
720 516	**GR**	A	450516	451516	452516	453516	459516
720 517	**GR**	A	450517	451517	452517	453517	459517
720 518	**GR**	A	450518	451518	452518	453518	459518
720 519	**GR**	A	450519	451519	452519	453519	459519
720 520	**GR**	A	450520	451520	452520	453520	459520
720 521	**GR**	A	450521	451521	452521	453521	459521
720 522	**GR**	A	450522	451522	452522	453522	459522
720 523	**GR**	A	450523	451523	452523	453523	459523
720 524	**GR**	A	450524	451524	452524	453524	459524
720 525	**GR**	A	450525	451525	452525	453525	459525
720 526	**GR**	A	450526	451526	452526	453526	459526
720 527	**GR**	A	450527	451527	452527	453527	459527
720 528	**GR**	A	450528	451528	452528	453528	459528
720 529	**GR**	A	450529	451529	452529	453529	459529
720 530	**GR**	A	450530	451530	452530	453530	459530
720 531	**GR**	A	450531	451531	452531	453531	459531
720 532	**GR**	A	450532	451532	452532	453532	459532
720 533	**GR**	A	450533	451533	452533	453533	459533
720 534	**GR**	A	450534	451534	452534	453534	459534
720 535	**GR**	A	450535	451535	452535	453535	459535
720 536	**GR**	A	450536	451536	452536	453536	459536
720 537	**GR**	A	450537	451537	452537	453537	459537
720 538	**GR**	A	450538	451538	452538	453538	459538

720 539	GR	A	450539	451539	452539	453539	459539
720 540	GR	A	450540	451540	452540	453540	459540
720 541	GR	A	450541	451541	452541	453541	459541
720 542	GR	A	450542	451542	452542	453542	459542
720 543	GR	A	450543	451543	452543	453543	459543
720 544	GR	A	450544	451544	452544	453544	459544
720 545	GR	A	450545	451545	452545	453545	459545
720 546	GR	A	450546	451546	452546	453546	459546
720 547	GR	A	450547	451547	452547	453547	459547
720 548	GR	A	450548	451548	452548	453548	459548
720 549	GR	A	450549	451549	452549	453549	459549
720 550	GR	A	450550	451550	452550	453550	459550
720 551	GR	A	450551	451551	452551	453551	459551
720 552	GR	A	450552	451552	452552	453552	459552
720 553	GR	A	450553	451553	452553	453553	459553
720 554	GR	A	450554	451554	452554	453554	459554
720 555	GR	A	450555	451555	452555	453555	459555
720 556	GR	A	450556	451556	452556	453556	459556
720 557	GR	A	450557	451557	452557	453557	459557
720 558	GR	A	450558	451558	452558	453558	459558
720 559	GR	A	450559	451559	452559	453559	459559
720 560	GR	A	450560	451560	452560	453560	459560
720 561	GR	A	450561	451561	452561	453561	459561
720 562	GR	A	450562	451562	452562	453562	459562
720 563	GR	A	450563	451563	452563	453563	459563
720 564	GR	A	450564	451564	452564	453564	459564
720 565	GR	A	450565	451565	452565	453565	459565
720 566	GR	A	450566	451566	452566	453566	459566
720 567	GR	A	450567	451567	452567	453567	459567
720 568	GR	A	450568	451568	452568	453568	459568
720 569	GR	A	450569	451569	452569	453569	459569
720 570	GR	A	450570	451570	452570	453570	459570
720 571	GR	A	450571	451571	452571	453571	459571
720 572	GR	A	450572	451572	452572	453572	459572
720 573	GR	A	450573	451573	452573	453573	459573
720 574	GR	A	450574	451574	452574	453574	459574
720 575	GR	A	450575	451575	452575	453575	459575
720 576	GR	A	450576	451576	452576	453576	459576
720 577	GR	A	450577	451577	452577	453577	459577
720 578	GR	A	450578	451578	452578	453578	459578
720 579	GR	A	450579	451579	452579	453579	459579
720 580	GR	A	450580	451580	452580	453580	459580
720 581	GR	A	450581	451581	452581	453581	459581
720 582	GR	A	450582	451582	452582	453582	459582
720 583	GR	A	450583	451583	452583	453583	459583
720 584	GR	A	450584	451584	452584	453584	459584
720 585	GR	A	450585	451585	452585	453585	459585
720 586	GR	A	450586	451586	452586	453586	459586
720 587	GR	A	450587	451587	452587	453587	459587
720 588	GR	A	450588	451588	452588	453588	459588
720 589	GR	A	450589	451589	452589	453589	459589

CLASS 730   AVENTRA   BOMBARDIER DERBY

West Midlands Trains has a mixed fleet of 3- and 5-car Aventra EMUs on order from Bombardier, for delivery 2020–21. The 3-car units will be used on suburban services around Birmingham, including on the Cross City line, while the 5-car units will be used on outer suburban and inter urban services from London Euston and in the West Midlands. Full details awaited.

Formation: DMS–PMS–DMS or DMC–MS–PMS–MS–DMS
Systems: 25 kV AC overhead.
Construction: Aluminium.
Traction Motors: Two Bombardier asynchronous of 250 kW.
Wheel Arrangement:
Braking: Disc & regenerative   **Dimensions:** 24.47/24.21 x 2.78 m.
Bogies: FLEXX B5000 inside-frame. **Couplers:** Dellner 12.
Gangways: End gangways.   **Control System:** IGBT Inverter.
Doors: Sliding plug.   **Maximum Speed:**
Heating & ventilation: Air conditioning.
Seating Layout:
Multiple Working: Within class.

Class 730/0. 3-car West Midlands area units.

DMS. Bombardier Derby 2020–21.   t.
PMS. Bombardier Derby 2020–21.   t.
DMS. Bombardier Derby 2020–21.   t.

730001	CO	490001	491001	492001
730002	CO	490002	491002	492002
730003	CO	490003	491003	492003
730004	CO	490004	491004	492004
730005	CO	490005	491005	492005
730006	CO	490006	491006	492006
730007	CO	490007	491007	492007
730008	CO	490008	491008	492008
730009	CO	490009	491009	492009
730010	CO	490010	491010	492010
730011	CO	490011	491011	492011
730012	CO	490012	491012	492012
730013	CO	490013	491013	492013
730014	CO	490014	491014	492014
730015	CO	490015	491015	492015
730016	CO	490016	491016	492016
730017	CO	490017	491017	492017
730018	CO	490018	491018	492018
730019	CO	490019	491019	492019
730020	CO	490020	491020	492020
730021	CO	490021	491021	492021
730022	CO	490022	491022	492022
730023	CO	490023	491023	492023
730024	CO	490024	491024	492024
730025	CO	490025	491025	492025
730026	CO	490026	491026	492026

730027	CO	490027	491027	492027		
730028	CO	490028	491028	492028		
730029	CO	490029	491029	492029		
730030	CO	490030	491030	492030		
730031	CO	490031	491031	492031		
730032	CO	490032	491032	492032		
730033	CO	490033	491033	492033		
730034	CO	490034	491034	492034		
730035	CO	490035	491035	492035		
730036	CO	490036	491036	492036		

Class 730/1. 5-car outer suburban units.

DMC. Bombardier Derby 2020–21.   t.
MS. Bombardier Derby 2020–21.   t.
PMS. Bombardier Derby 2020–21.   t.
MS. Bombardier Derby 2020–21.   t.
DMS. Bombardier Derby 2020–21.   t.

730101	CO	490101	491101	492101	493101	494101
730102	CO	490102	491102	492102	493102	494102
730103	CO	490103	491103	492103	493103	494103
730104	CO	490104	491104	492104	493104	494104
730105	CO	490105	491105	492105	493105	494105
730106	CO	490106	491106	492106	493106	494106
730107	CO	490107	491107	492107	493107	494107
730108	CO	490108	491108	492108	493108	494108
730109	CO	490109	491109	492109	493109	494109
730110	CO	490110	491110	492110	493110	494110
730111	CO	490111	491111	492111	493111	494111
730112	CO	490112	491112	492112	493112	494112
730113	CO	490113	491113	492113	493113	494113
730114	CO	490114	491114	492114	493114	494114
730115	CO	490115	491115	492115	493115	494115
730116	CO	490116	491116	492116	493116	494116
730117	CO	490117	491117	492117	493117	494117
730118	CO	490118	491118	492118	493118	494118
730119	CO	490119	491119	492119	493119	494119
730120	CO	490120	491120	492120	493120	494120
730121	CO	490121	491121	492121	493121	494121
730122	CO	490122	491122	492122	493122	494122
730123	CO	490123	491123	492123	493123	494123
730124	CO	490124	491124	492124	493124	494124
730125	CO	490125	491125	492125	493125	494125
730126	CO	490126	491126	492126	493126	494126
730127	CO	490127	491127	492127	493127	494127
730128	CO	490128	491128	492128	493128	494128
730129	CO	490129	491129	492129	493129	494129

Class 730/2. 5-car long distance units.

DMC. Bombardier Derby 2020–21.   t.
MS. Bombardier Derby 2020–21.   t.

PMS. Bombardier Derby 2020–21.   t.
MS. Bombardier Derby 2020–21.   t.
DMS. Bombardier Derby 2020–21.   t.

730 201	CO	490201	491201	492201	493201	494201
730 202	CO	490202	491202	492202	493202	494202
730 203	CO	490203	491203	492203	493203	494203
730 204	CO	490204	491204	492204	493204	494204
730 205	CO	490205	491205	492205	493205	494205
730 206	CO	490206	491206	492206	493206	494206
730 207	CO	490207	491207	492207	493207	494207
730 208	CO	490208	491208	492208	493208	494208
730 209	CO	490209	491209	492209	493209	494209
730 210	CO	490210	491210	492210	493210	494210
730 211	CO	490211	491211	492211	493211	494211
730 212	CO	490212	491212	492212	493212	494212
730 213	CO	490213	491213	492213	493213	494213
730 214	CO	490214	491214	492214	493214	494214
730 215	CO	490215	491215	492215	493215	494215
730 216	CO	490216	491216	492216	493216	494216

CLASS 745   FLIRT ELECTRIC   STADLER

This fleet of 20 12-car articulated Stadler EMUs was ordered by Greater Anglia in 2016 to replace its locomotive-hauled sets on Liverpool Street–Norwich services and Class 379s on the Liverpool Street–Stansted Airport route. The units will enter traffic from autumn 2019. The 12-car units are formed of two 6-car half units formed of three coupled articulated pairs. Full details awaited.

Formation (745/0): DMF–PTF–TS–TS–TS–MS–MS–TS–TS–TS–PTS–DMS or
(745/1): DMS–PTS–TS–TS–TS–MS–MS–TS–TS–TS–PTS–DMS.
Systems: 25 kV AC overhead.
Construction: Aluminium.
Traction Motors: Four TSA of 325 kW.
Wheel Arrangement: Bo-2-2 + 2-2-2 + 2-2-Bo + Bo-2-2 + 2-2-2 + 2-2-Bo.

Braking: Disc & regenerative	**Dimensions:**
Bogies: Stadler/Jacobs.	**Couplers:** Dellner 10.
Gangways: Within unit.	**Control System:** IGBT Inverter.
Doors: Sliding plug (one per vehicle).	**Maximum Speed:** 100 mph.

Heating & ventilation: Air conditioning.
Seating Layout: 1: 2+1 facing/unidirectional, 2: 2+2 unidirectional/facing.
Multiple Working: Within class.

Class 745/0. Fitted with First Class and café bar area for use on the London Liverpool Street–Norwich route.

DMF. Stadler Bussnang/Szolnok 2018–19.   t.
PTF. Stadler Bussnang/Szolnok 2018–19.   t.
TS(A). Stadler Bussnang/Szolnok 2018–19.   t.
TS(B). Stadler Bussnang/Szolnok 2018–19.   t.
TS(C). Stadler Bussnang/Szolnok 2018–19.   t.
MS(A). Stadler Bussnang/Szolnok 2018–19.   t.
MS(B). Stadler Bussnang/Szolnok 2018–19.   t.

TS(D). Stadler Bussnang/Szolnok 2018–19.   t.
TS(E). Stadler Bussnang/Szolnok 2018–19.   t.
TS(F). Stadler Bussnang/Szolnok 2018–19.   t.
PTS. Stadler Bussnang/Szolnok 2018–19.   t.
DMS. Stadler Bussnang/Szolnok 2018–19.   t.

745001	**GR** RR	413001 426001 332001 343001 341001 301001
		302001 342001 344001 346001 322001 312001
745002	**GR** RR	413002 426002 332002 343002 341002 301002
		302002 342002 344002 346002 322002 312002
745003	**GR** RR	413003 426003 332003 343003 341003 301003
		302003 342003 344003 346003 322003 312003
745004	**GR** RR	413004 426004 332004 343004 341004 301004
		302004 342004 344004 346004 322004 312004
745005	**GR** RR	413005 426005 332005 343005 341005 301005
		302005 342005 344005 346005 322005 312005
745006	**GR** RR	413006 426006 332006 343006 341006 301006
		302006 342006 344006 346006 322006 312006
745007	**GR** RR	413007 426007 332007 343007 341007 301007
		302007 342007 344007 346007 322007 312007
745008	**GR** RR	413008 426008 332008 343008 341008 301008
		302008 342008 344008 346008 322008 312008
745009	**GR** RR	413009 426009 332009 343009 341009 301009
		302009 342009 344009 346009 322009 312009
745010	**GR** RR	413010 426010 332010 343010 341010 301010
		302010 342010 344010 346010 322010 312010

Class 745/1. Standard Class only units for use between London Liverpool Street and Stansted Airport.

DMS. Stadler Bussnang/Szolnok 2018–19.   t.
PTS. Stadler Bussnang/Szolnok 2018–19.   t.
TS(A). Stadler Bussnang/Szolnok 2018–19.   t.
TS(B). Stadler Bussnang/Szolnok 2018–19.   t.
TS(C). Stadler Bussnang/Szolnok 2018–19.   t.
MS(A). Stadler Bussnang/Szolnok 2018–19.   t.
MS(B). Stadler Bussnang/Szolnok 2018–19.   t.
TS(D). Stadler Bussnang/Szolnok 2018–19.   t.
TS(E). Stadler Bussnang/Szolnok 2018–19.   t.
TS(F). Stadler Bussnang/Szolnok 2018–19.   t.
PTS. Stadler Bussnang/Szolnok 2018–19.   t.
DMS. Stadler Bussnang/Szolnok 2018–19.   t.

745101	**GR** RR	313101 326101 332101 343101 341101 301101
		302101 342101 344101 346101 322101 312101
745102	**GR** RR	313102 326102 332102 343102 341102 301102
		302102 342102 344102 346102 322102 312102
745103	**GR** RR	313103 326103 332103 343103 341103 301103
		302103 342103 344103 346103 322103 312103
745104	**GR** RR	313104 326104 332104 343104 341104 301104
		302104 342104 344104 346104 322104 312104
745105	**GR** RR	313105 326105 332105 343105 341105 301105
		302105 342105 344105 346105 322105 312105

745 106	**GR**	RR	313106	326106	332106	343106	341106	301106
			302106	342106	344106	346106	322106	312106
745 107	**GR**	RR	313107	326107	332107	343107	341107	301107
			302107	342107	344107	346107	322107	312107
745 108	**GR**	RR	313108	326108	332108	343108	341108	301108
			302108	342108	344108	346108	322108	312108
745 109	**GR**	RR	313109	326109	332109	343109	341109	301109
			302109	342109	344109	346109	322109	312109
745 110	**GR**	RR	313110	326110	332110	343110	341110	301110
			302110	342110	344110	346110	322110	312110

CLASS 755   FLIRT BI-MODE   STADLER

This fleet of 3- and 4-car articulated Stadler bi-mode units was ordered by Greater Anglia in 2016 to replace all of its older DMU fleets. The first units entered service in summer 2019. The design features a "power pack" in the middle that houses two diesel engines for the 3-car units and four diesel engines for the 4-car units. This has been given its own number, effectively making the units 4- and 5-car, although there is no passenger accommodation in the power pack car.

Formation: DMS–PP–PTS–DMS or DMS–PTS–PP–PTS–DMS.
Systems: Diesel/25 kV AC overhead.
Construction: Aluminium.
Engines: (4-car): Four Deutz V8 of 480 kW (645 hp), (3-car): Two Four Deutz V8 of 480 kW (645 hp).
Traction Motors: Four TSA of 325 kW.
Wheel Arrangement: Bo-2-2-2-Bo or Bo-2-2-2-2-Bo.
Braking: Disc & regenerative
Dimensions: 20.81/15.22/6.69 (PP) m x 2.72/2.82 (PP) m.
Bogies: Stadler/Jacobs.   **Couplers:** Dellner 10.
Gangways: Within unit.   **Control System:** IGBT Inverter.
Doors: Sliding plug (one per vehicle). **Maximum Speed:** 100 mph.
Heating & ventilation: Air conditioning.
Seating Layout: 2+2 unidirectional/facing.
Multiple Working: Within class.

Class 755/3. 3-car (plus power pack) units.

DMS(A). Stadler Szolnok/Siedlce/Bussnang/Valencia 2018–19. –/60(+4).
PP. Stadler Bussnang/Valencia 2018–19.
PTS. Stadler Szolnok/Siedlce/Bussnang/Valencia 2018–19. –/32(+7) 1TD 1T 2W.
DMS(B). Stadler Szolnok/Siedlce/Bussnang/Valencia 2018–19. –/52(+12).

755 325	**GR**	RR	911325	971325	981325	912325
755 326	**GR**	RR	911326	971326	981326	912326
755 327	**GR**	RR	911327	971327	981327	912327
755 328	**GR**	RR	911328	971328	981328	912328
755 329	**GR**	RR	911329	971329	981329	912329
755 330	**GR**	RR	911330	971330	981330	912330
755 331	**GR**	RR	911331	971331	981331	912331
755 332	**GR**	RR	911332	971332	981332	912332
755 333	**GR**	RR	911333	971333	981333	912333

755334	**GR**	RR		911334	971334	981334	912334
755335	**GR**	RR		911335	971335	981335	912335
755336	**GR**	RR		911336	971336	981336	912336
755337	**GR**	RR		911337	971337	981337	912337
755338	**GR**	RR		911338	971338	981338	912338

Class 755/4. 4-car (plus power pack) units.

DMS(A). Stadler Szolnok/Siedlce/Bussnang/Valencia 2018–19. –/60(+4). 41.4 t.
PTS(A). Stadler Szolnok/Siedlce/Bussnang/Valencia 2018–19. –/58(+4). 25.0 t.
PP. Stadler Bussnang/Valencia 2018–19. 28.5 t.
PTS(B). Stadler Szolnok/Siedlce/Bussnang/Valencia 2018–19. –/32(+7). 1TD 1T 2W. 26.4 t.
DMS(B). Stadler Szolnok/Siedlce/Bussnang/Valencia 2018–19. –/52(+12). 42.2 t.

755401	**GR**	RR			911401	961401	971401	981401	912401
755402	**GR**	RR			911402	961402	971402	981402	912402
755403	**GR**	RR			911403	961403	971403	981403	912403
755404	**GR**	RR			911404	961404	971404	981404	912404
755405	**GR**	RR			911405	961405	971405	981405	912405
755406	**GR**	RR			911406	961406	971406	981406	912406
755407	**GR**	RR			911407	961407	971407	981407	912407
755408	**GR**	RR			911408	961408	971408	981408	912408
755409	**GR**	RR	*GA*	NC	911409	961409	971409	981409	912409
755410	**GR**	RR	*GA*	NC	911410	961410	971410	981410	912410
755411	**GR**	RR			911411	961411	971411	981411	912411
755412	**GR**	RR			911412	961412	971412	981412	912412
755413	**GR**	RR	*GA*	NC	911413	961413	971413	981413	912413
755414	**GR**	RR	*GA*	NC	911414	961414	971414	981414	912414
755415	**GR**	RR			911415	961415	971415	981415	912415
755416	**GR**	RR			911416	961416	971416	981416	912416
755417	**GR**	RR	*GA*	NC	911417	961417	971417	981417	912417
755418	**GR**	RR	*GA*	NC	911418	961418	971418	981418	912418
755419	**GR**	RR			911419	961419	971419	981419	912419
755420	**GR**	RR			911420	961420	971420	981420	912420
755421	**GR**	RR			911421	961421	971421	981421	912421
755422	**GR**	RR	*GA*	NC	911422	961422	971422	981422	912422
755423	**GR**	RR			911423	961423	971423	981423	912423
755424	**GR**	RR	*GA*	NC	911424	961424	971424	981424	912424

CLASS 769   FLEX   BREL YORK/BRUSH

In 2017 it was announced that Porterbrook would be converting eight Class 319s into bi-mode "Flex" units for Northern, with two new diesel engines being fitted (one under each of the driving trailer cars) to drive ABB alternators. Subsequently orders have been placed by Transport for Wales for nine units and Great Western Railway for 19 units. The GWR units will be "tri-mode", with both AC overhead and DC third rail capability.

Work on the conversions is taking place at Brush Loughborough but the project has been beset by delays, with the first Northern units not due to enter traffic until early 2020. Identities of four of the TfW units is not yet known. All conversions are from Class 319/0 or 319/4 Phase 1 units. Full details awaited.

Formation: DMC–MS–TS–DMS.
Systems: Diesel/25 kV AC overhead/750 V DC third rail (GWR units only).
Construction: Steel.
Engines: Two MAN D2876 of 390 kW (523 hp).
Traction Motors: Four GEC G315BZ of 268 kW.
Wheel Arrangement: 2-2 + Bo-Bo + 2-2 + 2-2.
Braking: Disc.   **Dimensions:** 20.17/20.16 x 2.82 m.
Bogies: P7-4 (MS), T3-7 (others).   **Couplers:** Tightlock.
Gangways: Within unit + end doors. **Control System:** GTO chopper.
Doors: Sliding.
Maximum Speed: 100 mph (electric); 85 mph (diesel).
Seating Layout: 1: 2+1 facing (declassified); 2: 2+2/3+2 facing.
Multiple Working: Within class and with Class 319.

77291–381. DMC. Lot No. 31022 (odd nos.) 1987–88.
77431–457. DMC. Lot No. 31038 (odd nos.) 1988.
62891–936. MS. Lot No. 31023 1987–88.
62961–974. MS. Lot No. 31039 1988.
71772–817. TS. Lot No. 31024 1987–88.
71866–879. TS. Lot No. 31040 1988.
77330–380. DMS. Lot No. 31025 (even nos.) 1987–88.
77430–456. DMS. Lot No. 31041 (even nos.) 1988.

Class 769/0. Transport for Wales units.

769002	(319002)	TL	P		CF	77293	62892	71773	77292
769003	(319003)		P			77295	62893	71774	77294
769006	(319006)		P			77301	62896	71777	77300
769007	(319007)		P			77303	62897	71778	77302
769008	(319008)	TW	P		CF	77305	62898	71779	77304

Class 769/4. Northern units.

769424	(319424)	NR	P			77337	62914	71795	77336
769431	(319431)	NR	P			77351	62921	71802	77350
769434	(319434)	NR	P			77357	62924	71805	77356
769442	(319442)	NR	P		AN	77373	62932	71813	77372
769448	(319448)	NR	P			77433	62962	71867	77432
769450	(319450)	NR	P		AN	77437	62964	71869	77436
769456	(319456)	NR	P			77449	62970	71875	77448
769458	(319458)	NR	P			77453	62972	71877	77452

Class 769/9. Great Western Railway units.

769922	(319422)	P			77333	62912	71793	77332
769923	(319423)	P			77335	62913	71794	77334
769925	(319425)	P			77339	62915	71796	77338
769927	(319427)	P			77343	62917	71798	77342
769928	(319428)	P			77345	62918	71799	77344
769930	(319430)	P			77349	62920	71801	77348
769932	(319432)	P			77353	62922	71803	77352
769935	(319435)	P			77359	62925	71806	77358

769 936	(319436)	P	77361 62926 71807 77360
769 937	(319437)	P	77363 62927 71808 77362
769 938	(319438)	P	77365 62928 71809 77364
769 939	(319439)	P	77367 62929 71810 77366
769 940	(319440)	P	77369 62930 71811 77368
769 943	(319443)	P	77375 62933 71814 77374
769 945	(319445)	P	77379 62935 71816 77378
769 947	(319447)	P	77431 62961 71866 77430
769 949	(319449)	P	77435 62963 71868 77434
769 952	(319452)	P	77441 62966 71871 77440
769 959	(319459)	P	77455 62973 71878 77454

CLASS 777   STADLER

This fleet of articulated 4-car units was ordered from Stadler in 2017 by Merseytravel for the DC third rail Merseyrail suburban network, to replace Classes 507–508 in 2020–21. The fleet will be owned by Merseytravel. An option exists for up to a further 60 units. Full details awaited.

Formation: DMS–MS–MS–DMS.
System: 750 V DC third rail.
Construction: Aluminium.
Traction Motors: Six TSA of 350 kW (470 hp) per unit.
Wheel Arrangement: 2-Bo-Bo-Bo-2.
Braking: Tread & regenerative.   **Dimensions:** 19.00/13.50 x 2.82 m.
Bogies: Jakobs.   **Couplers:** Dellner 12.
Gangways: Within unit.   **Control System:** IGBT Inverter.
Doors: Sliding plug.   **Maximum Speed:** 75 mph.
Heating & ventilation: Air conditioning.
Seating Layout: 2+2 facing/unidirectional.
Multiple Working: Within class.

DMS(A). Stadler Szolnok/Siedlce/Altenrhein 2018–20. –/53.   t.
MS(A). Stadler Szolnok/Siedlce/Altenrhein 2018–20. –/39 1W.   t.
MS(B). Stadler Szolnok/Siedlce/Altenrhein 2018–20. –/39 1W.   t.
DMS(B). Stadler Szolnok/Siedlce/Altenrhein 2018–20. –/53.   t.

777 001	427001	428001	429001	430001
777 002	427002	428002	429002	430002
777 003	427003	428003	429003	430003
777 004	427004	428004	429004	430004
777 005	427005	428005	429005	430005
777 006	427006	428006	429006	430006
777 007	427007	428007	429007	430007
777 008	427008	428008	429008	430008
777 009	427009	428009	429009	430009
777 010	427010	428010	429010	430010
777 011	427011	428011	429011	430011
777 012	427012	428012	429012	430012
777 013	427013	428013	429013	430013
777 014	427014	428014	429014	430014
777 015	427015	428015	429015	430015

777016	427016	428016	429016	430016
777017	427017	428017	429017	430017
777018	427018	428018	429018	430018
777019	427019	428019	429019	430019
777020	427020	428020	429020	430020
777021	427021	428021	429021	430021
777022	427022	428022	429022	430022
777023	427023	428023	429023	430023
777024	427024	428024	429024	430024
777025	427025	428025	429025	430025
777026	427026	428026	429026	430026
777027	427027	428027	429027	430027
777028	427028	428028	429028	430028
777029	427029	428029	429029	430029
777030	427030	428030	429030	430030
777031	427031	428031	429031	430031
777032	427032	428032	429032	430032
777033	427033	428033	429033	430033
777034	427034	428034	429034	430034
777035	427035	428035	429035	430035
777036	427036	428036	429036	430036
777037	427037	428037	429037	430037
777038	427038	428038	429038	430038
777039	427039	428039	429039	430039
777040	427040	428040	429040	430040
777041	427041	428041	429041	430041
777042	427042	428042	429042	430042
777043	427043	428043	429043	430043
777044	427044	428044	429044	430044
777045	427045	428045	429045	430045
777046	427046	428046	429046	430046
777047	427047	428047	429047	430047
777048	427048	428048	429048	430048
777049	427049	428049	429049	430049
777050	427050	428050	429050	430050
777051	427051	428051	429051	430051
777052	427052	428052	429052	430052

CLASS 799   HYDROFLEX   BREL YORK/BRUSH

This hydrogen demonstrator unit was converted in 2019 from a Class 319 as part of a partnership between Porterbrook and the University of Birmingham. It is due to commence main line testing in spring 2020.

The Class 799 MS has been heavily modified and is now fitted with batteries, a hydrogen fuel cell and four hydrogen tanks. Hydrogen is stored in tanks at high pressure, from where it is piped into fuel cells where it is mixed with oxygen to create electricity to power the motors. The energy can also be stored in the batteries, these being used at times of high demand.

Formation: DMC–MS–TS–DMS.
Systems: Hydrogen/25 kV AC overhead/750 V DC third rail.
Construction: Steel.
Traction Motors: Four GEC G315BZ of 268 kW.
Wheel Arrangement: 2-2 + Bo-Bo + 2-2 + 2-2.
Braking: Disc.   **Dimensions:** 20.17/20.16 x 2.82 m.
Bogies: P7-4 (MS), T3-7 (others).   **Couplers:** Tightlock.
Gangways: Within unit + end doors. **Doors:** Sliding.
Maximum Speed: 75 mph.
Seating Layout: 1: 2+1 facing (declassified); 2: 2+2/3+2 facing.

Non-standard livery: HydroFlex (green, grey and white).

77291. DMC. Lot No. 31022. 1987–88.
62891. MS. Lot No. 31023 1987–88.
71772. TS. Lot No. 31024 1987–88.
77290. DMS. Lot No. 31025 1987–88.

769001   (319001)   **0**   P   LM   77291   62891   71772   77290

4. HITACHI IEP UNITS

CLASS 800 INTERCITY EXPRESS PROGRAMME
BI-MODE   HITACHI

In 2012 Agility Trains, a consortium of Hitachi and John Laing, signed a deal with the DfT to design, build, finance and maintain the next generation of InterCity rolling stock for the Great Western and East Coast Main Lines, principally to replace ageing High Speed Trains on these routes. A follow-on order in 2013 was placed for 30 9-car trains to replace the Class 91 and Mark 4 carriages on the ECML. This brought the total number of vehicles ordered to 866. Both GWR and LNER were originally planned to have a mix of 5-car and 9-car units which will be bi-mode and straight electric trains (although the EMUs also have one diesel engine fitted to each set). However, owing to delays with electrification works on the GWML, in 2016 it was announced that the 21 9-car electric Class 801 units for GWR would be built as 21 9-car bi-mode units, numbered instead in the Class 800/3 series.

The units are broadly based on the Southeastern Class 395s, but have 25–25.35 m length bodyshells. They are numbered in the Class 800 (bi-mode) and Class 801 (EMU) number series'. 12 trains (76 vehicles) were fully manufactured at Kasado in Japan before the new Hitachi factory at Newton Aycliffe, County Durham was up and running. The remaining trains are being assembled at either Newton Aycliffe or Kasado. New maintenance depots for the trains have been built at Stoke Gifford (Bristol), Swansea and North Pole (London, the former Eurostar depot) for the GWR sets and at Doncaster for the LNER units.

The first trains arrived for testing in 2015. 5-car units entered service on the Great Western Main Line in autumn 2017 and Class 800s entered service on the East Coast Main Line from spring 2019.

In 2015 GWR ordered a further 22 5-car and seven 9-car IEPs, designated Class 802/0 (5-car) and Class 802/1 (9-car). These are mainly used on Paddington–West of England services.

In 2016 GWR ordered a further seven 9-car Class 802s, TransPennine Express ordered 19 5-car Class 802s and Hull Trains ordered five 5-car Class 802s, for delivery 2019–20. The majority of the Class 802s were constructed at Pistoia in Italy, with some at Kasado.

Formation: Various, see class headings for details.
Systems: Diesel/25 kV AC overhead electric.
Construction: Aluminium.
Diesel engines: In the 5-car sets diesel engines are located in cars 2, 3 and 4. In the 9-car sets diesel engines are located in cars 2, 3, 5, 7 and 8.
Engines: MTU 12V 1600 R80L of 700 kW (940 hp).
Traction Motors: Four Hitachi asynchronous of 226 kW.
Wheel Arrangement: 2-2 + Bo-Bo + Bo-Bo + Bo-Bo + 2-2 or
2-2 + Bo-Bo + Bo-Bo + 2-2 + Bo-Bo + 2-2 + Bo-Bo + Bo-Bo + 2-2.

Braking: Disc & regenerative.	**Dimensions:** 25.35/25.00 m x 2.74 m.
Bogies: Hitachi.	**Couplers:** Dellner 10.
Gangways: Within unit.	**Control System:** IGBT Inverter.
Doors: Single-leaf sliding.	**Maximum Speed:** 125 mph.

Heating & ventilation: Air conditioning.
Seating Layout: 1: 2+1 facing/unidirectional; 2+2 facing/unidirectional.
Multiple Working: Within class and with Classes 801 and 802.

Class 800/0. 5-car Great Western Railway units.
Formation: PDTS–MS–MS–MC–PDTRBF.

PDTS. Hitachi Newton Aycliffe/Kasado 2013–17. –/56 1TD. 47.8 t.
MS. Hitachi Newton Aycliffe/Kasado 2013–17. –/88. 50.1 t.
MS. Hitachi Newton Aycliffe/Kasado 2013–17. –/88 2T. 50.3 t.
MC. Hitachi Newton Aycliffe/Kasado 2013–17. 18/58 1T. 50.6 t.
PDTRBF. Hitachi Newton Aycliffe/Kasado 2013–17. 18/– 1TD 2W. 51.7 t.

800001	**GW**	AT	*GW*	NP	811001	812001	813001	814001	815001
800002	**GW**	AT	*GW*	NP	811002	812002	813002	814002	815002
800003	**GW**	AT	*GW*	NP	811003	812003	813003	814003	815003
800004	**GW**	AT	*GW*	NP	811004	812004	813004	814004	815004
800005	**GW**	AT	*GW*	NP	811005	812005	813005	814005	815005
800006	**GW**	AT	*GW*	NP	811006	812006	813006	814006	815006
800007	**GW**	AT	*GW*	NP	811007	812007	813007	814007	815007
800008	**GW**	AT	*GW*	NP	811008	812008	813008	814008	815008
800009	**GW**	AT	*GW*	NP	811009	812009	813009	814009	815009
800010	**GW**	AT	*GW*	NP	811010	812010	813010	814010	815010
800011	**GW**	AT	*GW*	NP	811011	812011	813011	814011	815011
800012	**GW**	AT	*GW*	NP	811012	812012	813012	814012	815012
800013	**GW**	AT	*GW*	NP	811013	812013	813013	814013	815013
800014	**GW**	AT	*GW*	NP	811014	812014	813014	814014	815014
800015	**GW**	AT	*GW*	NP	811015	812015	813015	814015	815015
800016	**GW**	AT	*GW*	NP	811016	812016	813016	814016	815016
800017	**GW**	AT	*GW*	NP	811017	812017	813017	814017	815017
800018	**GW**	AT	*GW*	NP	811018	812018	813018	814018	815018

800019	**GW**	AT	*GW*	NP	811019	812019	813019	814019	815019
800020	**GW**	AT	*GW*	NP	811020	812020	813020	814020	815020
800021	**GW**	AT	*GW*	NP	811021	812021	813021	814021	815021
800022	**GW**	AT	*GW*	NP	811022	812022	813022	814022	815022
800023	**GW**	AT	*GW*	NP	811023	812023	813023	814023	815023
800024	**GW**	AT	*GW*	NP	811024	812024	813024	814024	815024
800025	**GW**	AT	*GW*	NP	811025	812025	813025	814025	815025
800026	**GW**	AT	*GW*	NP	811026	812026	813026	814026	815026
800027	**GW**	AT	*GW*	NP	811027	812027	813027	814027	815027
800028	**GW**	AT	*GW*	NP	811028	812028	813028	814028	815028
800029	**GW**	AT	*GW*	NP	811029	812029	813029	814029	815029
800030	**GW**	AT	*GW*	NP	811030	812030	813030	814030	815030
800031	**GW**	AT	*GW*	NP	811031	812031	813031	814031	815031
800032	**GW**	AT	*GW*	NP	811032	812032	813032	814032	815032
800033	**GW**	AT	*GW*	NP	811033	812033	813033	814033	815033
800034	**GW**	AT	*GW*	NP	811034	812034	813034	814034	815034
800035	**GW**	AT	*GW*	NP	811035	812035	813035	814035	815035
800036	**GW**	AT	*GW*	NP	811036	812036	813036	814036	815036

Names (one on each driving car):

800009	Sir Gareth Edwards/John Charles
800010	Michael Bond/Paddington Bear
800014	Megan Lloyd George CH/Edith New
800019	Joy Lofthouse/Johnny Johnson MBE DFM
800020	Bob Woodward/Elizabeth Ralph
800023	Firefighter Fleur Lombard QGM/Kathryn Osmond
800026	Don Cameron

Class 800/1. 9-car LNER units.
Formation: PDTS–MS–MS–TSRB–MS–TS–MC–MF–PDTRBF.

PDTS. Hitachi Kasado/Newton Aycliffe 2013–18. –/48 1TD 2W. 47.7 t.
MS. Hitachi Kasado/Newton Aycliffe 2013–18. –/88 1T. 50.5 t.
MS. Hitachi Kasado/Newton Aycliffe 2013–18. –/88 2T. 50.3 t.
TSRB. Hitachi Kasado/Newton Aycliffe 2013–18. –/72. 41.0 t.
MS. Hitachi Kasado/Newton Aycliffe 2013–18. –/88 2T. 50.3 t.
TS. Hitachi Kasado/Newton Aycliffe 2013–18. –/88 2T. 38.3 t.
MC. Hitachi Kasado/Newton Aycliffe 2013–18. 30/38. 49.1 t.
MF. Hitachi Kasado/Newton Aycliffe 2013–18. 56/– 1T. 50.6 t.
PDTRBF. Hitachi Kasado/Newton Aycliffe 2013–18. 15/– 1TD 2W. 51.7 t.

800101	**LZ**	AT	*LN*	DN	811101	812101	813101	814101	815101
					816101	817101	818101	819101	
800102	**LZ**	AT	*LN*	DN	811102	812102	813102	814102	815102
					816102	817102	818102	819102	
800103	**LZ**	AT	*LN*	DN	811103	812103	813103	814103	815103
					816103	817103	818103	819103	
800104	**LZ**	AT	*LN*	DN	811104	812104	813104	814104	815104
					816104	817104	818104	819104	
800105	**LZ**	AT	*LN*	DN	811105	812105	813105	814105	815105
					816105	817105	818105	819105	
800106	**LZ**	AT	*LN*	DN	811106	812106	813106	814106	815106
					816106	817106	818106	819106	

800 107	**LZ**	AT	*LN*	DN	811107	812107	813107	814107	815107
					816107	817107	818107	819107	
800 108	**LZ**	AT	*LN*	DN	811108	812108	813108	814108	815108
					816108	817108	818108	819108	
800 109	**LZ**	AT	*LN*	DN	811109	812109	813109	814109	815109
					816109	817109	818109	819109	
800 110	**LZ**	AT	*LN*	DN	811110	812110	813110	814110	815110
					816110	817110	818110	819110	
800 111	**LZ**	AT	*LN*	DN	811111	812111	813111	814111	815111
					816111	817111	818111	819111	
800 112	**LZ**	AT	*LN*	DN	811112	812112	813112	814112	815112
					816112	817112	818112	819112	
800 113	**LZ**	AT	*LN*	DN	811113	812113	813113	814113	815113
					816113	817113	818113	819113	

Class 800/2. 5-car LNER units.
Formation: PDTS–MSRB–MS–MC–PDTRBF.

PDTS. Hitachi Newton Aycliffe/Kasado 2018–19. –/56 1TD. 47.8 t.
MSRB. Hitachi Newton Aycliffe/Kasado 2018–19. –/72. 50.1 t.
MS. Hitachi Newton Aycliffe/Kasado 2018–19. –/88 2T. 50.3 t.
MC. Hitachi Newton Aycliffe/Kasado 2018–19. 30/38 1T. 50.6 t.
PDTRBF. Hitachi Newton Aycliffe/Kasado 2018–19. 18/– 1TD 2W. 51.7 t.

800 201	**LZ**	AT	811201	812201	813201	814201	815201
800 202	**LZ**	AT	811202	812202	813202	814202	815202
800 203	**LZ**	AT	811203	812203	813203	814203	815203
800 204	**LZ**	AT	811204	812204	813204	814204	815204
800 205	**LZ**	AT	811205	812205	813205	814205	815205
800 206	**LZ**	AT	811206	812206	813206	814206	815206
800 207	**LZ**	AT	811207	812207	813207	814207	815207
800 208	**LZ**	AT	811208	812208	813208	814208	815208
800 209	**LZ**	AT	811209	812209	813209	814209	815209
800 210	**LZ**	AT	811210	812210	813210	814210	815210

Class 800/3. 9-car Great Western Railway units. Originally to be built as
electric trains and numbered in the Class 801/0 series.
Formation: PDTS–MS–MS–TS–MS–TS–MS–MF–PDTRBF.

PDTS. Hitachi Newton Aycliffe/Kasado 2017–18. –/48 1TD 2W. 47.8 t.
MS. Hitachi Newton Aycliffe/Kasado 2017–18. –/88 1T. 50.1 t.
MS. Hitachi Newton Aycliffe/Kasado 2017–18. –/88 2T. 50.3 t.
TS. Hitachi Newton Aycliffe/Kasado 2017–18. –/88. 41.0 t.
MS. Hitachi Newton Aycliffe/Kasado 2017–18. –/88 2T. 50.3 t.
TS. Hitachi Newton Aycliffe/Kasado 2017–18. –/88 2T. 38.3 t.
MS. Hitachi Newton Aycliffe/Kasado 2017–18. –/88. 49.1 t.
MF. Hitachi Newton Aycliffe/Kasado 2017–18. 56/– 1T. 50.6 t.
PDTRBF. Hitachi Newton Aycliffe/Kasado 2017–18. 15/– 1TD 2W. 51.7 t.

800 301	**GW**	AT	*GW*	NP	821001	822001	823001	824001	825001
					826001	827001	828001	829001	
800 302	**GW**	AT	*GW*	NP	821002	822002	823002	824002	825002
					826002	827002	828002	829002	

800 303	**GW**	AT *GW* NP	821003	822003	823003	824003	825003	
			826003	827003	828003	829003		
800 304	**GW**	AT *GW* NP	821004	822004	823004	824004	825004	
			826004	827004	828004	829004		
800 305	**GW**	AT *GW* NP	821005	822005	823005	824005	825005	
			826005	827005	828005	829005		
800 306	**GW**	AT *GW* NP	821006	822006	823006	824006	825006	
			826006	827006	828006	829006		
800 307	**GW**	AT *GW* NP	821007	822007	823007	824007	825007	
			826007	827007	828007	829007		
800 308	**GW**	AT *GW* NP	821008	822008	823008	824008	825008	
			826008	827008	828008	829008		
800 309	**GW**	AT *GW* NP	821009	822009	823009	824009	825009	
			826009	827009	828009	829009		
800 310	**GW**	AT *GW* NP	821010	822010	823010	824010	825010	
			826010	827010	828010	829010		
800 311	**GW**	AT *GW* NP	821011	822011	823011	824011	825011	
			826011	827011	828011	829011		
800 312	**GW**	AT *GW* NP	821012	822012	823012	824012	825012	
			826012	827012	828012	829012		
800 313	**GW**	AT *GW* NP	821013	822013	823013	824013	825013	
			826013	827013	828013	829013		
800 314	**GW**	AT *GW* NP	821014	822014	823014	824014	825014	
			826014	827014	828014	829014		
800 315	**GW**	AT *GW* NP	821015	822015	823015	824015	825015	
			826015	827015	828015	829015		
800 316	**GW**	AT *GW* NP	821016	822016	823016	824016	825016	
			826016	827016	828016	829016		
800 317	**GW**	AT *GW* NP	821017	822017	823017	824017	825017	
			826017	827017	828017	829017		
800 318	**GW**	AT *GW* NP	821018	822018	823018	824018	825018	
			826018	827018	828018	829018		
800 319	**GW**	AT *GW* NP	821019	822019	823019	824019	825019	
			826019	827019	828019	829019		
800 320	**GW**	AT *GW* NP	821020	822020	823020	824020	825020	
			826020	827020	828020	829020		
800 321	**GW**	AT *GW* NP	821021	822021	823021	824021	825021	
			826021	827021	828021	829021		

Name (carried on alternative driving cars):

800 306   Allan Leonard Lewis VC/Harold Day DSC

CLASS 801 INTERCITY EXPRESS PROGRAMME
ELECTRIC   HITACHI

The Class 801s are electric units, but still have one diesel engine fitted per unit for emergency use.

Formation: Various, see class headings for details.
Systems: 25 kV AC overhead electric, plus one diesel engine per set.
Construction: Aluminium.
Diesel engines: In the 5-car sets the single diesel engine is located in car 2 and in the 9-car sets the diesel engine is located in car 8.
Engines: MTU 12V 1600 R80L of 700 kW (940 hp).
Traction Motors: Four Hitachi asynchronous of 226 kW.
Wheel Arrangement: 2-2 + Bo-Bo + Bo-Bo + Bo-Bo + 2-2 or
2-2 + Bo-Bo + Bo-Bo + 2-2 + Bo-Bo + 2-2 + Bo-Bo + Bo-Bo + 2-2.

Braking: Disc & regenerative.	**Dimensions:** 25.35/25.00 m x 2.74 m.
Bogies: Hitachi.	**Couplers:** Dellner 10.
Gangways: Within unit.	**Control System:** IGBT Inverter.
Doors: Single-leaf sliding.	**Maximum Speed:** 125 mph.

Heating & ventilation: Air conditioning.
Seating Layout: 1: 2+1 facing/unidirectional; 2+2 facing/unidirectional.
Multiple Working: Within class and with Classes 800 and 802.

Class 801/1. 5-car LNER units.
Formation: PDTS–MSRB–MS–MC–PDTRBF.

PDTS. Hitachi Newton Aycliffe/Kasado 2016–19. –/56 1TD. 47.8 t.
MSRB. Hitachi Newton Aycliffe/Kasado 2016–19. –/72. 52.1 t.
MS. Hitachi Newton Aycliffe/Kasado 2016–19. –/88 2T. 43.5 t.
MC. Hitachi Newton Aycliffe/Kasado 2016–19. 30/38 1T. 44.1 t.
PDTRBF. Hitachi Newton Aycliffe/Kasado 2016–19. 18/– 1TD 2W. 51.2 t.

801 101	LZ	AT	LN	DN	821101	822101	823101	824101	825101
801 102	LZ	AT	LN	DN	821102	822102	823102	824102	825102
801 103	LZ	AT	LN	DN	821103	822103	823103	824103	825103
801 104	LZ	AT	LN	DN	821104	822104	823104	824104	825104
801 105	LZ	AT	LN	DN	821105	822105	823105	824105	825105
801 106	LZ	AT	LN	DN	821106	822106	823106	824106	825106
801 107	LZ	AT	LN	DN	821107	822107	823107	824107	825107
801 108	LZ	AT	LN	DN	821108	822108	823108	824108	825108
801 109	LZ	AT	LN	DN	821109	822109	823109	824109	825109
801 110	LZ	AT	LN	DN	821110	822110	823110	824110	825110
801 111	LZ	AT	LN	DN	821111	822111	823111	824111	825111
801 112	LZ	AT	LN	DN	821112	822112	823112	824112	825112

Class 801/2. 9-car LNER units. Full details awaited.
Formation: PDTS–MS–MS–TSRB–MS–TS–MC–MF–PDTRBF.

PDTS. Hitachi Newton Aycliffe/Kasado 2018–20. –/48 1TD 2W.   t.
MS. Hitachi Newton Aycliffe/Kasado 2018–20. –/88 1T.   t.
MS. Hitachi Newton Aycliffe/Kasado 2018–20. –/88 2T.   t.
TSRB. Hitachi Newton Aycliffe/Kasado 2018–20. –/72.   t.
MS. Hitachi Newton Aycliffe/Kasado 2018–20. –/88 2T.   t.

TS. Hitachi Newton Aycliffe/Kasado 2018–20. –/88 2T.   t.
MC. Hitachi Newton Aycliffe/Kasado 2018–20. 30/38.   t.
MF. Hitachi Newton Aycliffe/Kasado 2018–20. 56/– 1T.   t.
PDTRBF. Hitachi Newton Aycliffe/Kasado 2018–20. 15/– 1TD 2W.   t.

801 201		AT	821201	822201	823201	824201	825201
			826201	827201	828201	829201	
801 202		AT	821202	822202	823202	824202	825202
			826202	827202	828202	829202	
801 203	**LZ**	AT	821203	822203	823203	824203	825203
			826203	827203	828203	829203	
801 204		AT	821204	822204	823204	824204	825204
			826204	827204	828204	829204	
801 205	**LZ**	AT	821205	822205	823205	824205	825205
			826205	827205	828205	829205	
801 206		AT	821206	822206	823206	824206	825206
			826206	827206	828206	829206	
801 207	**LZ**	AT	821207	822207	823207	824207	825207
			826207	827207	828207	829207	
801 208		AT	821208	822208	823208	824208	825208
			826208	827208	828208	829208	
801 209	**LZ**	AT	821209	822209	823209	824209	825209
			826209	827209	828209	829209	
801 210		AT	821210	822210	823210	824210	825210
			826210	827210	828210	829210	
801 211	**LZ**	AT	821211	822211	823211	824211	825211
			826211	827211	828211	829211	
801 212		AT	821212	822212	823212	824212	825212
			826212	827212	828212	829212	
801 213	**LZ**	AT	821213	822213	823213	824213	825213
			826213	827213	828213	829213	
801 214		AT	821214	822214	823214	824214	825214
			826214	827214	828214	829214	
801 215	**LZ**	AT	821215	822215	823215	824215	825215
			826215	827215	828215	829215	
801 216		AT	821216	822216	823216	824216	825216
			826216	827216	828216	829216	
801 217		AT	821217	822217	823217	824217	825217
			826217	827217	828217	829217	
801 218		AT	821218	822218	823218	824218	825218
			826218	827218	828218	829218	
801 219		AT	821219	822219	823219	824219	825219
			826219	827219	828219	829219	
801 220		AT	821220	822220	823220	824220	825220
			826220	827220	828220	829220	
801 221		AT	821221	822221	823221	824221	825221
			826221	827221	828221	829221	
801 222		AT	821222	822222	823222	824222	825222
			826222	827222	828222	829222	
801 223		AT	821223	822223	823223	824223	825223
			826223	827223	828223	829223	

801 224	AT	821224	822224	823224	824224	825224
		826224	827224	828224	829224	
801 225	AT	821225	822225	823225	824225	825225
		826225	827225	828225	829225	
801 226	AT	821226	822226	823226	824226	825226
		826226	827226	828226	829226	
801 227	AT	821227	822227	823227	824227	825227
		826227	827227	828227	829227	
801 228	AT	821228	822228	823228	824228	825228
		826228	827228	828228	829228	
801 229	AT	821229	822229	823229	824229	825229
		826229	827229	828229	829229	
801 230	AT	821230	822230	823230	824230	825230
		826230	827230	828230	829230	

CLASS 802   AT300   HITACHI

These units are technically they are very similar to the Class 800s. The GWR units have modifications to the roof-mounted brake resistors for operation along the Dawlish seawall.

Formation: Various, full details awaited.
Systems: Diesel/25 kV AC overhead electric.
Construction: Aluminium.
Diesel engines: In the 5-car sets diesel engines are located in cars 2, 3 and 4. In the 9-car sets diesel engines are located in cars 2, 3, 5, 7 and 8.
Engines: MTU 12V 1600 R80L of 700 kW (940 hp).
Traction Motors: Four Hitachi asynchronous of 226 kW.
Wheel Arrangement: 2-2 + Bo-Bo + Bo-Bo + 2-2 or
2-2 + Bo-Bo + Bo-Bo + 2-2 + Bo-Bo + 2-2 + Bo-Bo + Bo-Bo + 2-2.
Braking: Disc & regenerative.   **Dimensions:** 25.35/25.00 m x 2.74 m.
Bogies: Hitachi.   **Couplers:** Dellner 10.
Gangways: Within unit.   **Control System:** IGBT Inverter.
Doors: Single-leaf sliding.   **Maximum Speed:** 125 mph.
Heating & ventilation: Air conditioning.
Seating Layout: 1: 2+1 facing/unidirectional; 2+2 facing/unidirectional.
Multiple Working: Within class and with Classes 800 and 801.

Class 802/0. 5-car Great Western Railway units. Pre-series units 802 001/002 were built at Kasado and the remainder at Pistoia.
Formation: PDTS–MS–MS–MC–PDTRBF.

PDTS. Hitachi Pistoia/Kasado 2017–18. –/56 1TD. 48.0 t.
MS. Hitachi Pistoia/Kasado 2017–18. –/88. 50.9 t.
MS. Hitachi Pistoia/Kasado 2017–18. –/88 2T 51.1 t.
MC. Hitachi Pistoia/Kasado 2017–18. 18/58 1T. 51.5 t.
PDTRBF. Hitachi Pistoia/Kasado 2017–18. 18/– 1TD 2W. 51.3 t.

802 001	**GW**	E	*GW*	NP	831001	832001	833001	834001	835001
802 002	**GW**	E	*GW*	NP	831002	832002	833002	834002	835002
802 003	**GW**	E	*GW*	NP	831003	832003	833003	834003	835003
802 004	**GW**	E	*GW*	NP	831004	832004	833004	834004	835004
802 005	**GW**	E	*GW*	NP	831005	832005	833005	834005	835005

802 006	**GW**	E	*GW*	NP	831006	832006	833006	834006	835006
802 007	**GW**	E	*GW*	NP	831007	832007	833007	834007	835007
802 008	**GW**	E	*GW*	NP	831008	832008	833008	834008	835008
802 009	**GW**	E	*GW*	NP	831009	832009	833009	834009	835009
802 010	**GW**	E	*GW*	NP	831010	832010	833010	834010	835010
802 011	**GW**	E	*GW*	NP	831011	832011	833011	834011	835011
802 012	**GW**	E	*GW*	NP	831012	832012	833012	834012	835012
802 013	**GW**	E	*GW*	NP	831013	832013	833013	834013	835013
802 014	**GW**	E	*GW*	NP	831014	832014	833014	834014	835014
802 015	**GW**	E	*GW*	NP	831015	832015	833015	834015	835015
802 016	**GW**	E	*GW*	NP	831016	832016	833016	834016	835016
802 017	**GW**	E	*GW*	NP	831017	832017	833017	834017	835017
802 018	**GW**	E	*GW*	NP	831018	832018	833018	834018	835018
802 019	**GW**	E	*GW*	NP	831019	832019	833019	834019	835019
802 020	**GW**	E	*GW*	NP	831020	832020	833020	834020	835020
802 021	**GW**	E	*GW*	NP	831021	832021	833021	834021	835021
802 022	**GW**	E	*GW*	NP	831022	832022	833022	834022	835022

Names (one on each driving car):

802 008	Rick Rescorla/RNLB Solomon Browne
802 011	Sir Joshua Reynolds PRA/Capt. Robert Falcon Scott RN CVO
802 013	Michael Eavis CBE

Class 802/1. 9-car Great Western Railway units. Pre-series unit 802 101 was built at Kasado and the remainder at Pistoia.
Formation: PDTS–MS–MS–TS–MS–TS–MC–MF–PDTRBF.

PDTS. Hitachi Pistoia/Kasado 2017–18. –/48 1TD 2W. 47.7 t.
MS. Hitachi Pistoia/Kasado 2017–18. –/88 1T. 50.1 t.
MS. Hitachi Pistoia/Kasado 2017–18. –/88 2T. 50.3 t.
TS. Hitachi Pistoia/Kasado 2017–18. –/88. 41.0 t.
MS. Hitachi Pistoia/Kasado 2017–18. –/88 2T. 50.3 t.
TS. Hitachi Pistoia/Kasado 2017–18. –/88 2T. 38.3 t.
MS. Hitachi Pistoia/Kasado 2017–18. –/88. 50.3 t.
MF. Hitachi Pistoia/Kasado 2017–18. 56/– 1T. 50.6 t.
PDTRBF. Hitachi Pistoia/Kasado 2017–18. 15/– 1TD 2W. 51.7 t.

802 101	**GW**	E	*GW*	NP	831101	832101	833101	834101	835101
					836101	837101	838101	839101	
802 102	**GW**	E	*GW*	NP	831102	832102	833102	834102	835102
					836102	837102	838102	839102	
802 103	**GW**	E	*GW*	NP	831103	832103	833103	834103	835103
					836103	837103	838103	839103	
802 104	**GW**	E	*GW*	NP	831104	832104	833104	834104	835104
					836104	837104	838104	839104	
802 105	**GW**	E	*GW*	NP	831105	832105	833105	834105	835105
					836105	837105	838105	839105	
802 106	**GW**	E	*GW*	NP	831106	832106	833106	834106	835106
					836106	837106	838106	839106	
802 107	**GW**	E	*GW*	NP	831107	832107	833107	834107	835107
					836107	837107	838107	839107	
802 108	**GW**	E	*GW*	NP	831108	832108	833108	834108	835108
					836108	837108	838108	839108	

802 109	**GW**	E	*GW*	NP	831109	832109	833109	834109	835109
					836109	837109	838109	839109	
802 110	**GW**	E	*GW*	NP	831110	832110	833110	834110	835110
					836110	837110	838110	839110	
802 111	**GW**	E	*GW*	NP	831111	832111	833111	834111	835111
					836111	837111	838111	839111	
802 112	**GW**	E	*GW*	NP	831112	832112	833112	834112	835112
					836112	837112	838112	839112	
802 113	**GW**	E	*GW*	NP	831113	832113	833113	834113	835113
					836113	837113	838113	839113	
802 114	**GW**	E	*GW*	NP	831114	832114	833114	834114	835114
					836114	837114	838114	839114	

Class 802/2. TransPennine Express units.

PDTS. Hitachi Pistoia/Kasado 2018–19. –/56 1TD. 48.0 t.
MS. Hitachi Pistoia/Kasado 2018–19. –/86. 50.9 t.
MS. Hitachi Pistoia/Kasado 2018–19. –/86 2T 51.1 t.
MS. Hitachi Pistoia/Kasado 2018–19. –/88 1T 51.3 t.
PDTRBF. Hitachi Pistoia/Kasado 2018–19. 24/– 1TD 2W. 50.2 t.

802 201	**TP**	A	*TP*	DN	831201	832201	833201	834201	835201
802 202		A			831202	832202	833202	834202	835202
802 203		A			831203	832203	833203	834203	835203
802 204		A			831204	832204	833204	834204	835204
802 205		A			831205	832205	833205	834205	835205
802 206		A			831206	832206	833206	834206	835206
802 207	**U**	A	*TP*	DN	831207	832207	833207	834207	835207
802 208		A			831208	832208	833208	834208	835208
802 209	**TP**	A			831209	832209	833209	834209	835209
802 210	**TP**	A			831210	832210	833210	834210	835210
802 211	**TP**	A			831211	832211	833211	834211	835211
802 212	**TP**	A			831212	832212	833212	834212	835212
802 213	**TP**	A			831213	832213	833213	834213	835213
802 214	**TP**	A			831214	832214	833214	834214	835214
802 215		A			831215	832215	833215	834215	835215
802 216		A			831216	832216	833216	834216	835216
802 217		A			831217	832217	833217	834217	835217
802 218	**U**	A	*TP*	DN	831218	832218	833218	834218	835218
802 219		A			831219	832219	833219	834219	835219

Class 802/3. Hull Trains units. Due to enter traffic late 2019. Full details awaited.

PDTS. Hitachi Pistoia 2018–19.
MS. Hitachi Pistoia 2018–19.
MS. Hitachi Pistoia 2018–19.
MC. Hitachi Pistoia 2018–19.
PDTRBF. Hitachi Pistoia 2018–19.

802 301	A	831301	832301	833301	834301	835301
802 302	A	831302	832302	833302	834302	835302
802 303	A	831303	832303	833303	834303	835303
802 304	A	831304	832304	833304	834304	835304
802 305	A	831305	832305	833305	834305	835305

5. EUROSTAR UNITS

The original Eurostar Class 373 units were built for and are normally used on services between Britain and continental Europe via the Channel Tunnel. SNCF-owned units 3225/26 and 3227/28 have been removed from the Eurostar pool and withdrawn. As they are not now permitted through the Channel Tunnel they are not listed here.

The trailers from SNCF set 3203/04 were refurbished and renumbered to run with power cars 3211/12 (original power cars 3203/04 have been scrapped, as have the trailers from 3211/12).

Each Class 373 train consists of two 10-car units coupled, with a motor car at each driving end. All units are articulated with an extra motor bogie on the coach adjacent to the motor car.

All Class 373 sets can be used between London St Pancras and Paris, Brussels and Disneyland Paris. Certain sets (shown *) are equipped for 1500 V DC operation and are used for the winter service to Bourg Saint Maurice and the summer service to Avignon. All eight refurbished units are fitted for operation on 1500 V DC.

Seven 8-car Class 373 sets were built for Regional Eurostar services, but power car 3308 has been preserved at the National Railway Museum, York and the others have been scrapped.

The second generation Eurostar trains, the Siemens Class 374s, have now been introduced and have replaced most of the Class 373s. Eight sets have been fully refurbished and will be retained as part of Eurostar's long-term fleet – 3007/08, 3015/16, 3205/06, 3209/10, 3211/12, 3219/20, 3221/22 and 3229/30.

CLASS 373   "THREE CAPITALS" EUROSTARS

10-car half-sets. Built for services starting from or terminating in London Waterloo (now St Pancras). Individual vehicles in each set are allocated numbers 373xxx0 + 373xxx1 + 373xxx2 + 373xxx3 + 373xxx4 + 373xxx5 + 373xxx6 + 373xxx7 + 373xxx8 + 373xxx9, where 3xxx denotes the set number.

Formation: DM-MS-4TS-RB-2TF-TBF. Gangwayed within pair of units. Air conditioned.
Construction: Steel.
Supply Systems: 25 kV AC 50 Hz overhead or 3000 V DC overhead (* also equipped for 1500 V DC overhead operation).
Control System: GTO–GTO Inverter on UK 750 V DC and 25 kV AC, GTO Chopper on SNCB 3000 V DC.
Continuous rating: 12 x 240 kW (25 kV AC); 5700 kW (1500 and 3000 V DC).
Wheel Arrangement: Bo-Bo + Bo–2–2–2–2–2–2–2–2.
Lengths: 22.15 m (DM), 21.85 m (MS & TBF), 18.70 m (other cars).
Couplers: Schaku 10S at outer ends, Schaku 10L at inner end of each DM and outer ends of each sub set.
Maximum Speed: 186 mph (300 km/h).

Built: 1992–93 by GEC-Alsthom/Brush/ANF/De Dietrich/BN Construction/ACEC.

DM vehicles carry the set numbers indicated below.

Non-standard livery: 3213 and 3224 – Izy (green, white & purple).

† Refurbished.

At the time of writing the following sets were misformed: 3213 with 3224 and 3214 with 3223.
3213/24 is currently on hire to Thalys for the Paris–Brussels "Izy" service.

373xxx0 series. DM. Lot No. 31118 1992–95. 68.5 t.
373xxx1 series. MS. Lot No. 31119 1992–95. –/48 2T. 44.6 t.
373xxx2 series. TS. Lot No. 31120 1992–95. –/56 1T. 28.1 t.
373xxx3 series. TS. Lot No. 31121 1992–95. –/56 2T. 29.7 t.
373xxx4 series. TS. Lot No. 31122 1992–95. –/56 1T. 28.3 t.
373xxx5 series. TS. Lot No. 31123 1992–95. –/56 2T. 29.2 t.
373xxx6 series. RB. Lot No. 31124 1992–95. 31.1 t.
373xxx7 series. TF. Lot No. 31125 1992–95. 39/– 1T. 29.6 t.
373xxx8 series. TF. Lot No. 31126 1992–95. 39/– 1T. 32.2 t.
373xxx9 series. TBF. Lot No. 31127 1992–95. 25/– 1TD. 39.4 t.

3007	†*	**ES**	EU	*EU*	TI		3215	*	**EU**	SF	*EU*	LY
3008	†*	**ES**	EU	*EU*	TI		3216	*	**EU**	SF	*EU*	LY
3015	†*	**ES**	EU	*EU*	TI		3217		**EU**	SF	*EU*	LY
3016	†*	**ES**	EU	*EU*	TI		3218		**EU**	SF	*EU*	LY
3205	†*	**ES**	SF	*EU*	LY		3219	†*	**ES**	SF	*EU*	LY
3206	†*	**ES**	SF	*EU*	LY		3220	†*	**ES**	SF	*EU*	LY
3209	†*	**ES**	SF	*EU*	LY		3221	†*	**ES**	SF	*EU*	LY
3210	†*	**ES**	SF	*EU*	LY		3222	†*	**ES**	SF	*EU*	LY
3211	†*	**ES**	SF	*EU*	LY		3223	*	**EU**	SF	*EU*	LY
3212	†*	**ES**	SF	*EU*	LY		3224	*	**0**	SF	*EU*	LY
3213	*	**0**	SF	*EU*	LY		3229	†*	**ES**	SF	*EU*	LY
3214	*	**EU**	SF	*EU*	LY		3230	†*	**ES**	SF	*EU*	LY

Spare DM:

3999		**ER**	EU	*EU*	TI

CLASS 374   SIEMENS VELARO e320

8-car half-sets. These units are similar to the DB Class 407 ICE sets, with distributed power rather than a power car at either end like the Class 373s. The first sets entered service in November 2015, operating initially on the St Pancras–Paris route. They have also been used on the new St Pancras–Amsterdam service from 2018.

The initial order was for ten units (4001–20) and this was then increased by another seven (4021–34) in 2014. An option exists for a further six units.

Formation: DMF–TBF–MS–TS–TS–MS–TS–MSRB.
Gangwayed within pair of units. Air conditioned.
Construction: Aluminium.   **Control System:** IGBT Inverter.
Supply Systems: 25 kV AC 50 Hz overhead, 1500 V DC overhead and 3000 V DC overhead.
Continuous rating: 8000 kW (25 kV AC), 4200 kW (1500 and 3000 V DC).
Wheel Arrangement: Bo-Bo + 2-2 + Bo-Bo + 2-2 + 2-2 + Bo-Bo + 2-2 + Bo-Bo.
Lengths: 26.035 m (DMF), 24.775 m (other cars).
Couplers: Dellner 12.   **Maximum Speed:** 200 mph (320 km/h).
Built: 2012–17 by Siemens, Krefeld, Germany.

DM vehicles carry the full 12-digit EVNs as indicated below. For example set 4001/02 carries the numbers 93 70 3740 011-9 + 93 70 3740 012-7 + 93 70 3740 013-5 + 93 70 3740 014-3 + 93 70 3740 015-0 + 93 70 3740 016-8 + 93 70 3740 017-6 + 93 70 3740 018-4 + 93 70 3740 028-3 + 93 70 3740 027-5 + 93 70 3740 026-7 + 93 70 3740 025-9 + 93 70 3740 024-2 + 93 70 3740 023-4 + 93 70 3740 022-6 + 93 70 3740 021-8.

93 70 3740 xx1-c series. DMF. Siemens Krefeld 2012–17. 40/–. 58.0 t.
93 70 3740 xx2-c series. TBF. Siemens Krefeld 2012–17. 36/– 2T. 59.0 t.
93 70 3740 xx3-c series. MF. Siemens Krefeld 2012–17. 34/–(+2) 1TD 2W. 59.0 t.
93 70 3740 xx4-c series. TS. Siemens Krefeld 2012–17. –/76 2T. 53.0 t.
93 70 3740 xx5-c series. TS. Siemens Krefeld 2012–17. –/76 2T. 53.0 t.
93 70 3740 xx6-c series. MS. Siemens Krefeld 2012–17. –/76 2T. 58.0 t.
93 70 3740 xx7-c series. TS. Siemens Krefeld 2012–17. –/76 2T. 57.0 t.
93 70 3740 xx8-c series. MSRB. Siemens Krefeld 2012–17. –/32 2T. 58.0 t.

4001	**ES**	EU	*EU*	TI	4018	**ES**	EU	*EU*	TI
4002	**ES**	EU	*EU*	TI	4019	**ES**	EU	*EU*	TI
4003	**ES**	EU	*EU*	TI	4020	**ES**	EU	*EU*	TI
4004	**ES**	EU	*EU*	TI	4021	**ES**	EU	*EU*	TI
4005	**ES**	EU	*EU*	TI	4022	**ES**	EU	*EU*	TI
4006	**ES**	EU	*EU*	TI	4023	**ES**	EU	*EU*	TI
4007	**ES**	EU	*EU*	TI	4024	**ES**	EU	*EU*	TI
4008	**ES**	EU	*EU*	TI	4025	**ES**	EU	*EU*	TI
4009	**ES**	EU	*EU*	TI	4026	**ES**	EU	*EU*	TI
4010	**ES**	EU	*EU*	TI	4027	**ES**	EU	*EU*	TI
4011	**ES**	EU	*EU*	TI	4028	**ES**	EU	*EU*	TI
4012	**ES**	EU	*EU*	TI	4029	**ES**	EU	*EU*	TI
4013	**ES**	EU	*EU*	TI	4030	**ES**	EU	*EU*	TI
4014	**ES**	EU	*EU*	TI	4031	**ES**	EU	*EU*	TI
4015	**ES**	EU	*EU*	TI	4032	**ES**	EU	*EU*	TI
4016	**ES**	EU	*EU*	TI	4033	**ES**	EU	*EU*	TI
4017	**ES**	EU	*EU*	TI	4034	**ES**	EU	*EU*	TI

6. SERVICE EMUS

The following unit was used by Network Rail for ERTMS testing on the Hertford Loop. It has been heavily modified from its original condition, and now includes a toilet.

313 121   **Y**   BN   ZG   62549   71233   62613

7. EMU VEHICLES IN INDUSTRIAL SERVICE

This list comprises EMU vehicles that have been withdrawn from active service but continue to be used in industrial service.

Cl. 390	69133	69833	Virgin Trains Training Centre, Westmere Drive, Crewe, Cheshire (ex-unit 390 033)
Cl. 390	69633	69733	The Fire Service College, Moreton-in-Marsh, Gloucestershire (ex-unit 390 033)
Cl. 390	69933		Safety & Accident Investigation Centre, Cranfield University, Cranfield, Bedfordshire (ex-unit 390 033)
Cl. 508	64649	64712	Emergency Services Training Centre, Seacombe, Merseyside (ex-units 508 201/209)
Cl. 508	64681	71511	64724	The Fire Service College, Moreton-in-Marsh, Gloucestershire (unit 508 212)

8. EMUS AWAITING DISPOSAL

This list comprises vehicles awaiting disposal which are stored on the national railway network.

25 kV AC 50 Hz OVERHEAD UNITS:

Cl. 309	**RR**	WC	CS	71758
Cl. 365	**N**	X	ZN	65919
Cl. 365	**GW**	X	ZI	72290

9. CODES

9.1. LIVERY CODES

AL Advertising/promotional livery (see class heading for details).
BG BR blue & grey lined out in white.
C2 c2c (white with dark blue doors).
CN Connex/Southeastern (white with black window surrounds & grey lower band).
ES Revised Eurostar (deep blue & two-tone grey).
EU Eurostar (white with dark blue & yellow stripes).
FB First Group dark blue.
FU First Group "Urban Lights" (varying blue or uniform indigo blue with pink, white & blue markings on the lower bodyside).
GA Greater Anglia (white with red doors & black window surrounds).
GR New Greater Anglia (white/grey with black window surrounds & red & dark grey on the lower bodyside).
GV Gatwick Express Class 442 (red, white & indigo blue with mauve & blue doors).
GW Great Western Railway (TOC) dark green.
GX Gatwick Express Class 387 (red with white lining and grey doors).
HC Heathrow Connect (grey with a broad deep blue bodyside band & orange doors).
HE Heathrow Express (silver with purple doors and black window surrounds). Red advertising for Vodaphone.
HX New Heathrow Express (silver, grey & purple).
LD New London Overground (black upper bodyside with white, orange & blue lower bodyside stripes & orange doors).
LI London Northwestern Railway {interim} (dark green at unit ends and doors applied on **LM** light grey/black livery).
LM London Midland (grey & green with black stripe around the windows).
LN London Northwestern Railway (light grey, dark green & light green).
LO London Overground (all over white with a blue solebar, black window surrounds & orange doors).
LT London Transport maroon & cream.
LZ LNER Azuma (white with red window surrounds).
MY Merseyrail (all over yellow or all over grey (alternate sides)).
N BR Network SouthEast (white & blue with red lower bodyside stripe, grey solebar & cab ends).
NB Northern all over dark blue.
NC National Express white (white with blue doors).
NO Northern (deep blue, purple & white).
NR New Northern (white & purple).
NX National Express (white with grey ends).
O Non-standard (see class heading for details).
RM Royal Mail (all over red).
RR Regional Railways (dark blue/grey with light blue & white stripes, three narrow dark blue stripes at cab ends).
SB Southeastern blue (all over blue with black window surrounds).

SC Strathclyde PTE (carmine & cream lined out in black & gold).
SD Stagecoach/South West Trains outer suburban livery {Class 450 style} (deep blue with red doors & orange & red cab sides).
SE Southeastern suburban (all over white with black window surrounds, light blue doors and (on some units) dark blue lower bodyside stripe).
SN Southern (white & dark green with light green semi-circles at one end of each vehicle. Light grey band at solebar level).
SR ScotRail – Scotland's Railways (dark blue with Scottish Saltire flag & white/light blue flashes).
SS South West Trains inner suburban livery {Class 455 style} (red with blue & orange flashes at unit ends).
ST Stagecoach {long-distance stock} (white & dark blue with dark blue window surrounds and red & orange swishes at unit ends).
SW South Western Railway (two tone grey with a yellow lower bodyside stripe).
TF TfL Rail (white with blue doors & lower bodyside stripe).
TG Govia Thameslink interim {Class 387} (white with dark green doors).
TL Govia Thameslink Railway (light grey & white with light blue doors).
TP TransPennine Express (silver, grey, blue & purple).
TW Transport for Wales (white with a broad red stripe at cantrail level & red doors).
U Plain white or grey undercoat.
VT Virgin Trains silver (silver, with black window surrounds, white cantrail stripe and red roof. Red swept down at unit ends).
VW New Virgin Trains (white with a red swish at unit ends).
WI West Midlands Railway {interim} (gold at unit ends & gold doors applied on **LM** white/grey livery).
XR Crossrail (white with black window surrounds and a purple lower bodyside).
Y Network Rail yellow.
YR West Yorkshire PTE/Northern EMUs (red, lilac & grey).

9.2. OWNER CODES

A   Angel Trains
AT   Agility Trains
BN   Beacon Rail
CL   Caledonian Rail Leasing
CO   Corelink Rail Infrastructure
CT   Cross London Trains
E   Eversholt Rail (UK)
EU   Eurostar International
HE   Heathrow Airport Holdings
MQ   Macquarie Group
P   Porterbrook Leasing Company
QW   QW Rail Leasing
RF   Rail for London (Transport for London)

RM	Royal Mail
RR	Rock Rail
SF	SNCF (Société Nationale des Chemins de fer Français)
SR	ScotRail
SW	South Western Railway
SY	South Yorkshire Passenger Transport Executive
TF	Train Fleet (Department for Transport)
WC	West Coast Railway Company
X	Sold for scrap/further use and awaiting collection
XR	Crossrail

9.3. OPERATOR CODES

C2	c2c
DB	DB Cargo (UK)
EU	Eurostar (UK)
GA	Greater Anglia
GN	Great Northern (part of Govia Thameslink Railway)
GW	Great Western Railway
HE	Heathrow Express
LN	London North Eastern Railway
LO	London Overground
ME	Merseyrail
NO	Northern
SE	Southeastern
SN	Southern (part of Govia Thameslink Railway)
SR	ScotRail
SW	South Western Railway
SY	Stagecoach Supertram
TL	Thameslink (part of Govia Thameslink Railway)
TP	TransPennine Express
VW	Virgin Trains
WM	West Midlands Trains
XR	TfL Rail

9.4. ALLOCATION & LOCATION CODES

Code	Location	Depot Operator
AD	Ashford (Kent)	Hitachi
AK	Ardwick (Manchester)	Siemens
AN	Allerton (Liverpool)	Northern
BD	Birkenhead North	Stadler Rail Service UK
BI	Brighton Lovers Walk	Govia Thameslink Railway
BM	Bournemouth	South Western Railway
CE	Crewe International	DB Cargo (UK)

CF	Cardiff Canton	Transport for Wales/Colas Rail
CS	Carnforth	West Coast Railway Company
CY	Crewe South Yard	*Storage location only*
DN	Doncaster Carr	Hitachi
EC	Edinburgh Craigentinny	Hitachi
EM	East Ham (London)	c2c
EP	Ely Papworth Sidings	*Storage location only*
GW	Glasgow Shields Road	ScotRail
HE	Hornsey (London)	Govia Thameslink Railway
HT	Heaton (Newcastle-upon-Tyne)	Northern/LNER
IL	Ilford (London)	Greater Anglia/Elizabeth Line
LB	Loughborough Works	Brush Traction
LM	Quinton Rail Technology Centre (Long Marston, Warwickshire)	Motorail Logistics
LY	Le Landy (Paris)	SNCF
MA	Longsight (Manchester)	Alstom
NC	Norwich Crown Point	Greater Anglia
NG	New Cross Gate (London)	London Overground
NL	Neville Hill (Leeds)	East Midlands Railway/Northern
NN	Northampton King's Heath	Siemens
NP	North Pole (London)	Hitachi
NT	Northam (Southampton)	Siemens
NU	Sheffield Nunnery	Stagecoach Supertram
OC	Old Oak Common Crossrail (London)	Crossrail/Elizabeth Line
OH	Old Oak Common Heathrow (London)	Heathrow Express
RG	Reading	Great Western Railway
RM	Ramsgate	Southeastern
RY	Ryde (Isle of Wight)	South Western Railway
SG	Slade Green (London)	Southeastern
SL	Stewarts Lane (London)	Govia Thameslink Railway/Belmond
SO	Soho (Birmingham)	West Midlands Trains
SU	Selhurst (Croydon)	Govia Thameslink Railway
TB	Three Bridges (Crawley)	Siemens
TI	Temple Mills (London)	Eurostar
WD	Wimbledon (London)	South Western Railway
WN	Willesden (London)	Bombardier Transportation
WS	Worksop (Nottinghamshire)	Harry Needle Railroad Company
YO	Yoker (Glasgow)	ScotRail
ZA	RTC Business Park (Derby)	Loram (UK)
ZB	Doncaster Works	Wabtec Rail
ZC	Crewe Works	Bombardier Transportation UK
ZD	Derby Works	Bombardier Transportation UK
ZG	Eastleigh Works	Arlington Fleet Services
ZH	Springburn Depot (Glasgow)	*Closed*
ZI	Ilford Works	Bombardier Transportation UK
ZJ	Stoke-on-Trent Works	Axiom Rail (Stoke)
ZK	Kilmarnock Caledonia Works	Wabtec Rail Scotland
ZM	Kilmarnock Bonnyton Works	Brodie Engineering
ZN	Wolverton Works	Gemini Rail Group
ZR	Holgate Works (York)	Network Rail